Seamless Leadership

*'Seamless leadership' is a vital contribution
to grooming a future generation of leaders
that will guide our nation through turbulent
passages that inevitably lie ahead.*
– Neal Froneman – CEO Sibanye Gold

*This book captures our South African
leadership heritage well. A worthwhile read!*
– Herman Mashaba – Founder Black Like Me

*Better, more effective leadership is the one
thing every South African agrees we need.
What makes a great leader? Read this book.*
– Gareth Cliff

Seamless Leadership

Universal lessons from South Africa

Adriaan Groenewald

Jonathan Ball Publishers
JOHANNESBURG & CAPE TOWN

To my father, Louis Groenewald,
with whom I am undertaking this remarkable journey, which
includes inspiration from above, innovation and hard work.
We hope this will make South Africa and the world a better place.

AUTHOR'S NOTE
Information on companies reflects the state of affairs as at the date on which the interview was conducted.

Interviews originally published in *Business Report** between 2008 and 2014 include the following: Nick Badminton, Lt Governor Bell, Mike Brown, Zunaid Bulbulia, Bill Child, Gareth Cliff, Mark Cutifani, Brian Dames, Ian Donald, Adrian Gore, Chris Griffith, Tom Hamilton, Paul Harris, Michael Jordaan, Edward Kieswetter, Gary Kirsten, Chad Le Clos and Graham Hill, Julius Malema, Gill Marcus, Herman Mashaba, Heyneke Meyer, Sipho Nkosi, Bheki Sibiya, Dr Iqbal Survé, Mardia van der Walt-Korsten, Zwelinzima Vavi, Helen Zille, Jacob Zuma; and the following in *Star Workplace:* Raymond Ackerman, Gary Crittenden, Malusi Gigaba, Victor Matfield, Hlengani Mathebula, Roelf Meyer, Sizwe Nxasana, Gary Player, Terry Volkwyn.

**Business Report* is an Independent Media publication inside *The Star*, *The Cape Times*, *The Mercury* and *Pretoria News*.

Originally published in South Africa in 2015 by
JONATHAN BALL PUBLISHERS
A division of Media24 Limited
PO Box 33977
Jeppestown
2043

ISBN 978 1 86842 646 1
Ebook 978 1 86842 647 8

Twitter: http://www.twitter.com/JonathanBallPub
Facebook: http://www.facebook.com/pages/Jonathan-Ball-Publishers/298034457992
Blog: http://jonathanball.bookslive.co.za/

Cover design by MR Design
Design and typesetting by Triple M Design, Johannesburg
Printed and bound by Paarl Media, Paarl
Set in 10.5/15pt Rotis Serif Std

Contents

Foreword

It was back in 2010 that Adriaan and I first mooted the idea of doing something unique to foster a national conversation on leadership. Wherever we looked, it seemed as if every aspect of leadership had become an afterthought.

Not long after our initial discussion a bi-weekly feature on leadership was born, with Adriaan as lead contributor. This platform found its way into *Business Report*, the national financial daily that I have the privilege of editing.

At the outset, our goal was to push the boundaries and bring South Africans and the world at large an unvarnished dose of interviews and insights from leaders from all walks of life. From politics to business, to sports, to academia, to the arts – we said no leader should be off limits. And this is because, we thought, South Africans deserve to know what stuff their leaders are made of.

We also wanted to go back in time to reflect on the leaders' life stories – where they come from, what obstacles they have had to overcome, and how they hope to inspire the next generation of leaders.

These and many other questions have catalysed into this pertinent and timely book – *Seamless Leadership: Universal Lessons from South Africa.*

Generally, what is often unappreciated is the fact that South Africa's legacy is about nothing else but leadership. That legacy is borne out by the contribution that leaders like Nelson Mandela made to bring about change by heeding the call to rise above themselves. And yet, so little attention is given to leadership milestones that have taken the country from a hopeless state to a hopeful future.

In so many ways this book is about revealing the untold story of South Africa to the world. Put simply, that story is about the fact that South Africa is endowed with a diverse tapestry of leaders whose life experiences should inspire hope about our future as a nation. And where else in Africa do you find four Nobel Peace laureates – Chief Albert Luthuli, Nelson Mandela, FW de Klerk and Archbishop Desmond Tutu? Only in South Africa!

In bringing out this book, Adriaan has provided a mirror through which the current generation of South African leaders can look at themselves through the experiences of those featured within these pages. One of the first interviews we did for our leadership conversations project was with President Jacob Zuma in August 2010. In that interview, we got a rare glimpse at what was not generally in the public domain about the President. Such is the nature of the collection of the conversations contained in this book. Not only has Adriaan provided a treasure trove of insights about leadership in the South African context, he has also put together an illuminating spotlight about what may not generally be widely known about the leaders covered herein.

In any other country Herman Mashaba would by now be a household name. Not in South Africa. But here is a man whose life story brings to light the ingenuity of an ordinary entrepreneur who built a black hair care company out of nothing. How about Michael Jordaan? For a long time, he held the sole title of being the most active South African CEO on Twitter. This is someone who knew and understood what social media is, way before other business leaders did, when he was at the helm of First National Bank.

Adriaan also showcases a conversation that we both had with Dr Iqbal Survé, one of South Africa's leading businessmen. His 2013 purchase of Independent Newspapers, the largest publisher of English newspapers on the African continent, has not only made him a media mogul but a transformative force in what is still a highly contested space in South Africa.

This book gives you as the reader an unadulterated view into what has shaped some of the country's contemporary leaders, and that is the reason why its scope is not confined to business, but also features luminaries who have excelled in many other endeavours. Gill Marcus, former governor of the South African Reserve Bank, gives us a closer look at what constitutes her leadership philosophy, while the conversation with swimming sensation Chad Le Clos provides insights that were little known about this young man who shot into the spotlight at the London Olympics in 2012 to grab the baton from the American swimming super-hero, Michael Phelps.

So, from the boardroom to the swimming pool, this book goes wherever there is leadership.

Insights from all the stories contained inside the covers are, by and large, an acknowledgement of the breadth and scope of leadership experience that is found in South Africa. It is my hope that they will form a timeless reference for anyone seeking to understand why leaders are the way they are, or are not the way they are supposed to be.

I believe that inside each one of us there is a leader, waiting to seize the responsibility to build, inspire and challenge the status quo. These three tasks may seem so simple, yet they constitute some of the first things that leaders forget.

In this book Adriaan answers the question why leaders become leaders in the first place. His admiration of Nelson Mandela flows in part from a realisation that Mandela spent his life relentlessly pursuing the aim of bringing about a new reality as a leader – replacing despair with hope, and selfishness with magnanimity. This is what leadership meant to Mandela. In this book you will also learn how Mandela's leadership journey has helped shape the leaders profiled herein.

I know that this book marks just the beginning of a long conversation about leadership. Therefore, it should make it possible for you to start asking big questions about how you can contribute to this conversation. So it is a great privilege to introduce *Seamless Leadership* to you. Take time to immerse yourself in it, and it will provide you with more than just narratives about leadership, but real, practical and privileged understanding.

Ellis Mnyandu
Johannesburg, February 2015

Preface

A wise and visionary man once said this to me: 'One day you must show your fellow citizens the worth of belonging to this great nation, chosen above all others to fulfil a destiny peculiar to itself.' These words stuck with me like my own name, refusing to be erased from my memory.

It was 1984, and I was 17. For years I wondered about the meaning of those words. What peculiar destiny could this nation possibly have to fulfil? We were small, basically an emerging economy, with limited economic status, at the tip of a continent not always seen in a positive light. Many diverse issues threatened to come to a head: we seemed to be destined for serious conflict and even full-scale violence and war.

Then along came Nelson Mandela and other leaders from different arenas and achieved what without a doubt was perceived to be impossible – a relatively peaceful transition and a huge measure of unity across racial and political boundaries.

By this time I was in my early twenties, and by great good fortune I was relatively close to this miraculous occurrence. My uncle, General Tienie Groenewald, had joined with General Constand Viljoen and others to unite Afrikaners in an effort to secure their future. I remember how a friend and I visited my uncle's home almost every week to sit down and listen to developments around the negotiations, in which he was very involved. We listened in awe as he described the different characters in this national and international political spectacle. I heard about the different options for Afrikaners that were considered at the time, including war. I knew we were very close to a worst-case scenario; we really were!

On 22 April 1994, six days before South Africa's first-ever democratic elections, the US Ambassador to South Africa received a call from General Viljoen. He explained that they could not reach a compromise with the ANC and NP to sign a negotiated accord that would recognise the Afrikaners' wish for self-determination and that he had no option but to resort to violence. During a previous engagement the Ambassador had asked the General to inform him should such a situation arise.

The Ambassador asked for 48 hours. The answer was they didn't have 48 hours. He asked for 24 hours. Again the answer was they didn't have the luxury of even that. They settled on 8 hours. Within the allotted time the Ambassador came back to announce that signing by both the ANC and the NP would take place at 10 am the very next day, 23 April, at the Union Buildings, and it did. Interesting how much influence a US Ambassador had, or was it the US President? And who would have guessed he played such a prominent role in averting a national crisis?

What preceded this moment in South Africa's history is a story that could have gone so wrong; a story where humility and big picture thinking conquered ego; a story of great leadership; a story that every citizen in South Africa and beyond should be aware of and grateful for. If we don't know where we come from it is more difficult to appreciate where we are, 20 years into our democracy.

Does this mean South Africa was that close to more serious disruption, guerrilla war, even full-scale war or a blood bath? According to my uncle, Major-General Tienie Groenewald, there were plans in place that would without a doubt have changed the course of our country's history.

My uncle started his career as a pilot and climbed the ranks all the way to becoming Chief Director of Military Intelligence. As head of Branch National Intelligence Interpretation, his division interpreted all intelligence information evaluated by the intelligence departments on the security situation, banned organisations and anyone considered an enemy of the State at the time. It was done for President PW Botha's State Security Council and he was the first person ever to present to these Cabinet Ministers and other leaders on a regular basis. He saw Botha on Thursdays and often interacted with him and senior Ministers, including attending Cabinet team builds. He told me that when PW Botha was in a bad mood he presented and got out of there. When he was in a good mood he would often discuss certain challenging situations with him.

He observed that Botha relied heavily on those members in his Cabinet who could give philosophical inputs, because he was more of a doer, an operational leader. And he was not a man who could sit down and write a constitution; he wanted to use his experts. In this particular case they could not give him what he wanted, which according to my uncle was indicative of how poor the Cabinet make-up was in terms of expertise and leadership.

After a while my uncle asked to be released. He explained why: 'In two-and-a-half years, not once did we have to come back and say we were wrong in our interpretation. You reach a situation where you are quite influential and so I asked to step down.' Of course PW Botha asked why, and his answer was: 'Do you know how the J Edgar Hoovers and Hendrik van den Bergs are created? They are in a key position for too long and then they start manipulating the intelligence to influence decision making.' His philosophy was that intelligence was to interpret the situation and actions planned by the enemy but never to propose actions to be taken. That was the task of the commander or political decision maker.

Voluntarily stepping down from a powerful position says a lot about his character and value system, which was shaped in a family of ten children, seven brothers and three sisters. My grandfather was his tutor in many respects and my uncle believes he learnt more from him than from anyone else. His philosophy was one of never forcing you into anything. They had a Christian upbringing and of the ten children nine are still alive, married and with no divorces. They were and we still are a tight-knit family. My grandmother passed away at the age of 103. Of her my uncle says: 'She was the most beautiful woman that I have known in my life and a wonderful person.' I can attest, she was an amazing person.

After my uncle stepped down PW Botha asked him to get the Bureau of Information off the ground. This lasted until the beginning of 1990. It was during this period that my uncle realised the government did not have the faintest idea of where they were heading. They knew long ago that apartheid could no longer work, but they did not know what to do about it.

When De Klerk took over, my uncle decided on early retirement. Again the President wanted an explanation. The answer was clear and direct: 'You have many names one can compare you with, Mr President. In European history it would be Lord Chamberlain, who with his policy of appeasement was a great cause of World War II. In South African history, perhaps Piet Retief. It wasn't wrong for him to negotiate with the Zulu king. It wasn't wrong to make an agreement. But when he disarmed his people and placed them in a weak position, it not only led to his and his commando's death but to the biggest bloodshed in our history – the Battle of Blood River. And you, Mr President, have already neutralised your Defence Force; you have already placed yourself in the hands of the ANC, and your actions may lead to the biggest bloodbath this country has ever seen.' De Klerk did not take kindly to these words.

There was clear intelligence that indicated government was in a stronger position than they realised. While international and local pressure on the National Party to start negotiating intensified, according to my uncle the Russians were withdrawing all their support from the ANC because communism was under threat and they had to deal with their own challenges. They advised the ANC/SACP to 'negotiate and take what you can get'.

Not long after his retirement, an Afrikaner movement, the Boere Vryheidsbeweging (Boer Freedom Movement), asked my uncle to assist in creating unity amongst the Afrikaner people. They created a 'Committee of 23' and started liaising with different political and non-political organisations. They then formed a 'National Unity' committee and this body decided something drastic had to be done. The Unity Committee developed into the Afrikaner Volksfront (AVF). On the suggestion of Dries Bruwer, leader of the Transvaal Agricultural Union, a Committee of Generals was created, with General Viljoen as the leader. They went to Viljoen's farm and strategised. The approach decided on was three-pronged: mobilise, negotiate, and if needs be, resort to violence.

These leaders achieved the largest-ever mobilisation of Afrikaners and even other groupings that stood for self-determination. Political meetings happened across the country. Hundreds of thousands attended. The mobilisation phase was expanded to those black ethnic groups that supported self-determination, like the Zulus (IFP) and Bophuthatswana. This expanded alliance was called COSAG – Concerned South Africans Group. For a time there was complete unity in this group. According to my uncle it was the perfect example of what could be achieved when moderate leaders decided to negotiate peacefully.

The Generals agreed the mobilisation phase would be successful when the ANC made advances to them for talks, which happened. Jacob Zuma passed a message to Dries Bruwer that Nelson Mandela wanted to meet. The meeting was set up and both General Viljoen and my uncle attended. At the meeting Mandela said: 'I realise there is no way that the ANC can defeat the Afrikaner people. But there is also no way in which the Afrikaner people can defeat the ANC. If we continue on the road that we are walking now, we will end up in a situation very similar to the Middle East or Ireland. Isn't there a peaceful way out?' The response was: 'We want negotiations, so yes, we will talk.' Mandela appointed Thabo Mbeki and Jacob Zuma as ANC representatives and negotiations started in November 1993, while COSAG was moving along successfully in its negotiations with the NP government.

Alongside all of this the CODESA process took its up-and-down course. In December 1993 negotiations between the Generals and the ANC had reached a point where the signing of an accord on Afrikaner self-deter-mination was due on 21 December, but it didn't happen. In a meeting between COSAG, ANC and NP leaders, my uncle asked Joe Slovo whether the ANC would ever allow certain executive powers for the provinces. The answer was no, so he got up and walked out of the negotiations. He was followed by Chief Mangosuthu Buthelezi, Lucas Mangope and others. When this happened the signing of the accord between the Generals and the ANC became an uncomfortable matter. But fortunately talks with the ANC continued, and so did the mobilisation of Afrikaners country-wide.

By the time 20 April 1994 arrived there was a shortened version of the 21 December 1993 accord on the table, ready to be signed. It provided for the Afrikaner Volksfront to not use force and disrupt the elections, while on the ANC side they agreed to continue the negotiation on Afrikaner self-determination on the basis of constitutional principles agreed on and to set up mechanisms to achieve this, and also that when they continued after the elections, if they could not come to an agreement both parties would subject themselves to international mediation. This document is still valid. It became clear to the Generals that the NP would not sign the accord, and certain elements within the ANC felt that progress towards the elections had developed so far that there wasn't a need to sign anything. The Volksfront felt there was no alternative but to turn to violence. And this is when a call was made to the US Ambassador.

Dramatic plans were in motion, at first not for full-scale war. Because of my uncle's previous position he had insight into the National Key Points Register, a document containing all the relevant key points across South Africa, like Eskom and the SABC. He says: 'We had plans and identified the people that would occupy a critical number of these key points.' They would also take over certain towns controlled by the Conservative Party that they considered to be part of a possible Volkstaat. But they would have no military offensive outside these areas.

They knew that at least half of the Defence Force supported General Viljoen. But if the Defence Force was called upon they would have to act against their own people, who weren't committing any violence, and most Afrikaners wouldn't do this. There was a chance of this strategy developing into at least a guerrilla war, however, which required a base area from where they could operate. General Viljoen instructed my uncle to visit Jonas Savimbi, the political and military leader who founded and led UNITA in Angola. His highly secret mission: to garner his support for a base and more.

He travelled illegally in a light aircraft to Angola and met Savimbi from 3 am until 5 am. When asked if they could count on his support the Angolan's answer was: 'Inform General Viljoen everything I have is at his disposal, and if I gave him everything it wouldn't be a fraction of what he has done for us. I could never repay that man for what he has done for me.'

Then my uncle asked this question: 'If we had to kidnap the key political figures from the ANC and NP (Mandela, De Klerk, Ramaphosa, Meyer, and others), and fly them out to Angola to negotiate on our terms, would you provide us with those facilities?' Savimbi said he would. The Generals had knowledge of the movements of all NEC members, and the Cabinet was easy because they knew when it met. They even had at least two of Mandela's bodyguards as inside informants. My uncle admits they needed a bit more time to make sure these plans were absolutely foolproof, but they could have done it.

In the end, why did all this not happen? After all, the perception is that generals are trained for war and want it – a general who hasn't gone to war isn't a real general! Maybe our saving grace was that our generals had experienced war. My uncle explained: 'First of all, Generals know what war is. We also knew that once you start the path of violence there is really no end to it, and you create hatred, which would take generations to eradicate, as shown by the Middle East and Ireland.'

They also realised it would be a war between Afrikaner and Afrikaner. MK (the ANC's military wing) was no factor; it had no military significance whatsoever. The Generals believed that should they manage to push through the accord they would be establishing a base for peaceful negotiations in the future. What went wrong after the elections was the old problem of disunity amongst Afrikaners, and as a result they lost the power base that would have forced the ANC to continue the negotiations to find a political solution provided for in the Accord of 21 December 1993, which was part of the signed Accord of 23 April 1994. The ANC's question was always: Who do we make the agreement with? And of course the Volksfront became a political party that lost this aim of a Volkstaat after Viljoen retired.

Fortunately my uncle's warning to former President de Klerk did not materialise, though it came close. It is clear that what ultimately prevented the 'prophesied' blood bath was leaders on all sides, including the Generals, who could control their egos and consider the big picture, and who rose above personal agendas for the greater good. It is a leadership story that illustrates the need for unity in order to succeed, and that its lack will thwart positive movement or progress.

It was leaders like these who made the difference. And it is clear Nelson Mandela rose to the occasion, was true to his calling in life and tenaciously followed inspiration to push for movement towards national unity; to drive purposefully his belief that all human beings were created equal; to sacrifice all that he possessed for a country and world where all human beings can practise their God-given gift of free agency in order to learn and grow towards their full potential.

After all this happened I surprised myself by starting a career that included interviewing top leaders internationally about why and how they achieved success. With South African leaders, conversations revolved around how they led in this very complex environment, which truly is a microcosm

7

of the world. Whatever challenges exist somewhere on the planet, they somehow exist or have existed in South Africa in some form. South Africa is an extremely dynamic political, economic, and social place where leaders are tested on all levels and in every possible way.

So, for most of the lifespan of our 'new South Africa', born in the mid-1990s, I have interviewed and written about top political, corporate, entertainment and sports leaders. The journey has been fascinating on many fronts and has included interviews and associations with many who knew our icon, Nelson Mandela – President Zuma, Deputy President Motlanthe, Mathews Phosa, son-in-law Dr Kwame Amuah, Roelf Meyer (chief negotiator for the National Party in the 1990s), former DA leader Tony Leon, Dr Iqbal Survé (Mandela's doctor), DA leader Helen Zille, and many corporate and other leaders. And, of course, my uncle and my own father met Mandela on several occasions.

As we continue to uncover universal leadership processes, models and principles formed in the midst of our South African crucible, it becomes evident that we cannot study successful leaders or leadership in South Africa without also understanding the essence of those leadership attributes that Nelson Mandela symbolised. It is simply not possible to discuss great leadership with any group or individual in South Africa without discovering that their own leadership approach and thinking was somehow, whether obviously or at a deep subconscious level, influenced by the example and successes of Nelson Mandela.

As you read the interviews with other leaders in this book you will notice how many of them naturally refer to Nelson Mandela in some way. He is our nation's symbol of great leadership, the essence of the kind of leadership needed to be successful in this microcosm of the world called South Africa. And indeed, his leadership – and the positive leadership that in places in South Africa still exists – is the kind of leadership our planet needs. The world embraced Nelson Mandela in life on a large scale, but since his death our need for the essence of what his leadership symbolises has been all the greater.

So what is this peculiar destiny that South Africa must and will fulfil? When destiny and timing collide there is no stopping the movement that will explode. Nelson Mandela is a fitting example of this principle. The collision of his destiny and timing caused an explosion that resulted in a global phenomenon. Our destiny is to bring to the attention of the world that brand of leadership it so badly craves and needs. Collectively leaders of this and other generations have failed the people of this planet. Followers are disillusioned – and when a beacon of hope for better leadership is held up we gravitate towards it as the entire globe gravitates towards Mandela, or to the memory and feelings his leadership brought. The level of gravitation towards Nelson Mandela is a direct reflection of the hunger the world has for better leadership, and we are clearly very hungry!

We in South Africa have started veering off from the path of the essence of South African or Mandela leadership, because universally human beings often struggle to see and fully embrace the good in their own back yard. We have to be careful not to be distracted by this recent global Nelson Mandela frenzy to the point that we miss our destiny of continuing to take South Africa's leadership legacy to the next level, firstly as an example to the world and secondly proactively taking it to the world.

South Africans must elect and choose leaders that truly attempt to take our leadership legacy forward, so that we can fulfil our peculiar destiny, which means we have a collective responsibility as a nation.

Our South African leadership essence is one of unselfishly uniting around the creation of positive movement towards the perceived impossible, while fearlessly, openly embracing and confronting all perceived negatives, obstacles and constraints along the way. Furthermore, the essence of the universal process used by successful leaders in South Africa is one of extraordinarily high levels of thinking, feeling, desiring, embracing and becoming.

I am speaking here of leadership that understands that in order to get a situation out of a deep hole it needs to create an opposing pole equal to the depth of the problem – an impossible vision that over time is understood (thinking), felt (feeling), desired, embraced by most – and where followers and a country eventually become something greater. It is about creating impossible movement, against impossible resistance, towards becoming the impossible. As the great man said: 'It always seems impossible until it's done.'

It has taken me 29 years to process and understand an instruction given to me by a wise and inspired man. To all South Africans I therefore loudly proclaim that we belong to a great nation, chosen above all others to fulfil our peculiar destiny of demonstrating, beyond Nelson Mandela, this leadership that the world is craving. We understand contention and discord on a deep level because we have tasted it. We should therefore understand and strive for its opposite on a deep level, which is true unity, and then live it! We experienced movement from sure disaster to the perceived impossible of unity and growth, performance and improvement, so let us continue doing this, from the top down!

This book, emanating from the crucible of South Africa, is an attempt to bring to the attention of the world that brand of leadership it so badly needs. It is based not only on personal experience but on hundreds of interviews with very successful individuals, one-on-one sessions with senior executives, interactions with youth and so on.

In *Seamless Leadership* short chapters focus on a seamless leader's attitude towards certain principles, with added sections on principles learned from personal leadership conversations with individuals from different sectors of society, over many years [of my column in *Business Report* and *Star Workplace*], ranging from President Jacob Zuma to Helen Zille and Sizwe Nxasana to Mike Brown.

I do not necessarily hold these leaders up as perfect examples of seamless leadership, but as individuals who possess elements of this attitude, or whose interview highlights a certain seamless leadership principle. I also deliberately place names of 'competitors' next to each other throughout the book (Zuma/Zille; Nxasana/Brown), to drive home a principle. Though competition is part and parcel of society, those with a seamless leadership attitude tend to rise above it for the achievement of a much bigger purpose. I trust that this approach will open your eyes to an attitude towards life and leadership that brings much more satisfaction, joy, fulfilment and full potential for yourself, others and society at large.

CHAPTER 1

||||||||||||||||||||||||||||||||||||||||||||||||||||||||||||||||||||||||||||||||||||||||||||||||||||||

A leadership attitude for our times

WITH
- ❏ *Mark Cutifani*
- ❏ *Gareth Cliff*
- ❏ *Dr Iqbal Survé*

The world has changed dramatically since the 1990s, not only in economics, security, technology, attitudes, fashion, and politics, but also – and perhaps most of all – from the leadership point of view. Persistent economic and political volatility across the globe is accompanied by pervasive distrust between leaders, and between leaders and followers. It also seems that all too often the complex challenges leaders face outweigh their capabilities and expose the weaknesses in their leadership attitudes.

Are current leadership philosophies and development methodologies failing? At the very least it is reasonable to assume that they do not address the deep-rooted attitudes of leaders and how they approach their roles. All the efforts of authors and experts at putting forward sound leadership philosophies do not seem to have been persuasive enough for them to adopt an attitude that will really make organisations, society and the world a better place.

Gill Marcus, former Governor of the South African Reserve Bank, believes that, in the global financial tsunami, as she calls it, leaders must act for the greater good rather than for the good of themselves or their party or whatever entity they represent. Referring to the USA, she commented: 'Why is there such indecisive leadership? It is because there is national interest and party interest, at a time when we need decisive and coherent leadership, in the interest of all of us.'

For Marcus the biggest challenge leaders face globally, including here in South Africa, is confidence and trust: 'Nobody trusts any more, and yet this is crucial to solve the current global economic dilemma. If global leaders through the various institutions and meetings commit to doing something, it seems that the markets don't trust it is going to happen. We are experiencing a situation where citizens, particularly in the advanced economies, don't have confidence and trust in their leadership at any level, particularly political. Until trust and confidence is rebuilt, it will be very difficult to stabilise the global economy.'

What is going on? Why is there this lack of trust and confidence, when the world is flooded with leadership courses and literature containing advice on how to earn the trust of followers, and how to be a confident leader? Why do leaders struggle to win the trust of their people? Do followers sense incongruent motives – in other words, are leaders perceived as unauthentic – even though so much is written about authentic leadership? Are leaders not trained well enough? Are followers expecting too much?

I trust that reading this book will bring some clarity. Its purpose is to introduce a leadership philosophy whose time has come; that will take society to a better place and, if adhered to, change the world in a positive way; move it towards becoming more true to its intended destiny, a place where leaders and followers trust one another again; where the title of leader regains its rightful and honourable place in society.

You can see that I believe leadership to be an honour, not a right. It should not automatically be viewed as a synonym for 'privileged' or 'elite' or 'popular' or 'well known' or 'powerful'.

To introduce a message of such importance we have to start at the beginning and shift the reader's mind towards universal, 'big picture' thinking. Why is this so important?

So often, if not always, what helps and motivates us to resolve huge challenges in our personal lives, in business and in society, is the context of a much bigger picture, a goal, vision or purpose that frames the obstacle staring us in the face. This principle most certainly applied during the miraculous political transition of South Africa in the early 1990s. The dream of a better society outweighed individual and selfish agendas. This made it possible to overcome huge challenges and odds.

In life and leadership the following principle holds true: the further we see, the further we can go; the bigger the picture we see at any given moment, the bigger our dream and vision can be. In sum, greater context results in greater decisions. Therefore, if we hope to solve these potential global leadership crises, we need to start with the biggest and most universal picture possible, so that the context and motivation to confront the challenge can overshadow the task.

The big picture of life

Briefly, let's view life from a simple, logical angle; a big picture that hopefully makes sense to most, across differing beliefs. Embracing this picture could significantly influence your current approach to life and leadership.

There are over 7 billion people on the planet – and that's not counting the people who have already come and gone, and those of the future. Every one of these human beings enters this world through birth, and – sooner or later – leaves it through death. It is mind-boggling to contemplate that every one of these individuals is unique in the combination of their physical features, geography, language, beliefs, culture and much more. Why do all these different individuals exist on this planet? What is the purpose of being here? Perhaps, if we can establish what we have in common, we will find a clue and even answers to these important questions.

Not by chance, it seems, in between the two opposite ends of life – 'entry' (birth) and 'exit' (death) – each one of the billions of visitors to this earth experiences the following five fundamentals:

1. **Experience SITUATIONS:** From infancy through early childhood, early teens through teenage years, young adulthood through to old age, birth to death, from the minute we wake up every day until we go to bed, seven days a week, 365 days a year, we gain knowledge and – mostly – understanding through never-ending situations that cross our path. Some situations are unforeseen or outside our

control; some happen through our own doing. They come in shapes and forms that can be seen as either negative or positive.

2. **Experience PEOPLE (relationships):** The moment 7 billion of us were born we were surrounded – for better or worse – by people. It seems life cannot happen without other people, and situations mostly involve other human beings, directly or indirectly. In short, we are here together and not alone.

3. **Experience freedom of CHOICE (decisions):** Especially as we grow older, all of us have the freedom to choose how we react to innumerable situations. Then we also have a choice as to how to utilise the knowledge and understanding gained in our lives. We have to choose how we respond to human beings around us, to different relationships. And, we choose what our attitude is from situation to situation. All this happens within certain boundaries. Eventually we also use our knowledge and understanding to benefit ourselves or to benefit others and society, or both.

   The boundaries within which we exercise our freedom of choice are put there in several ways. First, there is society in general, in the shape of government and other institutions that create laws and rules within which we operate. When our choices take us outside these boundaries we usually experience some sort of reprimand, intended to bring us back within the boundaries. Second, our belief and value system, mostly by way of cultural background, religion or simply a belief in right and wrong and what lifestyle brings happiness and peace, also places boundaries in our lives. Then, thirdly, boundaries are also created in our own minds by way of personal perceptions about ourselves and what we can and cannot achieve. These personal perception boundaries in our own minds may be the most difficult boundaries to overcome. But more about this later.

4. **Experience OBSTACLES, challenges:** We all encounter challenges, trials, and obstacles of varying magnitude along the way, whether directly or indirectly (through others). It seems that these obstacles are placed here to help us grow character, to test us to the limit, to discover how we will choose, with the knowledge and understanding

gained. The outcome of situations over time also results in perceptions about ourselves, as mentioned above, which quite possibly become the greatest advantage or obstacle to achieving our full potential.

5. **Experience MOVEMENT:** Throughout all the situations, associations with people and obstacles that confront us, we end up making decisions so that we can move forward in life and in relationships. If we don't make decisions we will mostly stand still. When something or someone stands still, it will stagnate, or even die, literally in some cases. Movement comprises growth, development, improvement or change. Life on this earth is about movement. Movement is life.

I call these five commonalities the **SiPCOM Experience**, which in short captures the truth that all visitors to this planet continually experience Situations (experiences); People (relationships); Choices (decisions); Obstacles (or challenges); and Movement (growth, development). We cannot escape the SiPCOM Experience! And the 'COM' in SiPCOM reminds us that all people have this experience in COMMON.

Why these relentless situations? Why are we so intimately linked to other people? Why the freedom to choose? Why all these obstacles and challenges? Why must we move forward? Why are we on this planet?

How to make the best of our journey through life

Planet Earth is the place where we experience SiPCOM; where we are offered the privilege of implementing and practising the five COMmonalities; where we gain experience in these five categories. It all seems to be for a good reason: the world is a huge obstacle course or testing ground that offers its inhabitants an experience of a lifetime! You are thrust into a continuous (no turning back) cycle of gaining knowledge and understanding, through never-ending SITUATIONS, mostly involving other PEOPLE and requiring constant CHOICES (decision making), accompanied by regular OBSTACLES and challenges, in order to MOVE forward. It sounds like a 'Lord of the Rings' type of journey, doesn't it? The only way is forward, to some place (because one can't make worthwhile decisions without the context of some future), and the outcome can only be **personal growth, building character and relationships, learning to make decisions and experiencing movement or success.** Of course, the journey involves a risk of failure, too, especially when you add to the mix a conscious decision to make full use of opportunities rather than be an indifferent bystander. In short, SiPCOM is the perfect recipe for moving closer towards one's full potential.

Just from a logical perspective, it may be difficult to comprehend that this awesome, adventurous journey continues beyond the gateway that we call death. I believe that it has to, and that those of us who make the best of this part of the much bigger journey will be better prepared for whatever lies ahead.

How does one 'make the best' of this journey on Planet Earth? After all, we are here and we can only move forward. There is no turning back. We need to take full advantage of SiPCOM, which means we have to develop the abilities and skills to confidently engage situations, people, choices (decisions), obstacles or challenges, for movement within the context of this bigger picture. It will help if we can create a context, make what happens now – today – count, crucially by deciding where we want to move to, where we are going, where and how we want to 'end up'. In that way we become a 'forward thinker', a 'movement specialist'.

Create movement by becoming a forward thinker: Some situations are unforeseen or out of our control; others are expected or our own doing. We may as well try to determine or influence the 'own doing' part as much as we can, for the right reasons. Strangely enough, as we do this we end up giving more meaning and context to most of the unforeseen or 'out of our control' situations as well.

To take a very simple example, during grade 9 of high school years a decision must be made about what school subjects to take for the remaining three years. This falls in the category that is outside of the child's control, though not unforeseen, and there is no option but to make a choice; no alternative, except perhaps to drop out of school. A youngster who is fortunate enough to have done a bit of forward thinking by deciding where he or she wants to go in life, career-wise, because of some knowledge gained through exposure (more situations, more experience), will make wiser decisions. Those who know where they want to move to will possess the necessary context to make the situation and decision count, and in so doing allow seamless movement forward. In this instance the 'out of your control' situation is transformed into the 'own doing' category. It builds character, because the child moves forward with determination, actually wanting to make the decision as opposed to being forced to.

Compare the child who has no plans for the future. The 'outside your control' situation remains as such; it is not about wanting to make the decision so much as avoiding it: the choice of subjects may be those that will bring the most ease and comfort in the short term – the easier ones. This may have impacts later in life – but does it mean that an undecided child, or a late developer, is lost? Of course not. The consequences of the decision may yet turn into a character-building experience as he or she matures and realises that a chosen career cannot immediately be pursued because a bridging course is necessary. This happened to me and I think I turned out all right. However, I would still advocate the first option as the best one.

In this example we see the value of forward thinking and how it assists a child to move forward seamlessly, to make the best of a situation right now. In fact, we often speak about being present in the moment, in order to appreciate a situation to its fullest. Being a forward thinker helps us to live more effectively in the moment. Unknowingly this child is developing an ability to create movement in life, applying a universal skill that gives context and meaning to the situations, people, choices, obstacles and movement that comprise SiPCOM. If parents and teachers promote awareness of the fact that a universal skill is being developed, this will make it even more beneficial.

It is mostly our vision of the future – whether immediate or distant – that triggers and influences our decision making. I am hungry; what shall I have for breakfast (30 seconds into the future)? I want to get to work within 30 minutes; should I take the route through suburbs or on the highway? I want to be fit and slimmer in six months; shall I run or attend gym, or both? I want to meet someone special in my life; shall I accept that blind date or go online? I want to become the CEO of this organisation one day; shall I take on this next challenge as manager in another country or study further, or both? I want to have a happy family; should I work day and night to maximise earnings or cut down on the working hours and spend more time with the kids? If I pay this bribe once I will close this large deal in the near future and earn lots of money and acceptance soon after, but I also value honesty; what shall I do?

There are innumerable possible examples of how the desire to attain a goal – a future state, a dream, a vision, a destiny ... or, in short, where you want to end up – gives context to today's decisions and movement. As mentioned earlier, one can't make worthwhile decisions without the context of some desired future state. The clearer the future picture is, the clearer the decision making process. This means being a forward thinker is a critical skill in being a good decision maker and mover. Remember, the further we see, the further we can go; the bigger the picture we see at any given moment, the bigger our dream and vision can be; greater context brings greater decisions.

Make relationships meaningful: So we are here on this earth with others. We may as well make such associations as meaningful as possible. As they say, 'don't burn your bridges'. If we have no option but to live this life with other human beings and in the process we can't help but build relationships, why waste the opportunity? It wouldn't make sense.

How does one make relationships as meaningful as possible? Logically, if life becomes more meaningful when we make full use of SiPCOM, then relationships will become more meaningful when we somehow assist others to acquire the abilities to effectively engage SiPCOM, so that they too can build character more consciously. **To do this is to take a leap towards becoming a leader.** Life then becomes more meaningful both for others and for ourselves. It does not make sense for us to consciously experience SiPCOM and move towards our full potential in isolation. Help others to do the same and then life will have much more joy and fulfilment as we surround ourselves with people who experience joy and fulfilment themselves.

Hence, the core purpose of life is ... Together with others, to embrace situations, people, choices, obstacles and movement (SiPCOM) fully, as a forward thinker, to grow and develop one's own character, and build the characters of others and society, to experience full joy, fulfilment and potential in this life, and perhaps beyond.

I truly believe that all indicators point to the core purpose of living on this planet being to grow and develop the remarkable potential that has been planted inside every human being, including YOU. It is however up to us (choice) to gain knowledge and understanding about what exactly this potential can be and then make the decision to define that destiny or future potential – for ourselves, our marriage, our family, our career, our business, our community and even our country. And then, as we and others move towards the defined potential, learn to deal with the obstacles and challenges that will come our way as sure as night follows day. But, it starts with us.

In short, if all 7 billion (and more) human beings have SiPCOM in common, and if embracing and then sharing it results in their becoming leaders, then it seems our experience on earth is actually an intense leadership development programme for all of us. *We are here to continue learning to become leaders.* The aim of this book is to introduce to as many as possible an attitude that embraces and engages SiPCOM, consciously making full use of this earthly experience to evolve into thinking and acting like a leader, and then becoming one.

As more and more individuals are persuaded to adopt this attitude I am confident that the ripple effect will lead to an improvement of society at large. The kind of people we hope to multiply will ensure this world remains true to its destiny of being a worthy testing ground that assists human beings to become the best leaders they can be. I call this kind of person a **seamless leader**. By the way, the 'S' in SiPCOM reminds us of *Seamless* leadership.

And now, I passionately invite you on a seamless leadership journey.

Mark Cutifani – CEO Anglo American

Seamless Leadership Principles:
1. Look out for the seamless leader attitude that Cutifani possesses. Is it any wonder he is leading one of the largest mining houses in the world?
2. Try to see signs of his attitude towards SiPCOM. There are many to pick from, including:
   - Big picture thinking
   - Emphasis on people
   - Emphasis on creating movement

When I sat down with Mark Cutifani he was the leader of AngloGold Ashanti, the most widespread and balanced gold company in the world, with a presence in 25 countries and approximately 63 000 employees, half of whom were in South Africa. They generated about $9 billion a year, with approximately $3 billion cash with which to pay dividends, add to capital, etc. Shortly after our conversation he was elevated to global CEO for Anglo American.

As a gold company, what AngloGold Ashanti does is technically not simple as it mines some of the deepest mines in the world. There are challenges like safety, environmental management, community relationships, and a whole range of other complexities. Yet, while Cutifani was CEO they aimed to grow the business by about 25 per cent over the next three years and to be one of the top five mining companies in the world. Cutifani and his team aimed high, and it certainly seemed near impossible to achieve that without a very high level of commitment from the workforce. So, people had to be the most important assets inside AngloGold Ashanti, or not?

During his first meeting with staff, in his first week, he made a statement:

'People are not our most important assets.' Of course there was a deathly silence, and then he continued: 'People are more than assets. People *are* the business. I am not a chair, or a table, or even an ounce of gold or a building. These are all assets. I'm more than an asset; I'm a person that can contribute in various ways. At the end of the day, when we as managers sit back and reflect on why we are here, why we do what we do, we do it with people; it's for people. Every conversation we have is directed for and with people.' According to Cutifani, 'if you strip everything aside, leadership is about people, because people are the business'.

When a leader makes such a statement, everything he does must be in line with this ethos. What does he do by way of example to authenticate his strong belief in people? For Cutifani, symbols are very important in leadership, so he listed a few things he does on a daily basis as he heads for the office. For example, when he drives in he acknowledges every individual, including the security guard, with a friendly thumbs-up or wave. Then, he does not have a designated CEO parking space. He says: 'I am like everybody else. I come to work; I get paid for being here. If I am last in the morning and it means I have to walk 200 metres, that's okay. Like everybody else, I come here to do the best I can and go home to my family.' Walking from his car he acknowledges every person in the car park.

When Cutifani started as CEO it seemed like 'everybody walked head down, not acknowledging one another or saying hello,' but not long after he walked through the offices in such a way that he could greet everybody. Cutifani does not have a door to his office. If he is in his office anyone in the organisation may walk in and engage him. When he is in his back room it means he is doing something with or without someone where he prefers not to be disturbed. He insists that everybody calls him by his name and not '*Meneer*' or 'Sir'. He does not wear a tie, to go with the informal environment. He answers every email he receives from an employee within 48 hours, nine times out of ten. He does these little things very deliberately 'to demonstrate that AngloGold Ashanti is about people'.

What prepared Cutifani most for his overwhelming leadership task was all the experiences (and mistakes he made) over the years – and his ability to learn from these mistakes. But a very important influence on him as a leader has been his exposure to a researcher called Dr Elliott Jaques and his Requisite Organisation theory. According to Cutifani, Jaques acknowledges that 'leadership is about, firstly, capability and understanding of what the issues are, and being able to understand and solve or navigate through complex areas, to add value to those in the organisation that can't necessarily see where the pathway is'.

Cutifani likes this approach and adds that recognising capability and the ability of individuals to see and solve complex problems is a starting point to recognising talent within the organisation. He believes this ability is identifiable at a very early age – watch out for individuals who seem to solve complex challenges with relative ease! After identifying such individuals early in their careers a leader should try to give them as much exposure as possible so that they can develop a broad range of skills.

Cutifani comments: 'The real role of leadership is to make it very clear to people at all levels of the organisation what their role is, how they make a contribution and what they can do to make a difference within the organisation – and, very importantly, have them feel like they are making a contribution that is making a difference.'

To him leadership is also about articulating a vision and helping people feel what that vision is. But he adds: 'The ability, then, to put the people, the processes and the structures in place to actually align the work that happens on a daily basis, is the management part of leadership. And, if you don't have the management part of leadership, all you have is exhortation. If you have the management part you have the substance that backs it up and reinforces the role of the leader in being able to take the organisation through to delivering something special.'

Cutifani struck me as a leader with insight and wisdom. He seems to implement a leadership approach that is able to embrace and navigate through the complex times we live in. I wondered whether he was not at times frustrated when his employees or other leaders around him just couldn't see the bigger picture. His response was again indicative of a big picture thinker: 'Leaders are fully accountable for the impact they have on others. At the end of the day there is no point in getting frustrated, because I am accountable. What I have to do is think through how I can better land the message. Because the minute the leader starts blaming someone else, by for example saying "I can't get the message through," you are immediately saying the recipient is a dummy. The minute you think that, go and look in the mirror and come to grips with who the dummy is. Your job as the leader is to deliver the message. And leadership is patience.' If he cannot convince someone of his argument, then it is not well structured or he hasn't understood where the person is coming from. And, of course, 'their view may be right, which is why I can't convince them,' he adds.

About eight years ago Cutifani and his then management team were discussing a specific issue where half the management team got the point and the other half continued asking questions that he found annoying. Instead of listening he started lecturing. The more the team pushed back the louder Cutifani got. During a subsequent 360 feedback it surfaced that when he could not land the message he would get more difficult and start to lecture. He learnt that 'at the end of the day you are accountable for how you land the message. Lecturing isn't going to help. Take a step back, listen to the question and work with them on the question, and you may find that you get to a common landing a lot quicker.'

I believe that in South Africa we have extraordinary leadership challenges and we pride ourselves on our diversity. To successfully engage at least these dynamics, leaders must learn the art of avoiding 'restrictive leadership' by adopting its opposite, which is 'seamless leadership' – leading with a balanced big picture in mind, while, in an inclusive manner, confidently confronting barriers and boundaries to full potential of whatever entity. No doubt Cutifani is not perfect, and he and his management team will know this. But he certainly strives to demonstrate the qualities of a seamless leader.

Q&A

||||||||||||||||||||||||||||||||||||||||||||||||||||||||||||||||||||||||||||||||||||||||||||||||||||||||||||||||||||||||||||||||||||||||||||||||||||||||||||||||||||||||||

Q: Tell us something about your childhood that helped prepare you for leadership.

Cutifani: I was born and raised in an industrial town just south of Sydney, Australia, where coal mining was prevalent. I am a product of a mixed family. My father was Italian, a migrant at about 19 years of age, and he couldn't speak a word of the language. My mother is from an Irish background but Australian-born. Her family owned pubs. So you had a young Italian migrant and an Australian girl with an Irish background. Quite a volatile pairing. I was the oldest of three kids that had to be responsible, with dad working far away. Quite often when my parents had conversations or arguments they would talk at cross purposes, totally missing one another. I learnt to listen with different ears, to never take the words in the way they were expressed. It was the context and pieces around the conversation that mattered. I often found myself interpreting one parent's comments to the other, as the oldest child.

This cultural experience growing up may have prepared me for my current job and from a management point of view to try and listen to the conversation very carefully and to listen beyond the actual words, as spoken from the heart. As a leader, first understand what the real issue is, and then you can respond and provide the leadership to people and address the issues they need leadership for.

Q: Where does your value system come from?
Cutifani: Australia was a very racist society. As a kid growing up, the fact that my father was a very dark man meant that I was very different, and the Cutifani name was not that common either. In our town I was in a fight probably every other day for being called certain names. I think through those early years the issue of prejudice or the way you treat people, and that basic sense of humanity was something you sort of wished you had. What I went through was nothing, I would imagine, compared to what happened in other places in the world. But it had that much of an impact that, to me, everyone is an individual; they are different and in fact you should celebrate their differences. It is all about who we are and relationships. And my father was a friendly person with everyone. He just did not see issues of colour, race or whatever. My mother's family basically kicked her out of the family for marrying him. So we were somewhat isolated, it was just our family. Loyalty, honesty and trust were deeply seated.

Q: There seems to be less and less trust between leaders and followers the world over. Your comments?

Cutifani: First point I want to make is that you are not a leader if you have not established trust. So we have lots of people in leadership positions, but they are not leaders. Leaders build trust. And if you asked how one builds an effective organisation where people work together, it is when there is trust, which is the thing that binds. People in leadership positions make a mistake by acting like physicists – everything can be reduced to an equation, where the answer is correct, or it is an absolute that is well defined. Leadership is more than numbers or the facts that you deal with on a day-to-day basis. The other and critical part of leadership is the philosophy part, the sense that you are building people, and that you care; that they are part of the process, and that they are being listened to.

At the end of the day there are more people with a better standard of living in the world today than there have ever been. Yet one would say that we are seeing millions of people feeling disenfranchised, treated unfairly; leaders of major companies with their hands in the till; politicians we don't trust; and people are more unhappy than they were 10, 20 or more years ago. I think we are on the cusp of a change, and the change is around the sense that people in leadership positions are not listening; they are not responding to the social needs that people feel. Ultimately leadership is about getting the balance between the physicist and the philosopher, and building trust with people, which is the philosophy part that I think we have lost.

Q: Are we developing better leaders than in the past, or are we as a society missing something?

Cutifani: The challenge in many business schools is we have reduced leadership to a series of defined practices with expected outcomes. It's more than that. There is a soul in there somewhere. There is a heart. Leadership is listening and understanding the issues that drive people. In their own life they are looking for someone that's got a better sense of where we should be going and they are looking for leadership. What we are trying to do in AngloGold Ashanti with various programmes is to build relationships. I marvel at the ability Mandela had to get South Africans talking to each other. But my fear is that after him we reduced the relationships in this country to numbers. It's actually the sincerity, and the humanity and the relationships, and how we come together that matters. Real leadership is about both the relationships and the numbers.

Q: What is the impact of your leadership beyond this organisation?

Cutifani: From a mining industry point of view, I am the Vice-President of the Chamber of Mines. I think we as an industry have to listen more carefully to society; we have to work with the government and all key stakeholders in creating a different image and a different engagement process. I think we have to do a better job in society. So my role on the Chamber is about supporting us as an industry to achieve this while also improving our sustainability performance. And ultimately it is a better thing for our industry and for society. As a CEO my job is to make the world a better place.

I am also a spokesman for health matters for Business Leadership South Africa (BLSA). I was volunteered because I had a view on the health system. And, I serve on the advisory committees for several international universities, from Cape Town to Chicago to Brazil, and have now been invited to become an advisor on Columbia University's sustainability strategy group. So, education and developing and growing leadership, and changing the way industry works within society, is part of my contribution.

Q: And in one sentence, why do you do all of this?

Cutifani: I want to make a difference. I hope the world is a better place for my kids.

Gareth Cliff – Co-founder CliffCentral, Idols South Africa judge, and much more

Seamless Leadership Principles:
1. Notice the emphasis on the new follower that leaders have to deal with.
2. Look out for signs of seamless leadership in Cliff, together with other principles leaders need to be aware of as they strive to navigate themselves and their followers in this new world.

On 18 July 2013 my leadership session with the leader of a large law firm was interrupted because he had to go down to the lobby of their building to lead his colleagues in holding hands for Nelson Mandela, for 67 seconds. Of course, they – and what seemed to be the rest of South Africa – were following an initiative referred to as 'Hands Across South Africa', driven by Gareth Cliff of 5FM and SA Idols.

In his blog on 12 July Cliff had put forward an idea: 'Imagine a South Africa where everyone joined forces to work together towards a vibrant, integrated country.' Truth is that the level of unity equals the level of movement, or performance. Based on this principle alone our country's performance seems to indicate low levels of unity. Any initiative to improve this is therefore a good one. The #HandsAcrossSA call was 'Let's make some "Madiba Magic" happen! Whatever your age, race, gender or colour ... wherever you are ... whether you're at home or work, at school, college, university, shopping, or even in the car or taxi ... join hands across South Africa on Mandela Day, Thursday 18th July at 8:45 am for 67 seconds.'

The response to this call to all South Africans was overwhelming, to the point that Cliff, together with the legendary Professor Jonathan Jansen of the University of the Free State, decided to take it to the next level. In September 2013, following a more formal launch of #HandsAcrossSA, the call was: 'We felt the euphoria on Mandela Day, now let's give everybody a chance to keep talking; tell us what you are doing; we must all share in this responsibility. First of all take responsibility for yourself, and then we can start looking at how we can spread good messages, make positive changes, join projects that are already doing good things. And, everybody, let's just be part of a family that is moving forward rather than a family that is retrogressing.'

According to Cliff, South Africans have a desire to be part of something positive, as seen on Mandela Day. But a barrier to us uniting is in fact individual cultures that separate us rather than an overarching 'South African-ness' where we appreciate the diversity. It is a barrier, he explains, 'because it has become something one cannot criticise'. Another barrier, according to Cliff, is 'the fact that we are not honest with one another. In some cultures it is about not wanting to upset others, or feel awkward about a specific topic.' He feels many prefer to be diplomatic rather than honest, pretending all is okay rather than confronting the relevant issue.

I believe that leaders are in the business of creating movement. Cliff creates movement. Question is, what movement, and does #HandsAcrossSA answer this question? Often when I am presenting a slide show to an audience of some of the leaders I have engaged and the name of Gareth Cliff appears, a debate follows on whether someone like him is in fact a leader. Let us settle this once and for all. He has over 2 million listeners on his national morning show on 5 FM; he is a judge on SA Idols with millions of viewers; he has almost 600 000 friends on Facebook; he has over 500 000 followers on Twitter; he is an ambassador for the 'Step up let's lead' initiative, and much more. Is he a leader? Of course he is.

These days not only the young but even many older individuals are influenced by his opinions and views, which he makes known on a regular basis. Even hard-core lawyers followed his call for holding hands on Mandela Day. He does not lead a formal structure, like a political party, or a large corporate listed on the Johannesburg Stock Exchange, or even a state-owned enterprise. He is somehow surrounding himself with a following through another structure called social media.

Cliff seems to be a leader in the new reality, where the attitude of the so-called 'followers' is changing, or to a large degree has already changed dramatically. I have observed that many leaders are struggling to lead these new followers, to really understand them. And how can you lead effectively when you don't understand your follower and his/her attitude or outlook on life?

So who is this new follower, who has emerged at an alarming pace, competing for a voice for change and a new way of living, doing, leading? It is someone who is better informed than ever; someone with a view and opinion, even though at times it may be void of wisdom; someone who does not just respect authority blindly; someone who wants to be involved in decision making, yet also wants their leader to be strong and decisive; someone who may still be in the process of defining their own identity within an environment that moves forward at an ever-increasing pace; someone who wants to be successful 'yesterday'; someone who understands the world of social media, which creates a feeling and often reality of empowerment; someone who will never again be blindly mobilised by a politician, and perhaps any leader.

This new follower is being shaped by societal leaders like Cliff. He is on the fringe of influencing the 'new' attitude of those that CEOs and politicians attempt to lead. As an example, when Cliff proclaims assertively that the days of people accessing daily information through reading newspapers are over, then, whether this is true or not, it may very well become a reality because societal leaders like him say so. Thousands of followers who may still be reading newspapers daily start believing they are outdated and need to get with the times, to start tweeting. Or, if he states publicly that Julius Malema has become irrelevant, then this may very well become the reality. Cliff may argue that he simply reiterates what happens out there or what is already discussed privately around dinner tables and around the braai. But the mere fact that he confidently raises these views on powerful platforms changes the game, takes the trend to another level and adds momentum that leads to societal change.

Understand that his views are not only expressed on air, to disappear as soon as he walks out of the studio. They trend on Twitter and become a topic of discussion on Facebook and then even find their way into what used to be the main platforms for influencing, like newspapers and maga-zines. In short, as a leader you may want to consider following someone like Gareth Cliff in order to gain a better understanding of your own fol-lowers.

His personal aspiration is this: 'Show off the good and let them know they are not alone; and change the minds of the bad.' And then he adds this plea: 'Let's join hands and make it get better. The symbolism and feel-ing of what we did on Mandela Day was great! The feeling is what makes people get married. It is the feeling that makes people stand up for what they believe. Let's not pooh-pooh something like a bunch of people join-ing hands for a couple of seconds as a once-off gesture that does not have staying power. It stays in your head, it stays on your Facebook profile, it stays in your opinion on Twitter, and in the conversations you have with your own family, your teachers, students and friends.'

You may not listen to Cliff's show in the mornings, or follow him on Twitter; you may not agree with his sense of humour or his views on some issues. But you have to start taking him seriously as a leader and influencer in South Africa. He is becoming a real game changer on several fronts.

One thing is certain, that with the influence he has, all South Africans can be grateful for his burning desire for our country to be successful, that he wants to positively influence the future of this nation, which he believes is a wonderful one.

Dr Iqbal Survé – CEO Sekunjalo

Seamless Leadership Principles:
1. Look out for the seamless leader attitude that Dr Survé possesses.
2. Look out for signs of his attitude towards simplicity, universality, big picture context and much more.

He has to be one of the most discreet, influential, wealthy and successful individuals in South Africa. He is well-read, well-travelled and well-connected, with a clear sense of purpose to make a difference to the big picture. His aspirations are: 'To create a more just society in which one day I can say I played a role in its creation. I make no bones about my entrepreneurial drive which has made me a very rich man but I don't want to die a very rich man, I want to die as a man who used his resources in a small way and changed the world.'

Dr Survé explains further how he practically incorporates these aspirations into his daily life. Every day he affords himself a few minutes of meditation in the mornings and in the evenings, then asks himself the following questions: 'What good will I do today?' and then in the evening: 'What could I have done differently?' At the end of his life, he wants to be proud of his answers to these two questions, and feel 'that there is no deficit with respect to having made a difference in this country, the continent and the world'.

Sitting with this successful man was most interesting. He recently saved Independent Newspapers from its downward spiral under Irish reign; he regularly enjoys dinner with leaders like Bill and Hillary Clinton, as a founding member of their Clinton Global Initiative; he co-chairs the WEF Global Growth Company Board; he is a founding member of the BRICS

Business Council; he is a council member of the Global Agenda Council for Emerging Multinationals and the World Economic Forum; and he has accompanied all four South African presidents since democracy to global conferences and state visits. It sparked a feeling of hope for our continent and its potential, to know that leaders like Survé still back Africa, and put their money and energy where their mouth is.

He is not an ordinary leader and thinker and supports a different mind-set for leaders, which is probably exactly what we need in order to take this country and continent to the next level. Do not expect the status quo when he walks through the front door. If you do, you might as well walk out the back door.

The change of leader at the University of Cape Town (UCT) Graduate School of Business serves as an example. As Chair of the School he knew they needed someone who would create a programme to enhance leaders' capacity to manage complexity. This individual also needed to understand the social relevance of the content that is taught, the importance of entre-preneurship, and to improve on the School's ability to develop innovative thinking in leaders. They appointed Professor Walter Baets in 2009, and what movement has occurred at UCT Graduate School of Business since this change? They employ 25 more people than in the past; they have more money than they have ever had; they have all the accreditation from across the world that a business school needs; and their content ranks with the best out there, which is amazing considering the funding available to UCT compared with, for example, Harvard. The message to leaders is that what they needed the new Director to achieve reflects those attributes that are crucial for leaders who want to lead successfully in our country and continent, which is in a transformation phase – politically, economically, structurally and socially – against the backdrop of a global, complex village.

Survé believes that leaders of today have to be schooled in complexity management. Many would not necessarily name former President Mandela as a brilliant complexity manager. According to Survé, who knew Mandela well from several angles, 'his strength was that he was able to simplify complex issues so easily and disarm people in that simplicity because he was able to solve the relevant problem'. South Africa needs leaders who understand our extremes and difficulties, but 'who do not allow that to overwhelm their thinking, because the default position of all people is to choose a side you are most familiar with, based on where you come from, because that is how the brain naturally thinks,' explains Survé.

To perform in today's increasingly complex world a leader must train his mind to often choose that road that is opposite to the natural choice. We need leaders who can reframe the status quo rather than do what has always been done, 'thinking through the noise, challenges and seeing the answer, then working your way towards the answer through simple steps'. This, according to Survé, is where Mandela was so brilliant.

Survé has a very interesting and unique background and career that prepared him well for the current role he plays in Africa. This journey included being a medical doctor as part of a support team for the late Nelson Mandela, together with being an entrepreneur and philanthropist friend to the icon; being a 'mind-coach' for Bafana Bafana (when they did so well in the mid-1990s) and the Olympic team; developing post-traumatic stress disorder rehabilitation programmes in support of young people who were scarred through torture and imprisonment during apartheid; being a serious entrepreneur as founder and CEO for Sekunjalo, and much more.

With all his exposure and rich background, fortunately he is a leader who likes to share knowledge and information. There is a tendency to believe that by keeping information exclusive one has a competitive edge, he comments, but 'I actually don't subscribe to that. I think we should open up information, even to your competitors, and that is actually going to make you far more effective.' His advisors often get nervous when he publicly states what he plans to do. In his view it boils down to confidence, really believing in what you are doing.

This confidence becomes almost indestructible when informed by an ability to think simply and universally, in a way that successfully navigates through a very challenging, complex, fast-paced world, which can be compared to the roundabouts still seen in some public parks. Children get on to these structures and spin around, faster and faster. They then jump off, feel dazed and get back on again. The environment can be compared to this: it spins around and is getting faster all the time; everything impacts on everything; and if leaders don't discipline themselves to go to the centre but remain on the outskirts of this spinning environment they will eventually be flung off.

Survé agrees and adds: 'We all move away from the centre at times, be it when we buy a fancy sports car, a boat, becoming angry in times of stress. Holding the centre together is very important. Part of the movement I am trying to foster in South Africa is to get more leaders into that centre. There are those that become very wealthy and successful with their businesses, but in time they will suffer because they haven't taken the time to go to the centre.'

In South Africa and globally, going to the centre is not necessarily about holding a powerful position but rather about a powerful attitude that automatically manifests in certain behaviour, which in turn results in the development of certain attributes, which are eventually entrenched into the very character and being of a leader, forever. So-called success becomes synonymous with such a character.

Survé describes this kind of character with reference to leaders like Nelson Mandela, Kwame Nkrumah, Patrice Lumumba, and Albert Luthuli: 'These leaders have in common humanity, respect and dignity for all. They were fearless and were prepared to sacrifice their lives in pursuit of their beliefs. They were values driven and committed to a society which treated people with equality and dignity. They shared more than just the resources but also their thinking and did not have a sense of personal entitlement. They were visionaries in that they crafted the future according to their principles and values no matter how difficult the journey to get to that perfect future and that perfect world which had harmony and peace and dignity for all that lived in it.'

In short, this attitude is about a passionate desire to master universal principles and the 'big picture' context that governs and maximises everyday situations and experiences, relationships with people, decision making (choices), confronting of barriers (obstacles), and movement towards full potential of self, others and society. This is the attitude that Nelson Mandela adopted; this is the attitude Dr Iqbal Survé adopted; this is the attitude all leaders in South Africa, Africa and beyond should adopt if we are going to move this continent forward successfully.

CHAPTER 2

||||||||||||||||||||||||||||||||||||||||||||||||||||||||||||||||||||||||||||||||||||||||||||||||||||||||

A seamless leadership journey

WITH
- *Adrian Gore*
- *Terry Volkwyn*

It is important to understand right from the start that seamless leadership is not about becoming perfect in this life or holding a powerful position, but rather about a powerful attitude that automatically results in certain behaviour, which in turn results in the development of certain attributes, which are eventually entrenched into one's very character and being, forever. So-called success becomes synonymous with such a character.

The seed of seamless thinking and eventually leadership seems to be planted inside every human being. However, it also seems that very few leaders, if any, demonstrate this type of leadership to the full in this lifetime. We are human, after all. It often seems that some individuals are just ahead of others when it comes to the skill of leading, and they peak early in life. Those who continue positively on their leadership journey go on to do great things in this life. Unfortunately some early peakers run out of steam because no one is there to share the principle of the universal SiPCOM experience to motivate them to continue progressing.

Sadly, society at large does not necessarily see and agree on this bigger universal picture or purpose of life, and so not enough effort is being made to progress leadership instincts in our children. Our decisions on how to develop and educate children are based on limited information. What we mostly focus on in educational institutions is technical knowledge and skills. And of course gaining knowledge of any kind is a good

35

thing as it serves the core purpose of life. But we can do more and speed up the multiplication of seamless leaders by catching them early on their journey. Parents who lovingly take their responsibilities seriously will probably progress the seamless leadership abilities of their children.

Because seamless leadership defines the highest level of leadership thinking and attitude that can be achieved, and probably needs even more than this earthly experience can offer to fully mature, we are still un-covering different dimensions of it. The best we can do is to expose our fellow travellers to seamless leadership, and then the choice is theirs as to whether or not they want to adopt the philosophy. I borrow a word from my first publication, *Moving Towards Your Leadership Destiny*, which is TiLi – Take it or Leave it. Hopefully the simplicity, logic and truth of what is shared in this book will trigger the desire in many to take it on board.

Seamless leader attitude

A seamless leader is distinguished by a passionate desire to master uni-versal principles and big picture context that governs and maximises SiPCOM:

- ❏ life situations and experiences
- ❏ relationships with people
- ❏ decision making (choices)
- ❏ confronting of barriers (obstacles)
- ❏ movement towards full potential of self, others and society.

Seamless leadership is so much about attitude. Seamless leaders adopt a certain attitude about life situations, about people, about decision mak-ing, about obstacles, about movement, about universal principles, about society, about full potential, and about themselves.

William James, a pioneering American psychologist and philosopher, wrote, 'The greatest revolution of our generation is the discovery that hu-man beings, by changing the inner attitudes of their minds, can change the outer aspects of their lives.' Seamless leaders really believe this.

And Charles Swindoll – author, educator, and Christian pastor – said:

'Attitude, to me, is more important than facts. It is more important than the past, the education, the money, than circumstances, than failure, than successes, than what other people think or say or do. It is more important than appearance, giftedness or skill. It will make or break a company ... a church ... a home ... I am convinced that life is 10 per cent what happens to me and 90 per cent of how I react to it. And so it is with you ... We are in charge of our ATTITUDES.'

To illustrate further, a seamless leader attitude can function at different levels. For example, a junior manager in a bank, who manages frontline staff, can demonstrate a 'lower level' seamless leader attitude by seeing a bigger picture beyond her responsible area only. She may for example attempt to really understand the branch goals, or the entire bank's strategic objectives and how these will impact their community, and do all within her power to align her small division with the bigger picture, and strive to communicate the bigger picture to her staff. Such a leader is starting to show signs of seamless leadership.

A mine manager who sees the bigger picture of how his mine affects the broader community and passionately attempts to make a difference in that community – and not only to achieve production targets – demonstrates an important element of a seamless leader attitude.

The same goes for any leader. When we see a bigger picture than the one we are directly responsible for and we try to positively impact this picture, we start stretching our leadership thinking, we start leading beyond our boundaries towards the perceived impossible, which requires bigger thinking and stretching of not only one's own capabilities but those of one's followers as well. This is part of seamless leadership, because stretching people takes them closer to their full potential.

Of course in both these examples the respective leaders can shift their attitude up a few levels by embracing a full seamless leader attitude. As they do this their performance (movement) will be much more significant and bigger, because their thinking, their picture and purpose are much bigger and more universal.

The more evolved seamless leader will therefore view his or her responsible area within a picture that spirals bigger and bigger, until it embraces the core purpose of life. The mine manager will understand and work towards the full potential of his mine, the larger company they are part of, the community around them. He will even see the national and international picture of his industry. And of course, amidst all this he will see the universal picture of the core purpose of life, which means we will see every day how he treats his people with respect and strives to maximise SiPCOM in their lives; how he helps them to confront barriers to their full potential. His decisions will mostly be unselfish, and will be made after considering the biggest possible picture, starting with individuals around him.

This is the power of a universal seamless leader attitude – it brings together the big picture and the immediate picture of self and those around us; and, it determines the principles and values through which we do this. In other words, a seamless leader who truly grasps the **universality** of SiPCOM will not only see the bigger picture but will also demonstrate through day-to-day interactions that situations are a privilege; that people are most important; that choices and decisions are critical; that obstacles and challenges are part of life and in fact contribute towards character building; and that movement is inevitable, and it is always the goal.

All leaders, whether ordinary or even great, will implement principles that govern and facilitate decision making and ensure movement and removal of barriers to the potential of themselves and their organisation. By the same token they will also assist others to move towards their full potential, because this is what happens when someone is part of positive movement.

It thus follows that many ordinary leaders are in a way serving the universal SiPCOM experience and by default doing good anyway. But more often than not their day-to-day actions are not necessarily aligned to the spirit of SiPCOM and the true attitude of a seamless leader. Perhaps they see the big picture, but drive towards it in the wrong way or for the wrong reasons (motives); or they may even lead in the right way with the right motives, but fail to see the bigger picture. Seamless leaders bring all of this together.

More and more in today's challenging and complex world, when leaders do not adhere to the bigger universal SiPCOM picture and purpose, the seamless leader way, then their motive may easily be corrupted or even replaced by a lower and more selfish purpose – for example, wanting power, or profit and wealth, or a large company for the sake of having one, or wealthy shareholders, or being in political power, or public recognition, and so on. It could even be all of the above, as these motives have an addiction of their own and easily feed off one another. Such motives are not higher, universal and timeless ones, although in today's so-called sophisticated yet materialistic and selfish world they are highly regarded and respected by many.

Perhaps here is where the incongruity lies; perhaps this is one of the core reasons why distrust between leaders and followers is being exposed like never before. Perhaps some leaders who act out certain philosophies, like 'servant leadership', are – deep down – pursuing the weaker motives that society seems to respect and handsomely rewards. No matter how hard they try, those around them sense that something is not right; that their leader is not genuine; that he, or she, leads two lives. Actions and motives are not aligned at the core.

Fortunately though, achievement driven by lower motives and values does not necessarily mean total disqualification, because when such leaders can be 'converted' to seamless leadership, the sky is the limit. They simply need to understand that seamless leadership abilities are inside them, based on their track record of successful movement, and that these need to be identified and fine-tuned or 'course corrected'.

Why do individuals like Bill Gates become huge philanthropists? We know that many doubt their motives and suggest that it is easy to give away $5 billion when one still has $5 billion left. But in the context of seamless leadership, I believe that these individuals start sensing a higher purpose to life. Instinctively they start connecting their actions and leadership to the core purpose of life and their seamless leadership instincts.

Don't think that I believe building a huge and profitable organisation is wrong. In fact, seamless leaders multiply anything under their care to its full potential, but it is then built on sound motives and foundation. And, more often than not, their influence extends beyond that area under their care and responsibility – as the examples of Adrian Gore and Terry Volkwyn show.

Stages of the seamless leader journey

The self-image: As obvious as this statement may seem, the truth is that our understanding of our own self-image is the basis of all our expectations, values, performance and attitude in life. Therefore, understanding our own self-image is the first stage in a seamless leader journey.

Leadership Psychology (L-Psych for short) tells us that all our instincts and human drivers boil down to our deep-rooted beliefs about what we possess (possessions) and where we feel we belong (belonging). The secret to understanding our self-image is to understand all our negative as well as positive 'belonging' and 'possessions'. It is humanly impossible to fully appreciate our positive attributes and potential until we have developed the wisdom to confront our negative belonging and possessions.

Mastering seamless leadership processes: The second stage of the seamless leader journey is about mastering processes that govern seamless leadership. To process all situations is a basic universal instinct that is common to all humankind.

One of the imperatives of human behaviour is the following principle: *'It is humanly impossible to perform above our believed values, standards and beliefs'*. Negative values, standards and beliefs are our real shackles. These shackles can only be removed by compliance with principles of change that are always process driven.

Multiplication: The instinct to multiply is a basic driver of human behaviour. It speaks to the human instinct to create movement. Each of us is designed to be a multiplier of positive attributes, more seamless leaders and in fact anything that has been placed under our care (see chapter 7). The fact that many of us allow ourselves to be bound by prejudices and negative barriers, and that some of us multiply only for selfish purposes is the saddest thing around.

The seamless leadership journey results in a seamless leader attitude that makes life an exciting and infinitely valuable journey. Is it an easy path? Of course not. All the top leaders I have met have a 'no gain without pain' attitude. They also provide ample evidence that the higher our thinking and broader our context, the greater our determination to change for the better by enduring whatever price we have to pay to reach the full potential of ourselves, others and society.

Another use for the SiPCOM acronym highlights the elements of the seamless leadership journey – Self-Image, Processes and Multiplying.

Adrian Gore – Founder and CEO Discovery Group

||||||||||||||||||||||||||||||||||||||||||||||||||||||||||||||||||||||||||||||||||||||||||||||||||||||||||||||||||||||||||||||||||||||||||||||||||||||||

Seamless Leadership Principles:

1. Look out for the seamless leader attitude that Gore demonstrates. Is it any wonder he has been leading Discovery so successfully for so long?
2. Try to see signs of his attitude towards SiPCOM. There are many to pick from, including:
   ❏ Always think ahead
   ❏ Be authentic and instil in others a strong sense of purpose
   ❏ Have a purpose, pursue it, and lead people towards it, all the while adhering to a set of values
   ❏ You can be at your best when experiencing problems.

||||||||||||||||||||||||||||||||||||||||||||||||||||||||||||||||||||||||||||||||||||||||||||||||||||||||||||||||||||||||||||||||||||||||||||||||||||||||

Imagine that you and your company have the following record of achievements: you were chosen as South Africa's best entrepreneur; recognised as the most admired person in your industry; CEO of the year; finalist in Moneyweb CEO's CEO of the Year competition; consistently in the top 20 of the Deloitte's Best Company to Work For Survey; in the top 10 of *Fortune* Magazine's Most Admired Company to Work For; in the top 10 of the most admired leaders; billions in turnover since the company started 18 or so years ago; and of course you are highly profitable. If I were to ask you how you think this was done; what the foundation of the success of such a company and person could have been, what would be the simplest answer you could come up with?

I asked Adrian Gore this exact question. His answer: 'I think one of the key drivers of my and the company's success is being a team. We have put together a remarkable team of people – incredibly smart, dedicated, loyal, and I think what has been good for us is that we built a company with a purpose, to make a change to the environment. That whole energy that we have created is self-perpetuating.'

What else could have given rise to his remarkable career in a very challenging South African environment? His answer: 'Maybe two things. I am an optimist. It manifests in the fact that I am a bit of a dreamer. I keep thinking ahead; thinking about how I can make a change; pushing ahead ... I work at being positive. I have an innate belief that you can make a difference. The second thing is that I have a sense of urgency – if you are going to get something done you'd better do it today because quite quickly you just don't get the chance to do it ... I know that in everyone there is greatness, but most people don't realise how quickly life passes them by.'

In the late 1980s Gore was a young man in his late twenties working for another large corporate in an industry that was in crisis. He had the idea of launching a product to combat some of the challenges, which they did. He approached a financial institution with the idea of forming a company with a sort of American style – specialist, focused, with a different ethos. They liked the idea and agreed to inject the seed capital into it – R10 million. In March 1992 he began with a desk, a chair and a rented office.

He was rather young ... and perhaps one of the virtues of being young is that you are too ignorant to be scared, although when he started the company his daughter was just born and he would lie in bed and wonder if they could really get the idea going. Generally, though, there was a feeling that nothing could stop them. He feels the same today. With the right people, a solution to any problem can be found. There is an innate feeling in his company that no matter what is thrown at them, they will find a way through it.

Gore is intrigued by leadership, not in the academic sense, but he enjoys leading people, if the purpose is noble. 'As a leader you have to be authentic; you have to have a real purpose, or else people see through you. People are not motivated by just success or money. If they believe they are in an organisation that has a noble purpose they will push harder; they will be motivated. I think any great leader has to do that. Maybe this is the difference between being a leader or a manager. Managers just execute; leaders give a strong purpose as to why they do it.'

What has motivated his employees is building a business that impacts on people positively. Apart from being very gratifying, it is from this type of culture that business follows – earnings, sustainability, and so on. The other great motivator is achievement. Money is simply an accounting method, telling you that you are making progress. When people are at the bottom of the slope moving upwards, learning, progressing, they are motivated and it is contagious.

He is adamant that any person can accomplish great things and become successful. It is a choice. As CEO he attends induction sessions with new employees where he asks the question: 'Is there greatness within you?' and every single person answers yes. He has never met someone who doesn't believe there is something special inside them! He always asks a follow-up question to the effect of: 'Have you used this greatness?' following which attendees always answer no. He then asks them what they are waiting for ... but the honest answer is that people are just waiting around and they don't get it done. I asked him why some manage to tap into their greatness and others don't. He believes once again that most people believe life is forever; that they will eventually get around to it.

A question that I believe is at the heart of the challenge to transfer leadership capability is: 'Do you have a conscious leadership model?' Gore's answer was an emphatic no. How then did he transfer leadership – for instance, if his son approached him with a request to teach him to be a better leader, what would he do? Gore pondered: perhaps there was something superficial about following a certain model ... but then: 'If you have a purpose and you decide to pursue it and lead people towards it and you follow a good set of values, you are going to be a good leader.' (This sounds like a model to me.) First, he would ask his son if his purpose was good, then he would urge him to be positive and make time short, because those are the things that galvanise people. But he believes there is no canned leadership style: great leaders have a uniqueness about them.

'A leader needs to grow at the same rate as the company he is in,' Gore says. In other words, sharpen the saw. He has endeavoured to sharpen his saw by reading widely and ensuring he knows what is happening; he analyses and argues points with himself to continually develop his mind. He believes that getting immersed in people and understanding the problems you are facing is probably the biggest developer of your brain. He stays physically fit by training twice a day, and he never misses.

Despite all this, he is the first to admit that he has weaknesses. He feels that he is a procrastinator; an obsessive person (perhaps his exercise programme is a manifestation of this); he is intellectually arrogant – he thinks he knows things.

Even the best leaders make mistakes: I wanted to know how he would react when this happened to him. First of all, he likes to wait to the very last moment, when every bit of information is available, before making a decision. He is convinced that while it is tough emotionally, logically it is the smartest thing to do: 'When you make the decision it's the richest you can make, and therefore if it's wrong you feel completely free to admit having done the wrong thing.' His team debates things intensely and very seldom makes cavalier decisions: 'I easily go back on decisions. I don't have this religious view that you have to stick to a decision because you made it. I have had some amazing turn-arounds in my thinking.'

Gore gave a real gem of advice to someone who wanted to know how to deal with challenges in his small business: 'You are at your best when you are having problems. When things are going incredibly smoothly you become complacent and bad habits tend to creep in. I am not suggesting you should revel in difficulties, but if I think of the difficult times we had, we've been at our best in those times. I have found that when you have problems there is a moment in time when you turn and face it, and you sort of accept it emotionally and intellectually, and you take a run at it; that's when you are at your best. When you are running from the problem, not only does it catch you and eat you up, but it is also very demotivating. How you motivate yourself is to attack the problems. When companies are small they have problems; when companies are big they have problems. The art of leadership is to use problems to fuel motivation.'

In his own words: 'Good leadership inspires others to lead!' How true this is.

Terry Volkwyn – CEO Primedia Broadcasting

Seamless Leadership Principles:

1. Look out for Volkwyn's movement towards seamless leadership.
2. Try to identify signs of a seamless leader attitude in this piece. There are many to pick from, including:
   - ❏ It's all about the people
   - ❏ Values are very important
   - ❏ Create an empowering environment
   - ❏ Strive towards 'leading beyond'.

The journey of this leader is an amazing one. She was raised in a simple Free State family as the youngest of three daughters. Dad, a gold miner, actually wanted her to be a boy – hence the spelling of her name. Mom was the strict one; Dad was the one who helped with homework and consistently reminded them that they could do anything they wanted. This belief implanted in her had an obvious effect throughout her life, though her mother's phrase, 'if you don't do it right, don't do it at all' is something she often hears herself repeat as she engages staff. When she uttered this phrase out loud I could almost see her transform from CEO to a motherly appearance.

Early in her career she landed up at the *Rand Daily Mail* and later became a sales rep without a car. She demonstrated resilience, drive and loyalty to her parents' teachings by making use of buses and her feet over long distances, in order to get to prospective customers. Being in the print media environment opened her eyes to what was really happening in the South African political arena. She started asking questions and developed some resistance towards the ignorant, with whom she would debate political issues. When she visited her parents they would find her in the 'servant' quarters leading conversations about politics.

When Volkwyn moved into the broadcasting field, Talk Radio 702 was a natural fit as it was viewed as a somewhat rebellious station at the time. She joined as a sales person and slowly moved up the ranks. In the earlier stages of her leadership career she was brutally tough. Fortunately as time went on she rubbed shoulders with great mentors; interestingly, she also consciously learnt from bad examples how *not* to lead.

A pivotal moment in her career as a leader was attending a programme on 'Leadership for radio' in the USA. Some of her instinctive feelings about how to lead were defined during the course, and on her return to South Africa she very successfully implemented, with more confidence and academic support, certain managerial and leadership practices.

For Volkwyn it was always about the people and so she started studying behaviour and personality types in order to understand individuals. Even today she tries hard to align individual abilities with the right roles. Perhaps this skill was necessitated by an environment where she had to mobilise powerful household names like John Robbie, Jeremy Mansfield and Jenny Crwys-Williams. Feeling intimidated by these and other influential presenters has long been replaced by mutual respect.

She strives for balance – family, exercise, diet – and strongly believes in leading oneself effectively before leading others effectively. Values are important – and to her a value is not a value unless you are willing to lose money over it.

Volkwyn seems to have evolved from being just tough, to adopting a remarkably balanced and authentic leadership approach: 'We can challenge managers, bosses, even her! It is very empowering. On a personal level she is tough as nails but cares about all of us. She does not bear a grudge, which is great. Finally, she has a sense of humour,' said a member of staff.

I reflected on the comments by employees and from experience know that most leaders would only dream of being described in this way. It was extremely reassuring to discover that the leader behind the LeadSA movement, intending to inspire a leadership culture in South Africa, is herself respected, loved and admired. It gives LeadSA authenticity, an essential ingredient in the success recipe of an initiative of this nature.

I believe Volkwyn has now arrived in a leadership space that I call 'leading beyond'. In other words, she demonstrates leadership beyond the boundaries for which she is held accountable. It requires incredible courage, maturity and faith to do this. It also takes time, of course, but is very liberating. In essence she has permitted the highly evolved leadership instinct that goes with the seamless leader attitude to mature to the point where it triggered a burning desire to achieve even broader excellence for herself and Primedia Broadcasting; to assist others and society to move closer to full potential.

This attitude allowed her to be more in tune with the world around her and so connect with the hearts of her employees by aligning them to broader societal needs, to give them a sense of higher purpose. In this space, shareholder satisfaction becomes a by-product of something much greater. Her mature view had to be sold to management and the board. It was challenging, but thank goodness she did not give up and her colleagues had the courage and faith to buy into it, placing them on that higher road towards maturing their own seamless leader attitudes.

Ultimately all South Africans may benefit from the courage she has shown by 'leading beyond' to launch LeadSA.

||||||||||||||||||||||||||||||||||||||||||||||||||||||||||||||||||||||||||||||||||||||||||||||||||||||||

CHAPTER 3

Seamless leader attitude to processes and decision making

WITH
- *President Jacob Zuma*
- *Helen Zille*

One of the universal principles of seamless leadership is respect for and mastery of a process that governs and maximises situations, people relationships, choices, confronting of obstacles and movement towards full potential of others, society and self. All movement and life is process driven, as are all human relationships. It follows that to the extent that we master process, we will be empowered to master life situations and human relationships around us.

To be the master of 'all processes' is humanly impossible, but the principle remains true – successful movement in all situations and relationships is governed by successful process. As we grow in our ability to master positive processes, we will grow a healthy confidence and faith as well.

Nothing moves without going through a *process*. Life may be defined as a succession of processes. Without process we can achieve nothing! Blinking our eyes is a process. Planning is a process; so is achieving. Moving from point *a* to point *b* is a process.

One of the foundation stones of a seamless leader attitude is the discipline to recognise that in every situation in life the first thing we need to do is to process the situation – that is, think it through, which may mean breaking it down into simpler components to understand what makes it tick. Inability to do this generates anxiety, fear and doubt. People tend to grasp at instant answers without making allowance for the imperative to process the situation before jumping to conclusions. I believe that most of our problems and unhappiness are caused by failure to follow effective processes in making decisions and addressing challenges.

We all know people who never seem to think things through; they simply react to them. Acquiring the ability to process situations confidently and successfully is itself a process! One must take the time to develop the necessary confidence.

The process necessary to incur positive movement in a specific situation may be different to the process required in another situation or set of conditions. An example would be to travel by sea or by air. Obviously each mode of travel requires different processes, modes of transport, preparation and planning, etc.

However, all movement has certain things in common which are natural to all movement. Movement is life. Life is movement. Seamless leaders seek profitable (successful) movement against the backdrop of a positive value system and SiPCOM. In other words, positive movement is getting worthwhile things done and moving barriers in the process.

We move things in our hearts and minds as well as in the physical world. Take away somebody's ability to move physically and it may cause great pain and anguish. But take away the ability to move in the heart and the mind and we take away life.

In order for us to increase our capacity to process positive movement (become movement specialists), we need to more fully understand the nature of movement. For our purposes the underlying universal law can be expressed as follows: **All movement is governed by the integration of motivation, direction and supporting structure.** In each movement we may find uniquely different motivations (driving energy, reasons, aspirations, desires), directions (plans, goals, objectives, strategies, etc) and varieties of structure (resources, facilities, systems, organisation, etc). However, all movement (and life in general), whether negative or positive, is governed by processes of some kind or other.

Whether the situation is emotional, mental or physical, movement in any direction requires the intervention of process. Whether the movement is negative or positive, it still requires process.

Two key process categories

From a positive perspective, there are two key process categories that require our attention. The first process category is the overarching one, which is that all movement and life is process driven. The second process category is that of human relationships and the processes that drive these.

To the extent that we master process, we will be empowered to master life situations and human relationships around us. To be the master of 'all processes' is humanly impossible, but the principle remains true – successful movement in all situations and relationships is governed by successful process. As we grow in our ability to master positive processes, we will grow a healthy confidence and faith as well.

Seamless leader confidence is trust in processes that work

Most of us realise instinctively how important it is to come across as confident on our journey through life. So, what do we often do? We act out, through body language or verbally, what we perceive confidence to be.

Most human beings, if not all, are not nearly as confident as they project. In fact, I believe that there are huge misunderstandings about what confidence is. When is someone confident? Are those individuals or leaders who outwardly come across as confident actually confident? How is confidence really developed?

The Green Mile is a film that played on the circuit many years ago, and I have often used it to define the concept of confidence. Tom Hanks plays the role of a 1930s prison officer, supervisor of death row, and Michael Clark Duncan plays the role of a black man falsely convicted as the killer of two young girls. He comes across as uneducated, shy and lacking in confidence. Tom Hanks's character discovers that the prisoner has a healing power whereby he somehow absorbs other people's pain or illness into his own body and then releases it again.

In the film the wife of a senior correctional services manager, outside the prison, contracts brain cancer. Tom Hanks's character and his team decide to secretly take the prisoner to the home of the manager, who

51

is not aware of the prisoner's ability, to try and heal his wife. A scene unfolds where this supposedly shy, uneducated, unsure man walks towards the front door of the house while the manager points a shotgun at him. The prisoner confidently moves forward until he is very close to the manager. He slowly and confidently takes the gun from him and says in a deep voice: 'I just want to help.' He walks past the manager into the home while the wife groans in pain in the background. The manager runs up from behind shouting at the prisoner to leave his house. The prisoner confidently and gently tells him: 'You be quiet now,' and he walks up the stairs. Everyone follows him. He heals the wife, and the story continues as the prisoner returns to his old self – shy and unconfident.

It's fiction, of course, but this is an excellent example of the principle that confidence is essentially about trust in processes (abilities, skills) that work. When this black man of the 1930s entered the realm of the healing process in which he had absolute trust, he suddenly came across as being outwardly confident. Those around him couldn't help but follow him. He became the leader, even though the social environment at that time did not provide for someone in his shoes to lead. Was he self-confident? No! Did he have trust in a healing process that had worked in the past? Yes! The result? He came across as confident while trusting the process.

A person who is well qualified and has a great deal of experience in the field of marketing will come across as very confident in a discussion on the topic. Is the individual self-confident? Not necessarily! He simply has trust in marketing processes and principles, like the prisoner on death row had trust in a healing process. How confident will this same marketer come across if the topic changes to that of finance? Probably much less so. The chartered accountant will suddenly take over and come across as more confident, because he or she trusts financial processes and principles.

Many individuals are recognised by society as 'confident' and 'successful' leaders because of position or title and certain material possessions. Often these people are in fact confident in the context of a certain technical field of expertise – they have mastered principles and processes in law, medicine, engineering, or business, for example, but they are not necessarily confident or even happy when one measures them outside of their expertise or comfort zone.

Examples of this are too many to mention. But think of a successful attorney whose home environment is in shambles; a financial director who is in that position because of his technical expertise, but fails dismally in people issues; well-known business individuals who are already in their third or fourth marriage; highly profitable or successful individuals who have alcohol problems, and so on.

As illustrated above, I have come to the conclusion that you can only become a seamless leader if you develop confidence (acquire trust in principles and processes) in the two key process categories – life processes and human relationship processes. Seamless leaders acquire trust in principles and processes that govern interaction with people and they acquire trust in principles and processes that govern life.

Bystanders often look at seamless leaders and see outward assurance, self-belief, success and happiness, not realising that what they see is a consequence of these leaders' striving to acquire trust in these different universal principles and processes, while being acutely aware of their own weaknesses and shortcomings.

This unique combination reflects a humble confidence as opposed to an arrogant confidence.

The converse is also true. The essence of a lack of confidence (fear, doubts, panic, despondency, envy, etc) is caused by a lack of trust in process. If I am faced with a crisis situation at work, I will experience confidence in direct proportion to my trust in being able to process the situation successfully. Such trust may be the consequence of years of training and experience; it could also be augmented by spiritual peace of mind and faith.

To be stuck in the middle of the process is to stop moving positively. Human nature tends to jump the chain (steps) of process and to seek a resolution before the full process is completed. Impatience (or stupidity!) may be defined as 'jumping the process chain'. If the representative teams involved in the historic CODESA negotiations on the democratisation of South Africa had insisted on 'jumping the chain' instead of working through the process, they might have generated untold bloodshed and suffering.

The piece on President Zuma shows how much value he places on being obedient to a process-driven discipline in all the decisions he makes. Many may believe he is making core mistakes in a number of areas, but he strives nevertheless to be 'decisive-in-process'.

An attitude of 'decisiveness-in-process' is not just a requirement for the leader of a country, but for all of us who want to be successful in our careers, at home or in any area of life. As seen in the interviews with President Zuma and Helen Zille, confidence in the 'decisive-in-process' approach hinges largely on the principle of trust.

The Destiny Chain

The Destiny Chain is about successfully activating and managing the universal law of movement: 'All movement is *process* governed by integration of *motivation, direction and structure*'. This is what Seamless Leaders do, often subconsciously.

My experience in years of leadership counselling and interviews with hundreds of top performers in our society provides considerable backing for the authenticity of the following steps governing successful process, especially relating to human relationship and organisational performance (movement). This is the Destiny Chain process. Think of SiPCOM as you review this process:

1. Define the situation that you want to move carefully and factually.
2. Define the possible obstacles or barriers (negative expectations and perceptions) arising out of the situation. Be honest and thorough in doing this. Be especially diligent in defining the negative emotional barriers (expectations and perceptions), not just the logical concerns.
3. After completing the list of negative obstacles or barriers, to shift your own attitude and see the context more clearly, list all the possible positive elements, expectations and perceptions that may flow from the situation. Doing this also stops you from becoming fixated on the perceived negatives.
4. Define positive aspirations (desires), what you want from the situation (forward thinking mode); where you want it to move to.
5. Define the direction(s) or actions you need to take to successfully

realise your aspirations and address the negative obstacles and barriers (expectations and perceptions).

6. Define the structure(s) and supporting organisation, resources, etc needed to successfully pursue your directions (plans).
7. Evaluate and re-evaluate (assess, measure, hold accountable) the above steps continually.
8. Adjust plans or act tough when necessary.
9. Always re-focus on the long-term vision and positive aspirations.

The above process is known as the Destiny Chain because of its tried and tested ability to shift attitude and then generate positive movement towards a better destiny, at all levels. Note that steps 4–6 activate the law of movement by dealing with motivation, direction and structure. Interesting how the law of movement falls slap bang into the middle of the Destiny Chain process, and how everything revolves around it (more in chapter 6). The process may require training and coaching, but it is most certainly worth the effort.

The best form of decisiveness is being 'decisive in process', which is how a seamless leader operates. The SiPCOM acronym finds a further use in Si*tuation* P*rocessing* = CO*nfident* M*ovement.*

President Jacob Zuma – President of South Africa

Seamless Leadership Principles:

1. Look out for the discussion of decision making, being a 'decisive-in-process' leader.
2. Try to identify where President Zuma aims to demonstrate a seamless leadership attitude.
3. Try to identify more seamless leadership principles.
4. Note that our President is presented in an objective, unemotional way, in accordance with the spirit of seamless leadership.

I once attended a function where Jacob Gedleyihlekisa Zuma was the special guest. He sat two tables away from me during an evening event shortly before he became President and because of my interest in leadership I watched him closely – how he laughed at himself while Trevor Noah made jokes about him; how people gravitated towards his table; how attendees approached him freely despite the extraordinary controversies that surrounded him at the time. As a typical 'distance critic', influenced by media and analysts, I had certain views about our President. Who didn't, or doesn't? And, not long after he became President I felt prompted to write an open letter to him, challenging him to initiate a national debate on values in order to create more unity, not knowing at the time that I would eventually personally meet him.

Business Report Editor Ellis Mnyandu and I enjoyed the rare opportunity of sitting across from President Zuma in the comfort of his Pretoria residence, Mahlamba Ndlopfu, looking him in the eye while holding an intense leadership conversation.

Attempting to write about him as a leader places a heavy responsibility on one's shoulders, because there are diverse and very strong, even negative views regarding President Zuma the person, the politician, the struggle hero, and the leader. I regularly address groups on the topic of leadership and leaders in society, and more often than not they say he comes across as 'approachable, inclusive, consultative, amicable, a good listener, but too indecisive'. The question is – has he changed, or, is this still the perception some have of him?

When I met him at the end of 2011 I did find him approachable, for a president – the proof being that we got to interview him in his home for an hour. Also, the *Business Report* Leadership Platform follow-up questions e-mailed to him personally were answered very swiftly. In his presence, both Mnyandu and I quickly felt comfortable, and he certainly came across as warm, considering our conversation was at 6 pm after a very long and hectic day. The President was still in his business suit, with no sign of fatigue.

Coincidentally, one of his staff described a telling difference between him and his predecessor: in six months she entered the presidential home once when former President Mbeki was the head of state. With President Zuma she finds herself there weekly as he regularly allows for meetings there. This is not necessarily about a right or wrong approach, but it demonstrates how engaging he wants to be.

When one sits with President Zuma face-to-face rather than viewing him through the television screen or the eyes of ruthless cartoonists, comedians or analysts, he is much more charismatic and impressive. We found that during the interview, while of course remaining aware that he was the President, we felt comfortable enough to converse with and even interrupt him. He is human and one senses he has not lost contact with this reality.

Is he a decisive leader, or not? This has always been a question on people's minds and needs to be unpacked because of its importance and relevance not only to President Zuma but to all prospective seamless leaders.

'Well, people have a right to make a criticism of whatever type. It is their democratic right,' Zuma commented, but he also added that such critics 'can't produce one thing that I did not take a decision on. It is actually one of these perceptions people talk about that becomes a reality.

They can't tell me I did not decide on this or that matter. They live in the world of excitement; once there is an issue I must act immediately and if I don't I am indecisive.'

The so-called 'decisive leader' who always makes quick decisions will have to accept the risk of the shotgun approach – he will get some decisions right and some wrong. This is the kind of leader who 'thinks on his feet'. Those around the leader may view him as decisive when decisions are accurate – and of course in such instances there is quick movement, which temporarily satisfies followers. However, when decisions are inaccurate the leader causes damage, backtracks with excuses and quickly loses credibility. People then hastily refer to him as irresponsible and even an autocrat. In politics such decisive leadership can certainly lead to dictatorship, especially against the backdrop of Africa, with its reputation for dictators.

Of such an approach President Zuma says: 'I don't believe you must take a decision on your feet, because if you do this you are often not absolutely correct – there is something you did not check.'

An indecisive leader somehow freezes and puts off decisions because of fear, inexperience, inability to comprehend a complex situation, or whatever reason. The motive for withholding a decision is not consciously part of a process. In fact, a person who is indecisive will never – or at least, should never – end up in a responsible leadership position.

A 'decisive in process' leader trusts the process that leads to a more comprehensive solution and always attempts to see the bigger picture. He or she consults widely to get buy-in. Such a leader is more concerned about doing what is right than being perceived as decisive, and trusts the principle of: 'It is one thing to be right, yet another thing to be the right time.' This is a leader who really covers most angles before making a decision, as required by the steps in the Destiny Chain process. In fact, sometimes the process prompts the leader to refrain from acting at that moment, which decisive decision, though sometimes confusing to others, often proves to be correct.

A seamless leader adopts the 'decisive in process' approach, realising at the same time that while the disadvantage of this approach is that decisions do sometimes take longer, they are correct more often than not.

I believe that the seamless leader instinct inside President Zuma prompts him towards the 'decisive in process' approach, though there are other factors at play that seem to influence him towards being indecisive at times. In his opinion, 'Having been in public life for quite a while, people would by now realise I don't take a decision without really applying my mind. That does not in any way say you are indecisive. It is the wrong application of the expression, that you are indecisive if you don't take a decision now. Take a hasty decision and you are going to be apologising all the time. I believe you need to think. If you have got to take a decision, even if matters are clear after you have done something wrong, I have to apply my mind, because you are a human being. I am not taking a decision about a bag that I must pick up and go.'

A clash with the Public Protector at the time of the interview provided an example: 'In this instance I wrote and explained the allegation, and then asked for a response. And he must respond. I must consider this because at the end, if I take a decision it is one that is going to live with you for your life. I am dealing with a human being here. Ever since I received the report from the protector I interacted with the people concerned, with the Public Protector. At one point I even announced that I alerted the Speaker what I was doing. So it is not as if I am sitting indecisively. I am taking due process, so that when I come to finality I will be able to explain my decision at every level, even if somebody questions the decision.'

More often than not a seamless leader adopts the 'decisive in process' approach because of the backdrop against which he leads. It can hardly be denied that President Zuma faces a challenging backdrop, even a dilemma. South Africa requires decisive leadership; citizens understandably want to see societal ills and challenges resolved speedily. On the other hand, the President has to act as a 'decisive in processes' leader. He must consult widely and consider the big picture, because South African society is extremely diverse, and aspirations of Alliance partners can be at opposite ends of the continuum. Also, the ANC way is for him to align decisions with policies from its National Executive Committee. And by the way, because the ANC is such a dominant party, its very diversity, the collective wisdom of the NEC and its counterbalances within may very well be South Africa's safeguard against becoming a dictatorship. If this is so,

South Africans need to be grateful that President Zuma leans towards the 'decisive in process' approach; that he wants to unite because he senses the totality of South Africa's political and social landscape.

However, we are still faced with the dilemma that as he respects this back-drop and attempts to perform as a 'decisive in process' leader he will inevitably take longer to make decisions and often be perceived as indecisive.

The real question is whether or not it is possible for President Zuma to ever be perceived as decisive, considering the dynamics described above. What do we want as South Africans: a 'decisive in process' leader who respects the overall South African dynamics, at times making slower decisions and coming across as indecisive, but – within the bigger picture – achieving some improvement of societal challenges; or a decisive leader who disrespects the backdrop against which he leads and probably becomes more of a dictator, but (if we are very lucky) makes change, or at least perceptions of change, happen at a faster pace? We can't have it all. Or can we? Is there a way for President Zuma, or future presidents of South Africa, to remain a 'decisive in process' leader, yet somehow also come across as decisive to followers?

When all is said and done, President Zuma is the 'CEO' of this extremely complex organisation called South Africa Pty (Ltd). As one CEO of a large corporate explained, 'South Africa is a microcosm of the world. It is the real experiment.' President Zuma agreed fully with this view: 'To run South Africa is a big challenge. It is not a simple matter. South Africa is a complex country because of its history, because of its people. When we talk about unity in diversity we summarise what South Africa is. You find the smartest people in the world are from South Africa. But you also have a huge population that was deprived of an education because of the apartheid system, which makes the country complex with highly sophisticated people, but also people who are really down-to-earth, poorest of the poor – and they all have views. How do you handle these?'

According to President Zuma, the greatest challenge for South Africa's leader is to harmonise and unite all this diversity into one direction. He believes we therefore need a leader 'who understands South Africa very well'. As things currently stand he will continue leading in an environment where dilemmas and dichotomies are par for the course, where it may very well be impossible to please all citizens and where his often 'decisive in process' leadership at times, perhaps unfairly so, portrays indecisiveness.

Making sense of difficult questions such as this and then bringing about movement that initially seemed unlikely is the reality of leadership, and President Zuma has to achieve this on the largest scale imaginable. As he says: 'That's precisely the reason why it is not everybody who is a leader.'

In a leadership context, logic demands that there has to be forward thinking: a vision. And, the more complex the dynamics of the entity one wants to move, the more compelling the vision should be, so that followers want to be 'there' rather than 'here'.

The question is, therefore, what is the vision and would the leadership philosophy of President Zuma add value to the task at hand?

Firstly, the vision, which President Zuma described as follows: 'Our vision was enunciated 100 years ago when the ANC was formed. The vision of a united and democratic society came into being. As the years went by, this crystallised into the building of a non-racial, united, non-sexist, democratic and prosperous society. The Freedom Charter firstly, and later the Constitution of the Republic, are the foundation documents which spell out the national vision. We want a society where everybody has access to basic human rights, and to a better life with water, electricity, housing, proper roads, quality education, quality health care and a host of other simple things which will improve the lives of our people.'

This is the vision, straight from our leader's mouth. Some may feel that they are not consciously aware of this vision, as communicating it incessantly is just as important as coming up with it. President Zuma admits communication must improve: 'Yes, I agree that we need to communicate more and more about what we are working to achieve, and also our achievements as a nation.'

However, it is also true that the attitude of the recipient of the communication often determines how well the message is received. According to President Zuma, 'We have achieved a lot over the years, but unfortunately there is a culture of dwelling on the negatives and failing to see how well the country has done, from a pariah to a vibrant, stable democracy.'

In large organisations weak communication is *always* one of the obstacles to getting buy-in, understanding, passion and movement towards the vision. Now just imagine how challenging it is in a country as diverse and complex as South Africa. As President Zuma states: 'It is not just government alone that must communicate. The media, business, labour – all sectors must learn to see the positives that exist and share these with the country and the world'.

More and more it seems that to fully own a vision it must connect at a mental and emotional level. To achieve emotional ownership it has to be appealing. For this to happen one must truly value those components that make up the vision because what one truly values connects with the heart and then it becomes appealing. And to own it mentally, there must be confidence in how one believes it will be achieved (the plan). In this way values, vision, behaviour, strategy, the mind and heart are integrated into one great whole.

What kind of leader or leadership is needed to get people to this vision? Let's start with President Zuma's own philosophy: 'My philosophy is I should lead in the collective, consult as I think it is important. At times people want to know why I consult so much. It is absolutely important to take everybody on board. Because if you have consulted you have a chance that you have a decision that will be defended by a collective, rather than a decision that will be defended by you only. And if you are a leader you must create that positive, collective leadership. It must not be lost. You must not be the one who thinks other people should create it. And you create it by the way you interact. You must allow someone to put across a view, and you engage, and you hear them. Then you hear other elements that help you see the picture differently. In other words, in very friendly discussions, somebody must actually come to a view without you forcing them into a view. I think it is an important thing to do.'

Real, meaningful, emotional, lasting buy-in and alignment only happens when there is inclusion, involvement, participation, good communication. One cannot click one's finger or order someone to be officially aligned and on board. It therefore seems that theoretically President Zuma's leadership philosophy should be the right one for the job at hand.

However, while the collective leadership philosophy is definitely the way to go in today's complex society, there is a potential dilemma in such an approach. A collective leader must possess effective authority (also known as trust), which in turn hinges on adherence to an unwritten pact between leader and follower. Firstly the leader commits to counselling widely and wisely before making an important decision; then, followers commit to accepting and sustaining the decision. A leader cannot always consult several stakeholders with varying opinions and then make a decision that satisfies all parties. So, for this collective philosophy to work, leader and followers must respect and trust one another and ultimately sustain the end decision, even if it does not align with their own view. Participants must accept that the leader, who is perhaps the only one to see the entire picture, has in all likelihood made the right decision, driven by the right motives.

This does not seem to work seamlessly in real life; certainly not in South Africa or most other so-called democracies. Why do people not adhere to this unwritten pact? Perhaps it is just not within the DNA of opposition politics and even the democratic system. Or, is there not sufficient trust or respect between followers and leaders? Also, do citizens trust and respect the office or position of President? Do they trust and respect the democratic process through which he was elected, which is the same process through which future presidents will be elected?

In general, followers (and often the leader as well) find it difficult to separate the person from the position that he or she holds. While the person, who is only human, makes mistakes and can be criticised, often followers confuse freedom of speech with freedom to treat the leader with disrespect, and in the process denigrate the office of president. Admittedly it is a fine line that separates the two sides, but I wonder if this principle is given enough thought. You see, the more citizens downgrade the office of the president the more they downgrade the effective authority of this position. Perhaps signs of disrespect can be seen in the way the President is addressed in media headlines and articles; or the type of cartoons that are allowed in the press; and so on. One can write a hard-hitting article but still refer to President Zuma rather than Zuma only, for example.

Ultimately, the challenge with collective, consultative, open leadership is that the leader's authority and power to lead could weaken, especially when his 'office' and the 'pact' are not adhered to. Disunity, rivalry, and division could become the order of the day. Such a situation then speaks to the following principle: in leadership the level of unity equals the level of performance – 50 per cent unity = 50 per cent performance; 100 per cent unity = 100 per cent performance. Therefore, when unity walks out the back door, so does performance. Of course a given in this situation is that the leader must earn respect and realise at all times that every action he takes, word he utters or does not utter, impacts on the perception of whether he truly lives and breathes the vision. It is a heavy and very visible burden to carry. This could very well be where President Zuma has gone wrong.

Society's evolution towards collective leadership is starting to raise some interesting leadership dichotomies and questions for debate. You see, it is not collective leadership only that we should strive for, but seamless leadership, which most South Africans got a taste of during the Mandela era.

President Zuma's appeal to South Africans, from the heart, is that 'our history has proven that when united around a common goal we can succeed. The common goal is to build a great country with jobs, safer communities and many other social needs.' And this leads us to the question, if we agree with this goal, are we on board? Some may feel guilt-ridden for not being inspired by the vision: surely all should want such a society?

One of the key pillars of a seamless society is unity. President Zuma gives the ANC's perspective: 'Our theme as government is that "working together, we can do more". Government cannot do everything on its own. We must work together to eradicate poverty, unemployment and other social ills facing our society. Nobody must be a bystander. It is a collective responsibility. We need the support of every South African. We need ideas and action from everybody to build a non-racial, non-sexist, democratic and prosperous South Africa.'

To the question 'Is it possible to unite South Africa's diversity into one direction?' the answer has to be yes. This is why initiatives like the National Development Plan and LeadSA, which attempt to unite South Africans around common values, are so important. However, in President Zuma's own words, 'We must accept that it will not be easy to achieve all the things we want to achieve and we cannot achieve them as fast as we want, but if we believe in ourselves and our abilities collectively, we will achieve our goals.' Indeed, when he makes the right calls everyone benefits; should he succeed everyone succeeds; should he fail, everyone fails. Anyone who wants him to fail is driven by selfish motives and does not possess a seamless leader attitude.

In leadership, what seems like one's worst hour can give birth to one's greatest opportunity to rise and do the impossible, make a mark, stand and be counted. President Zuma may be in his worst hour. Is he going to show the necessary courage and seamless leadership to turn the tide in his favour? It will be challenging and daunting, a path of courage – uncompromising, unselfish, brave leadership.

Helen Zille – Leader of the Democratic Alliance

Seamless Leadership Principles:

1. Look out for Zille's comments on decision making.
2. Try to identify where she demonstrates a seamless leader attitude.
3. Try to identify more seamless leadership principles, including:
   - ❏ Learn to defer gratification
   - ❏ Allow empathy to become a spark for action
   - ❏ Take time to diagnose a problem accurately
   - ❏ Move out to the fringe
   - ❏ Keep on keeping on
   - ❏ Reflect on your mistakes.

Many compare Helen Zille to Margaret Thatcher, Britain's Iron Lady. Well, after meeting and spending time with her I suggest, as a somewhat informed person, that you erase most of that perception from your mind.

Her parents raised her to take responsibility very seriously; to learn to defer gratification – not to do what you feel like doing but what needs to be done. In her own words: 'I've never asked myself whether I feel like doing something or whether it is not more expedient to do A rather than B. If something has to be done it has to be done.' Combine such an outlook and value system with the ability to work extremely hard and to act tough when required, and then throw in the factor of being a woman, and it could be easy to fall into the trap of drawing comparisons with the notorious English Prime Minister.

In a nutshell though I would summarise Zille as someone who was raised and almost programmed to act on a sense of justice, doing what's right; who feels compelled to make the world a better place, driving towards solutions that improve people's plight.

An attribute that stands out very clearly is that of empathy. She feels for people and the conditions under which they suffer. This empathy drives Helen to action; almost triggers something inside her that she herself can't control. She moves unstoppably into gear to create movement, change, and improvement. Energy comes from somewhere inside her and she bites into the problem like a bull terrier and does not let go. I am even willing to stick my neck out and state that 'winning votes' hardly crosses her mind when she is in this mode, if this is at all possible for a politician.

Zille believes that 'diagnosing a problem is the key to solving it'. You cannot find the desired solution when the problem was diagnosed incorrectly in the first place. She believes many people are guilty of this: it is often the 'fundamental mistake that is made in policy formulation in South Africa and also in interventions. People define the problem incorrectly and then, like the age-old example of a doctor who does a heart transplant instead of taking out the appendix, they implement the wrong solution.' She further believes that when one diagnoses a problem, especially when it is a big one, the next step is to break it up into smaller solvable components.

One of the greatest quotes I have heard over the years is by Dr Gary Hamel, who says: 'The future begins not at the core but at the fringe.' Seamless leaders don't just manage from the core, or they don't simply remain in secure territory, the way things have always been done. They move out to where there is a clearer view of the real and often daunting challenge. When they have the challenge clearly defined they come up with pioneering, innovative, ground-breaking ways to overcome it. This takes courage, because the solution is so often unpopular and controversial!

I believe that if the DA wants to make a significant impact on South African politics, Zille will have to be a 'fringe' leader. So in my first interview with her, I asked her whether that was how she would identify herself. Her answer: '..."fringe" leaders are people who think ahead and look back from a vantage point of 10 or 20 years into the future. They say that on the basis of that perspective what will have been the right decision now? So you are not thinking from the core where you happen to be now but you are thinking from a very different perspective, looking back over history as you think and anticipate it may unfold, and say what will have been the right decision today. That is why I got so involved in the Black Sash and other organisations many years ago. It certainly wasn't core then but very fringe ... The hallmark of a leader is to decide what the problem is, what you have to do about it, pointing in a direction and then being decisive and having the courage to do it.'

When Zille moves out to the fringe of South African politics the real leadership challenge she sees 'is to overcome race and ethnicity as a mobilising factor. We have to get to the politics of shared values, shared policies, trumping identity. At the moment it is the other way around ... We will never grow as a party if we can't get support from black people, and we can only get support from black people when they feel we are articulating their ideas and their values, which we are in many instances, but the power of race holds people in to voting in a certain direction. It is as if certain parties own certain people on the basis of their race and ethnicity. Unless we can crack that we are going to have permanent built-in majorities and minorities in South Africa. We will never have a viable democracy because we can only have a proper democracy when government can change hands through the ballot box.'

Interestingly enough, she says such a challenge has never been overcome in any other country with deep ethnic divisions.

Ultimately she believes 'there are no silver bullets here. We have to keep on keeping on, showing people that we care and that we are absolutely committed and that our policies are best for all South Africans.'

Talking about her leadership style, she said 'the issue is not having one style but having good enough judgement to know what is appropriate in different situations. That is the key test of a leader – to have the discretion and the judgement to know what is appropriate in complex situations and move forward to a new level. This can only be developed over time and with experience and with good capacity to reflect on your mistakes – to understand what went wrong and why, and then to be able to draw on that experience in the next situation.'

Like many leaders she works on her weaknesses, like for example being untidy, which leads to often having to look for things. She diagnosed this issue and realised that a reason could be that she always moves forward and never looks backwards. When she has done something she moves on to the next thing and does not look back long enough to 'file' the paper component of the situation, which can lead to problems in the future.

Despite her incredibly pressured schedule, which she is comfortable with, she seems to have a sense of gratitude about life. Her mayoral body-guard asked her how she was doing fairly late one evening, following a hectic day, and her answer was something along the lines of: 'I am very happy and blessed.' I asked Zille to explain this answer: 'I suppose I do feel blessed because so many things are right in my life. I have an extraordinary husband; I have two wonderful children; I have a dry home that does not leak when it rains; I have extraordinary colleagues; I have an excellent team; I have a family who really care for me and I have good friends. So I feel deeply blessed all the time.'

When all is said and done, is Zille the leader destined to change the face of politics in South Africa? Is she going to be the one to change the up-to-now unbreakable pattern of voting across traditional, racial, ethnic lines? Is she what South Africa needs right now?

She most certainly continues to prove that she is a great leader and demonstrates several seamless leader attributes. There is no doubt that Zille is impacting the South African political landscape.

A more recent Q&A

Q: I saw you about four or five years ago so I am interested in what you have learned about leadership over these past few years. I think it's been a rough ride - it's not easy. Does anything stand out?

Zille: I think the thing that stands out for me the most is how important the team is and how you have to put really smart people into the team, who are prepared to tell you the things you don't want to hear; who are prepared to take risks in their own turf and make mistakes; and who are driven to see results. Picking the right people for the team is the key thing.

Q: Corporate leaders would agree with you. I guess some people have a better gut feel for that than others – what have you learned about yourself in regards to this? Have you made mistakes?

Zille: Oh yes, everyone makes mistakes – I learn far more from my mistakes than I do from my successes. I've learned to be a better judge of situations and of issues. I've learned to be far more considered when I get angry and I've learned to count to ten in a far better way than I did before. I have more discretion than I used to have, put it that way. I've come to understand how to do succession planning and how best to do that – it wasn't really on my radar five years ago but now it certainly is. I've also come to realise what elements of an organisation make it work and I make sure they do work, but I let the people that I entrust make that work and I don't look over their shoulders. Trust is a very important ingredient in the function of an organisation – it's got to be real trust between the components that make the thing work.

Q: Do you think that's more difficult to achieve in politics than perhaps in business?

Zille: I'm not sure. We certainly have a very high level of trust in our party between the critical elements. There are always the inevitable tensions between individuals which can sometimes spill over but at a core level there's deep trust.

Q: What have you sacrificed over the last three to five years, and I'm not just talking about not seeing family – if you're involved in politics surely it must affect even who you are? It's been an intense few years. Have you changed?

Zille: I wouldn't say I have sacrificed. I hope I've grown. I hope I am less affected by the turmoil that I face every day. I'm less affected by negative comments. I'm less affected by controversy. But I think in a good sense. I don't think I have become blunted – I've just learned what to take seriously and what not to take seriously. I've put things into perspective. I've learned what it means to say 'take it from whence it comes'. I know who to take seriously and who not to take seriously. I know when an insult is an insult or when it's easily ignorable or the advice is good advice. So I've learned to be very discerning – I suppose that's part of discretion. What I have lost is my voice, from speaking on platforms all the time, and singing and other things I suppose that come with the territory. I think the thing that I've lost the most is time with my children – not now, but when they were younger – now when I look back I think I should have spotted this, or seen that coming or been aware of that – but I wasn't and thankfully they are very well-adjusted young men and they're flying and they have wind beneath their wings and we've got a great relationship. But I suppose that's my biggest regret.

Q: What a school of life you've been through – no one can imagine it unless they've been there. You're in the middle of everything that affects everyone in the country.

Zille: Yes, but I love issues and I love challenges. That's what keeps me motivated and gives me a sense of purpose, what keeps me going. It was much harder being a teenager than where I have been the past 10 years – much harder. When you're a teenager you need affirmation badly and your whole concept of self is defined by the affirmation that you either get or don't get from other people. It's a very difficult space and as you get older it worries you less and less and then you find your own sense of purpose and you find your own yardsticks and you do what you believe is right and that's fine.

Q: You certainly believe in integrity – I have no doubt about that.

Zille: Politics should be a space where the people with the most integrity are drawn to. Unfortunately it isn't always the case, but there are a lot of people with real integrity in politics. It isn't a space where sharks swim to feed necessarily, and if it is a place where sharks swim to feed and if the sharks get to the top, then the voters put them there. The truth is that people get the government they voted for, which therefore is the government they deserve. Politics is about power and power is simply the ability to make things happen and democracy is just one way of organising how power is attained, how it's exercised, how it's called into account and how it's rotated. The ability to make things happen can be used to further your own interest or in the broader interest, and if people are empowered to decide who has power to make things happen, then they must decide in whose interests people exercise power. They must make those judgements, and in a democracy, if corrupt politicians make it to the top, it's the voters that put them there. It's really critical to have politicians of integrity because otherwise the entire power system becomes corrupted. I believe it's an absolutely integral part of any representative system. It is a specific feature that I look for in the people that I put into positions.

Q: You've managed to keep yours intact?
Zille: I hope so, but you mustn't ask me that, you must ask other people who I work with – ask my party, ask my colleagues. I hope I say what I do and I do what I say.

Q: For how long should you stay in this position? You've mentioned succession – so obviously your intention is not to stay there forever – but why is it that opposition leaders stay there for as long as they do – they stay even longer than a President who often stays for just a term or two? What's the difference – why should there not be proper succession planning, have a term or two and then move out?
Zille: Well they should – and those that don't wither on the vine. But the difference is that one is prescribed in the constitution and the other isn't. We have constitutional term limits in South Africa for a president but for no one else – and it shouldn't really matter for anybody else. Why should a party with five public representatives have term limits for its president – it's up to them whether their party flourishes or fails. Nothing hangs by it – I mean Bantu Holomisa doesn't have access to state institutions that he can manipulate to his own ends, which is the reason you put term limits on presidents. So if the United Democratic Movement thinks that Holomisa is the right person to take them forward irrespective of whether they've lost in every election since they were formed, and they've gone backwards – because you can't win after two or three elections in a context like South Africa, if you keep going backwards – if they still want him then that's their business. Nothing else hangs on it. Two terms as prescribed by the constitution for a president is 10 years. Now next year (2014) in May, I will have been leader of the DA for seven years. So it's not as if I've had term

after term after term. In other countries they don't even have term limits for their presidents. Maggie Thatcher I think had four terms; Angela Merkel (Germany) is going now for a record third term in office, maybe even a fourth term, I have to work that out. In those contexts where it's impossible for the leaders to manipulate the constitution because the constitution is so strong and because the institutions of the constitution are so strong and independent and there are so many checks and balances – term limits for a president are not really that significant. Voters can change their mind, and institutions will not tolerate executive interference.

In an emerging democracy where institutions are really vulnerable, term limits for a president are very important. Having said that, you need two terms in order to make any kind of impact in government. So I think two terms is a fair reflection of what voters should allow in an administration if they want to see results properly, but my position has been quite clear to my party. I've said the minute someone comes along who can do this job better than me – i.e. grow the party and hold it together, because those two things are critically important simultaneously – I will be the first to step down. I would like to continue working for our cause because I have done it my whole life; I would like to continue doing that in one capacity or another, but certainly the leader that can take us forward is the one we want. The leader who can make the greatest progress is the one we want. We poll all the time. We will know when the time comes.

Because I said this year that I was ready to step down and make way for Mamphela Ramphele and that whole deal was on the cards and then she decided not to go ahead with it, it's left people with the impression that I want to step down pretty soon. That's completely untrue. I'm happy to continue doing this job, I love it. I'm full of energy for it, I have appetite for it. But I'm not married to it and I'm not determined to hold onto it if someone can do it better. I felt that Mamphela might be able to grow our party better than I could in next year's election – it didn't turn out that way, perhaps retrospectively we were right not to go through with that deal. I'm here and I'm happy and I'm up and at 'em.

Q: Some leaders have said to me – isn't it time for a leader of colour? I'm wary of asking that question because you have several leaders of colour running your party; I've met two of them. You just mentioned now that you were willing to let Mamphela Ramphele take over, so I guess you would say to me it's not a colour issue at all, it's a competence issue, and it's who's right.

Zille: Put it this way – the DA has more black voters than any other opposition party in South Africa, certainly more than all the black-led parties in South Africa. Even if there wasn't a single white, coloured or Indian voter we would still be the biggest opposition party. When I became the leader of the party from being in the position of a Councillor in the City of Cape Town, I said my plan was to build many platforms for many voices and many faces in the party. I've done my best to build up those faces and to magnify those voices. We are the most diverse party South Africa has ever had. We've got the most diverse leadership any party in South Africa has ever had. I consciously create platforms for all the other leaders in this party – consciously – and enable them to drive their issues, drive their profile. That's my succession plan.

Q: It's amazing how the perception may still exist among some that it's a white party. I don't know why that remains.

Zille: I've made it my absolute business to change that but the reason it hangs on is primarily because we've allowed our opponents to define who we are. That's why we ran our 'Know Your DA' campaign, because I was sick and tired of being told who we are by the people. I said: 'This is who we are.'

Q: After all these interviews with leaders over the past 15 years, one thing I have discovered is that leaders are in the business of movement. So you give a leader some responsibility and they must move it from where it is to some place better. In the process I uncovered the universal law of movement and that universal process leaders use to create movement. With that backdrop, just summarise what you've moved since you became the leader of the DA.

Zille: Tony Leon moved us into the official opposition. I moved us into becoming a party of government. So people have stopped seeing us as just a party of opposition, though they think we are a very good opposition

– that is Tony's legacy. He created the platform for me to be able to move the DA to becoming a party of government. And people see that now we're in government, we run the place competently. That's been the big movement.

Q: From a city to a province ...

Zille: And 28 local authorities now throughout South Africa. We've also moved into becoming the most diverse organisation in terms of membership votes and leadership and next year we'll get more black votes than all the other minority votes put together. And we have become a party that has majority black membership too.

Q: I'm interested in how you keep that unity in the party, because even recently there was speculation about disunity. That will always come before the elections, but how do you actively and consciously keep that unity – because it is a place of power and agendas and no doubt there's more happening in the DA than the public may even know?

Zille: I do it by trying to be as accessible as I can and keeping the conversation as open as we can. The more open we are with each other, the less room there is for conniving in corridors. The second way we do it – we have very carefully worked-out systems and processes that everyone agrees with in terms of legitimacy and fairness, and everyone sticks with the process. That mitigates power struggles and conflict within the organisation. The reason other opposition parties can't succeed is because they can't develop those structures and systems and processes we have developed. And it's those that can take an intense contest of competition and rivalry and turn it into a cohesive process that succeed, and that's what we've done. Let me give you an example. If any organisation – all of its senior people – had to compete every five years for each others' positions, I don't know if they would survive. But in politics, you've got a job, if you're lucky, for five years and then you've got to compete for your job again, against colleagues who are your friends and your caucus mates and everything. You know, it's a recipe for conflict. And especially if you're a diminishing party – it's a recipe for internal mayhem. And yet we have our Electoral College systems, our selection panel systems, our membership systems, and they work and help to mitigate the inevitable conflict and competition that comes up in political parties. That's what COPE didn't have, it's what the UDM doesn't have – none of the other opposition parties have – and to be frank, nor does the ANC. But what the ANC manages to do is use the politics of patronage as the kind of centrifugal force to hold things together.

Q: Do you have a values belief? I know you have a work ethic like few – but how do you make sure that that becomes part of the culture and filters all the way down, because the DA is just getting bigger and bigger?

Zille: Our values are absolutely critical. We stand for the open society and we stand for the opportunity-driven society and that has very profound implications for an organisation and for our entire culture. We believe fully in the rule of law, not the rule of individuals. We believe fully in non-racialism in a serious way. We believe in an open market economy to create jobs and beat poverty. But above all, the open society is premised on Karl Popper's idea that you must always look for reasons that you may be wrong rather than proof that you are right. And that has a very profound impact on the culture of this organisation because within that context you welcome people with different ideas; you welcome people who challenge you; you welcome people who approach things differently and you welcome the debate around the issues. And then when you reach agreement through proper processes because you believe in due process, everyone goes with it and seeks to make it a success. That's a profound culture within an organisation. If we ever start mobilising on the basis of race or turning the organisation into a cult of personalities or if we have people subverting the system in their own interests, then it will belie our values and our culture. That's why we put huge effort into training all our public representatives, putting them through a tough values test, actually; that's why we do our young leaders programme every year, because we have to keep our values and understanding of our vision as part of what we do.

Q: What leadership lessons did you learn through the discussions with Dr Ramphele?

Zille: What I learned from that experience was that you're generous to a point and then you say, no, no more. And then you know what your best alternative to a negotiated agreement is. You know where you've got to draw a line in the sand.

Q: What would you do first if elected President?
Zille: If I was elected President I would appoint the right people in the right places. I would put the right Ministers in and I would make sure we had DGs in who could really do the job.

||||||||||||||||||||||||||||||||||||||||||||||||||||||||||||||||||||||||||||||||||||||||||||||||||||||||||

CHAPTER 4

Seamless leader attitude to combining 'success' and values

WITH
- ❏ *Gary Kirsten*
- ❏ *Sizwe Nxasana*
- ❏ *Brian Dames*

The importance of values in our personal, family and work environments cannot be overstated. They play a crucial role as a catalyst, tool and universal principle of change and movement in seamless leadership.

The Oxford Dictionary defines values as follows: *'One's principles or standards; one's judgment of what is valuable or important in life'.*

Seamless leaders understand and truly believe that our values strike deep into the very soul of human behaviour. They understand it is not necessarily what we say that is a true reflection of our value system, but what we believe to be 'real' in the deepest part of our being. Our behaviour, especially when we are on our own, is a direct reflection of our true value system. Most of us would claim that we value being a fair and compassionate person. Yet if we are suddenly confronted by a hungry robber attempting to take our food by force, then our personal value system may be in tatters at that moment. The reality of the threatening situation may also threaten our declared values. In other words, one may feel resentment and hatred rather than compassion towards the man.

This is an extreme example but it makes an important point. We need to recognise that our positive values must be conditioned into our very soul or else we will default automatically to negative values, depending on the pressure of the situation. All of us are in fact driven by a set of values that is a mixture of both positive and negative. This is a major reason why people perform so differently in life. Some have a well-entrenched positive value system while others default very quickly to negative and reactive values.

The point is that believed values are an imperative of human behaviour. All our perceptions and actions are driven by our perceived deep-rooted values, whether these are positive or negative. The normal day-to-day expressions of human conduct such as anger, frustration, criticism, vindictiveness, envy, misunderstanding, negativity, lack of respect, are all mostly expressions of a negative value system. But the converse is also true; that the many expressions of loyalty, compassion, unity, patience, tolerance and passion for excellence are also an expression of our positive value system.

The value system of a seamless leader is closely aligned to SiPCOM. Consider the values listed above – loyalty, compassion, unity, patience, tolerance and passion for excellence. These are closely linked to a deep-rooted respect for situations, people, choices, obstacles and movement.

But how does one balance values with success? Success has so many definitions! During a radio show I presented several years ago, a listener called in and asked the panel to define success. Needless to say, every definition given was different – good answers, no doubt, but different nevertheless. Our experience is that although 'successful' individuals' definitions of success often differ slightly there are similarities, whether one talks about personal or leadership success.

For now we will refer to success as either 'profitable' or 'profitable & happy' living, the latter being the ideal. What we mean by 'profitable' living is someone who aspires towards something they want and even obtains it by investing what it takes – be it time in the gym to lose 30 kg or in studies to acquire a degree, or capital and energy in a business venture for a specific financial return.

But, on the journey of achievement this specific profitable person may do it at the cost of something or someone they value most. In other words, he or she may invest time to achieve an aspiration only to look back and find their spouse and children are not there with them, almost as it were a 'profit & loss' (P&L) scenario – profit in building a successful business or country, but loss of happy relationships. Such a leader could even appear on the list of extraordinary leaders. But, they have failed at making the best of one of the five core similarities of life (SiPCOM) – association with people and building worthwhile relationships.

What we mean by 'profitable and happy' living is the achievement of aspirations without losing what is valued most in life. That is, a P&H (Profitable & Happy) result rather than a P&L (Profit & Loss) result, as in attaining a successful business as well as happy family relationships. Such people know what they want in life, what they value most and strive to achieve in both areas.

If you possess a mature seamless leader attitude, your wants and aspirations will be aligned not only with yourself but also with significant others, the organisation you are part of and even society at large.

I know of an individual who rose through the ranks of a global company (one of the largest in the world) to end up at head office in Germany, reporting to the global executive team, at a relatively young age. His family followed him there. He travelled a lot. His wife was desperately unhappy, so he gave up his promising career, came back to South Africa and started his own business. He made a decision to lead a P&H life rather than a P&L life.

A profitable and happy (successful) person can usually answer with confidence at least the following four critical questions: 1) What do I really want in life? 2) How will I get to what I want? 3) What resources, skills, etc will I need to get to the 'how'? 4) What do I/significant others/ society value most in life? Answering these questions honestly, aiming towards and achieving the 'want', while aligning with what one values most, equals real success and elements of seamless leadership principles. Such a leader applies some of the dynamics of forward thinking and movement.

Not only a person but also an organisation, division, branch or any entity can choose the profitable & happy road. A seamless leader and team will openly and honestly answer these same questions about their responsible area: 1) What do we as a family/business/department/organisation/country really want to achieve? 2) How will we get to what we want? 3) What will we need (resources/skills/systems) to get to the 'how'? 4) What do we as a team of individuals value most?

Of course when members of a team are individually on the profitable and happy path they will more fully understand that the same principles apply to the team or organisation. There are obviously more principles needed for an organisation to be successful, such as measurable actions, holding every leader accountable, and so on. But, with a team of individuals who understand and apply these principles in their own lives, measurement and accountability come naturally.

Profitable and happy individuals apply, often subconsciously, the same criteria to others as to themselves, and so move from leading themselves to leading others, hence moving even closer towards a seamless leader attitude. In other words, when they deal with others they find out from them what they really want; how they want to get there; what they need to get there; and what they value. They can then align their own answers with the answers of others. Because of this attitude they tend to generate feelings of passion and enjoyment in themselves and others. You can sense this in their presence. What a significant difference it makes to someone personally as well as those around them when they are enthusiastic, confident and passionate!

Some years ago I had the privilege of being a judge on the 'Boss of the Year' panel. What stood out clearly in the finalists was the passion and enjoyment they had for their job and life. What impressed me even more was the passion and enjoyment that radiated from each one of the nominators while the panel interviewed them. It was clear that these finalists had managed to transfer their enjoyment for the job and life over to their staff (more on this in chapter 5).

When all is said and done, a profitable and happy leader usually starts developing an attitude of approval, admiration and acceptance of universal principles and processes that empower both leader and co-workers to become profitable and happy. And, the more you focus on and master these universal (always applicable) principles and processes, the more you think like a seamless leader, which boosts your capacity to feel in control and be positive about challenges no matter what the situation.

You will also be less sensitive about personal feelings and image because you will be so busy measuring your actions against universal standards rather than against what others think. In other words, a seamless leader does not have emotional hang-ups. Focusing on universal principles and processes, rather than emotional self-involvement, tends to allow you to be more teachable, to develop a fine sense of humour, to be more relaxed. It provides you with emotional space to respect and listen to others.

Profitable and happy leaders who have moved closer towards seamless leadership enjoy being exposed to ideas that improve their own performance. They want to know why and how other people do well, not to compete but to discover or broaden their own understanding of success principles even further, in order to more accurately measure their own performance against these. I seldom find individuals with such a mentality unapproachable. In fact they are surprisingly teachable and balanced!

So, we need to make a choice. Do we want to be a leader with a profit and loss (P&L) mentality – we know what we want; know how we are going to get there; know what we need to get there, and then go for it no matter what? Or, are we going to be a profitable and happy (P&H) leader who evolves into a seamless leader with a 'WE' attitude – we know what we want; know how we are going to get there; know what we need to get there; know what we value most in life; and then go for it?

If we don't make a conscious decision towards the one or the other, the default mentality will unfortunately more often than not be P&L.

Seamless leaders choose the P&H route because striving to answer these four questions is part of mastering the universal principles that govern and maximise the ability to confront and move barriers to full potential. Answering these questions lies at the heart of movement dynamics and being a forward thinker. It forms part of the Destiny Chain process mentioned in chapter 2. It incorporates SiPCOM.

To summarise, one of the ways to achieve full potential is to know ourselves or the situation we are supposed to lead and then define the state of 'full potential' – **What do I/we really want to achieve?** Then plan how to get there – **How will I/we get to what I/we want?** This is followed by deciding what is needed to get to the destiny – **What will I/we need (resources/skills/systems) to get to the 'how'?** And then following the moral compass, a decision about what we value most – **What do I/we as a team of individuals value most?**

Gary Kirsten – former Coach for national Indian and South African cricket teams

Seamless Leadership Principles:

1. Look out for Kirsten's emphasis on values in his own life and those of the players.

2. See how Kirsten followed P&H principles.

3. Try to identify more seamless leadership principles and signs of a seamless leadership attitude. There are many to pick from.

Michael Jordaan, former CEO of First National Bank, said this of national cricket coach Gary Kirsten: 'I had a beer with him in India to chat about leadership which turned into a three-and-a-half hour conversation. We spoke exactly the same language, even though we came from such different disciplines.'

After a conversation with Kirsten I understood this comment. He is an avid reader and student of leadership, people and ways to get them to achieve their best, which is exactly what he accomplished with the South African team. According to him, quality leadership is that ingredient that 'makes a difference to a team, an organisation and a family'. There have been three vehicles through which he has worked to understand leadership. One was through research, by reading many books – leadership, management, business, autobiographies and much more. Another vehicle was the influence of an executive coach who shadowed him in India and gave him feedback on a daily basis, resulting in personal growth. Third, of course, he had views of what a great coach is all about from the perspective of being a professional cricketer for 17 years. The information he acquired from these vehicles was invaluable. However, as Kirsten explained, 'I felt I could present this information to the individual in the right way.

For me that is one of the qualities of leadership. It's not about the new information or any intellectual property. It's how you deliver it.' His personal experience was that the quality of information delivery to him as a player determined to what extent he bought into what his coach said.

Many believe that coaching is 80 per cent luck and timing, in terms of the team and talent the coach inherits, and only 20 per cent or less is about the skill of the coach. Kirsten agrees. But at that level a great coach with a leadership approach can take a 60 per cent team and turn them into an 80 per cent team, which is the difference between being the best in the world on a consistent basis and always coming close. We all know that this was exactly the movement that the advent of Kirsten as coach brought about. How, is the real question, and the answer should make any leader out there sit up and take note.

To start with, Kirsten felt that he could tweak something in the Protea team, 'otherwise I wouldn't do it'. He recognised that he inherited a very good, experienced, high-performing team, with an experienced captain – but what contributed to the 10 per cent tweak? He explained: 'In leadership you live your values on a daily basis. A lot of those values will then be infiltrated into the team culture. From a leadership perspective it was a lot about who I was every day towards those players and the environment. By doing that, was I able to influence the environment in a positive way that would give them the 10 per cent tweak?' So here is the first secret, and it isn't rocket science. Kirsten looked at himself first and asked himself the difficult question: 'Am I offering everything of myself to set up this environment for success?' It was firstly an intimately personal journey. Once he felt he was moving in the right direction he could authentically pose the same question to every player 'to make sure our environment was foolproof'. This sounds so simple, but what a difference such an attitude would make in any organisation! In my opinion very few leaders manage to achieve this.

Kirsten's approach created an environment where players were not playing for any one person but for the group, the team. 'When you get people playing for each other you have a very powerful force that goes way beyond individual credibility and success. The success will come, but players are playing for a bigger cause.' For him, 'If you cannot create that in any team, organisation or group of people I don't believe you can really lead the people forward.'

When Kirsten became the leader of our national team he pulled them together because they all knew some tweaking had to be done. They created their own language together, which in essence meant standards of behaviour – or values. Kirsten saw his job from then on as fairly simple: live the valued standards of behaviour and make sure these find their way into everyday conversations with the players. In other words, not a day went by that he did not refer to or somehow mention the values to players or a player. Another example was the word 'care' – they cared for one another, and heard the word 'care' every single day of their lives. But he realised: 'I needed that language that everyone bought into: not my language – their language, their content. And it was my responsibility to deliver the content in the most appropriate way.' He had to add value to this outcome and ensure individuals in the team understood their responsibility in relation to what they wanted to achieve. He added: 'I am right in there. This is my massive responsibility.'

Very importantly, 'If they are showing behaviours that don't reflect the values then I check in with them, because that's their words, not my words. I have to check in on the behaviours.' Kirsten was wary of placing the values or words on a wall, 'because it is easy to put those words up and then walk away. The words are crucial, but if the words become your organisation's language then the behaviours of the people in that team should be a reflection of the words. It has to be lived out by the leaders.'

Adopting these values made it possible for team members to 'live in harmony as a group of people, because we all bought into that system'. Kirsten believes it cannot work in any other way. One set of values is the way! And, over and above this, someone can bring their attitude, energy and commitment along to add value.

All the above constitutes most of the 10 per cent tweak and represents what takes a team to being the world champions; crossing the line and closing the loop on what must be done.

When leaders knew I was sitting down with Kirsten many wanted to know how he united the team; how he managed to get individual egos to become submissive to the team. In summary, his model could therefore partially be:

1. Authenticate yourself – make sure you are on a personal journey of improvement as a leader and person.
2. Challenge your team members to do the same.
3. Unite the team around their own language, values and standards of behaviour.
4. As the leader, live these values to be the example.
5. Import the values and standards into your everyday language.
6. Somehow measure the behaviour.
7. Hold team members accountable when they don't live the standards.

Q&A

Q: Someone wondered why you accepted a job where you will be fired in four years. Seriously, being a coach is a career that is exceptionally unsure.
Kirsten: There is no long-term plan, because it is so results orientated. You sign a contract for two years, or whatever, and that could be it. I manage this by not focusing on trophies, even though I am measured by it and accept it and the responsibility that comes with that. I rather focus on leading people and helping them be the best they can be, and creating an environment for people to be as successful as they can be. If that brings trophies and success then I am grateful for that.

Q: Do you look for more in players, other than the obvious talent and certain skills?
Kirsten: Yes I do. But we are somewhat restricted as resources are limited. We only have certain very talented players around. So, it is not as if I can say I have five guys from whom to pick for one position, who are highly talented and can make it at international level, and I can now pick the one that fits into the team value system, culture. That's what I would love to be doing. Sometimes we don't have five but two or one. So you have

to take that individual and work with him; try to get the best out of him; make sure your critical mass in your team is up in such a way that the majority of the individuals buy into the team value system and what it stands for. In any team one is going to have mavericks who feel it is their show, that the team needs them, because they are the high performers.

Q: How do you handle that?
Kirsten: They can be very destructive. In my limited experience there are two ways of dealing with it. You have to get that guy on your side or you have to try and create an environment where your senior players get him on side, because it might not always be able to be you. Ultimately you don't necessarily need the player completely on side. You just have to have him not be destructive, or the cancer in the team. If he starts trying to win people over or lobbying people over to a way of doing things then you are in trouble. If he keeps to himself, pretty quiet, performs well, doesn't get involved too much, not destructive, critical mass is up and you don't really need him in a leadership position, he's accepting enough of the culture, I can work with such a guy.

Q: One would think a national coach should preferably be from the same country so as to feel an allegiance towards country, yet you transcended this principle in India. How did you do that?
Kirsten: Whatever team, organisation or group, you have to understand that environment you are going into; what you need to do; how you need to shift as an individual; not how the people around you need to shift. So I need to understand that space, then ask: 'Within my leadership philosophies, what do I need to do, say or be to these individuals, based on who they are as people?' That was an incredible learning experience for me in India and South Africa, two very different cultures. I felt that the needs and requirements for the South African team were very different to the requirements of the Indian team, within who I am as a person and my coaching philosophies. I ended up leading very differently.

Q: Summarise your leadership philosophy?
Kirsten: What can I do in my personal capacity, mentally, physically,

emotionally, spiritually, within my power, as an individual, to positively influence a group of individuals to create an environment where people are happy and enjoy what they are doing and thrive, are highly successful.

Q: You seem to be calm under pressure. How do you do that?
Kirsten: I think I hide it. I think we always feel it. What is important for me is when you become a person of influence, as a leader, people are looking at you; they watch you; follow your lead. So if you have poor body language and panic in it, yet you are an inspirational leader to people, by definition you are going to make your subjects panic as well, because you are inspiring as a leader. So if you have high intensity, panic, or whatever, I think it is going to affect your players. But there is also an upside in that when you show great intensity that will come through into the team. I have always gone for the theory of just remaining neutral. The downside is that people criticise you for not caring enough. I'll take that hit. At the end of the day my influence is what happens behind closed doors.

Q: Favourite leadership books?
Kirsten: Jim Collins, *Good to Great*; Pep Guardiola's *Another Way of Winning*; Bill Walsh, *The Score Takes Care of Itself: My Philosophy on Leadership*.

Sizwe Nxasana – CEO First Rand Group

Seamless Leadership Principles:

1. Look out for Nxasana's emphasis on values in his own life and that of the organisation, together with the principle of giving direction.

2. Try to identify more seamless leadership principles and signs of a seamless leadership attitude. There are many to pick from, including:
   - ❑ Develop a strong moral compass
   - ❑ One can never communicate enough
   - ❑ Listen more
   - ❑ Create a common understanding of values and direction of the business
   - ❑ Leaders are there to make decisions.

We live in a very delicate society where even leaders who honestly try to be above reproach in their conduct are apt to land in troubled waters. Certain factors (positive and negative at times) in our highly democratic society cause them to find themselves on the front or inside pages of newspapers where, by association, they are positioned as unethical.

One such factor is the emergence of a culture where we confront issues through the media rather than with the relevant parties direct. If one camp feels like they are starting to lose ground they try to bring themselves back into the race by involving the media.

A culture of selfish materialism and self-preservation has also reared its head. This means leaders often don't make decisions for the good of an organisation but for self-gain. These and many other factors are barriers to a seamless society, and if not brought under some level of control will make it less and less attractive to lead organisations in the future.

Today, perhaps more than at any other time in the world's history, leaders need a strong moral compass to navigate themselves and their organisations; some sure way of knowing what is right and what is wrong.

Together with this, when a high-pressure situation emerges, they need a technique that places them in a space where they can pause and quietly measure their and their organisations' actions against moral values that they believe in; a benchmark or standard that they will not compromise.

If this technique does not exist consciously, or if their moral compass is weak, leaders risk failing to notice in time when confronted with traps – sometimes obvious and other times disguised – that exist in a very ambiguous moral society. There are situations where the moment can be so big that the leader is sucked into it without stopping to review the morality of the situation. The danger is when the possible outcome and recognition associated with that moment appears more attractive than the promptings or warnings of a weak conscience (that quiet voice) that may be guided by a 'convenient' or unclear moral compass.

What or who is your moral compass? Although all of us have this built-in 'quiet voice' or conscience, most of us have adopted our moral values from someone, directly or indirectly. It could be a parent, an uncle, a coach, or a spiritual leader or God. It may be important to know consciously where your beliefs come from, so that you can compare or measure or if necessary apply a technique that may involve asking a question to bring you back to your roots. Is the alternative simply to choose convenience, fluctuating between different sets of moral values, depending on the situation?

Often when a difficult situation confronts Sizwe Nxasana, he asks himself: 'What would my mother have told me about this particular situation?' When he asks himself this question he invariably finds an answer. This, I believe, is one of his techniques of calling up his moral compass; of measuring against those valued standards that he truly believes in.

Nxasana is a tall man with 'presence' and it is easy to be impressed by him. After matriculating in Durban he started working for the KwaZulu-Natal government while deciding what to do with his life, then eventually opted for a B Com degree at Fort Hare University, followed by post-graduate studies in accounting to eventually become a professional chartered accountant. Thereafter he worked outside of the accounting profession, but came back into it.

He started his own practice, called Sizwe & Company, in 1989, which grew and eventually merged with other firms to become one of the largest black-owned accounting firms in South Africa. In 1998 he made a huge leap, not only industry-wise but size-wise when he jumped from his accounting practice to the telecommunications industry as the CEO of Telkom, leading this giant organisation for almost eight years. Another milestone in his career came in 2006 when he made a leap from telecommunications to the financial sector and joined First Rand Group. At the end of 2009 he took over fully as the Group CEO of the entire First Rand Group.

His several unique leadership experiences have helped form an approach to dealing with people that reflects universal truths:

1. Communication: as other great leaders have mentioned before, one can never communicate enough.
2. Listen more, with a belief that others in the organisation can contribute: leaders sometimes think that their positions necessitate them talking all the time, delivering messages. Instead they need to create an environment where they listen to their people and stakeholders generally.
3. Create a common understanding of values and direction of the business. This makes it easier for people to relate to the organisation. Having a shared sense of values also makes it easier to deal with people issues and to act more consistently.

Nxasana is a great believer that leaders are there to make decisions, and that they will make mistakes in the process. But, it is also important to understand that one cannot have all the information before making a decision. The leader is to discuss, debate, collate information and use intuition to make decisions. And, before making a decision, ensure the right motive guides you – the best interest of the organisation. If the decision ends up as the wrong one the leader can take the rap and learn from it.

Genuinely considering whether a decision is in the best interest of the organisation is another technique of pausing and consulting one's moral compass. If things go wrong and the leader can with humility apologise, followed by a clear explanation of how the decision seemed to be in the best interests of the organisation at the time, stakeholders will more often than not be reasonable in their judgement.

Would Nxasana's mother ever have realised that she was raising her son to one day lead tens of thousands of people in organisations like Telkom and First Rand Group; that she would continue forming part of Nxasana's moral compass? How powerful one's upbringing is – in fact, how powerful mothers can be in raising seamless leaders.

Brian Dames – former CEO Eskom

Seamless Leadership Principles:
1. Notice Dames's own value system.
2. Look out for the comments on a need for values in order to transform an organisation.
3. Try to identify more seamless leadership principles and signs of a seamless leadership attitude in Dames.

Brian Dames, CEO of Eskom until 2014, grew up in Kimberley. His father sold life policies for Metropolitan and his mother was a teacher. His home environment was a disciplined one and church was very much a part of their upbringing. The family moved to Cape Town where his one brother and sister were already studying and Dames needed to start his first year at varsity, to major in physics and computer science. The move was not ideal for his mother. She fell ill and they buried her the day after Dames and his brother graduated. She was adamant that she would continue to work until they completed their education.

One of the siblings in their family had constant health problems, which was a central feature in the family affairs. Mom and Dad often had to focus on caring for this child, leaving the others to function independently. Their values were clear and they could therefore look after themselves within these parameters. Dames can cook for himself, clean the house ('if he has to' he says), he can iron his clothes, and much more.

It seems that these and other personal experiences grounded Dames. Not only does he have a very close relationship with his family, but he also developed a clear sense and appreciation of life and knows what his own values are – to live for people around him and not for himself; making his own decisions within certain boundaries; a sense of responsibility;

caring for the less fortunate; working hard; staying real; interacting with people at all levels.

His career started at Koeberg as a nuclear physicist and he enjoyed it so much that he thought he would do nothing else. A management programme at Stellenbosch changed this perception and he became interested in management and leadership.

A year later he was picked as one of only two candidates in the Eskom organisation to attend a full-time two-year MBA programme in the USA, with his family accompanying him. That experience changed his career away from the fascinating scientific path to a challenging yet rewarding future in leadership.

Following much-publicised controversies, the Eskom CEO position became vacant. A common perception is that putting one's name in the hat for this position sets one up for failure. Dames wrestled with whether he should go for the opportunity or not. After discussions with his family they encouraged him to put his hand up.

Throughout his career he had had the opportunity to take on difficult challenges and turn these situations around. The question on most South Africans' minds was whether this 'good guy' with depth of character could lead Eskom out of the muddle it found itself in. Being a good guy was obviously not enough.

At the time of entering the race for the top job, Dames felt that Eskom needed strong leadership; someone who could boost morale and create some sense of stability, direction and vision. Employees and other stakeholders were anxious, angry, and mistrustful, had little confidence in Eskom leadership and had no sense of pride in working for the organisation.

While the situation was precarious, to say the least, Dames started doing all within his power to lead within his circle of influence. Part of his approach was to build a healthy relationship with the Chairman and Board of Eskom.

His first actions as CEO were to engage the Exco team to establish clear expectations, understanding what he wanted and what other people wanted; he opened up the Exco and brought in broader management to engage them as well; clear, quick decisions were made early, which included structural change such as closing the executive dining room; they engaged nearly all the staff to introduce Dames so that he could share expectations, give perspective and communicate company results, and they launched a strategic review process that involved some 100 managers, who, within certain guidelines, had to produce an answer to the question of what it was that Eskom wanted to create. The output was presented to the Board and the company adopted a new strategic direction; this direction was then communicated to all staff before Dames went away on holiday end 2010; at the same time they engaged externally with government leaders, like premiers and mayors in several provinces, and with the unions.

The plan was for this inclusive strategic review process to evolve into a Leadership Academy to systematically prepare and grow leaders, close development gaps and expose the leadership pipeline to the world of leadership. Executive management also started focusing on giving employees the freedom to do their jobs, with clear expectations as to what behaviours were expected from them, and trusting them to do what they had to do.

Dames believes that leadership is what makes the difference. When he graduated, Bishop Tutu was Chancellor at the university. He encouraged graduates to prepare themselves to lead one day and emphasised that 'it is not about you but how you are going to serve the country; it is not about how much you can accumulate'. This advice always stuck with Dames.

He believes that as a leader you must first open yourself up and understand your strengths and weaknesses, not only to know yourself but also to assist others in getting to know you. Only after opening yourself up should you set clear expectations for leadership behaviours that set the tone and culture of the organisation. Dames defined six clear and simple leadership objectives and behaviours: 'I expect leaders to grow people; I expect them to have open and transparent communication; I expect them to be coaches; I expect them to live the vision; I expect them to create a sense of passion, energise people; to make decisions and take people with them.'

Dames rates his managers against these leadership behaviours and expects this same discipline from every other manager. He also believes in the need for a leader to sit down with his immediate reports and discuss their development, strengths and weaknesses, career opportunities, and so on. As he says: 'We all deserve quality time from our superiors.'

For most leaders, changing culture is the most difficult thing to do, often because they don't really grasp the following truth about it: culture stems from consistent, shared behaviours, which in turn stem from deep-rooted values and beliefs. So many leaders fall into the trap of trying to change culture by trying to change behaviours. They often discover too late that they are wasting a lot of resources and valuable time on the wrong approach.

Broadly speaking, behaviours are the tip of the iceberg. The right approach is to understand and address that larger part of the culture iceberg that is below the surface, i.e. values and beliefs. As leaders, connecting with our people at this level is more meaningful and more likely to influence long-term behaviour change. If not done this way that iceberg called culture could sink your ship – be it Eskom or South Africa. Finding a way of answering the following questions will help:

1. Collectively, what are the deep-rooted personal values and beliefs of my workforce?
2. Collectively, what positive and negative values and beliefs are currently being portrayed in the behaviours of leaders and employees of our organisation?
3. Collectively, what values and beliefs do all of us desire to inculcate into this organisation?

Involving all levels of one's organisation in answering the above three questions brings the guessing game to an end, because leaders need not make assumptions about why their people continue acting in a certain way. Then the real work and courageous leadership starts by using this insight to actively drive the internalisation of the desired values (point 3), while eliminating from the culture those values, beliefs and behaviours that limit potential for growth.

An example of needed behaviour change mentioned by Dames was the sensitive issue of safety, which most mines and construction companies also struggle with. Changing negative safety behaviours is part and parcel of needing to change the underlying culture and context within Eskom. Changing culture takes incredible courage and conscious effort, because the desired outcome is a deep, lasting change rather than a superficial, short-lived change.

Dames adopted a video lecture by Professor Sumantra Ghoshal that he showed across Eskom. In the lecture, the Professor explained that every year, in July, he would go to Kolkata, India, for almost a month to visit his parents. But, in downtown Kolkata in July the temperature is over 100°F with humidity of 98 per cent. He would spend most of his time indoors resting and conserving energy.

In contrast, he explained that he used to live in Fontainebleau, France, 40 miles south of Paris. 'Around it is the protected forest of Fontainebleau, which is one of the prettiest forests in all of Europe. You enter the forest in spring, with a firm desire to have a very leisurely walk and you cannot. There is something about the smell of the air, about the trees, that will make you want to run, jog, jump up, catch a branch, to throw a stone, to do something. You will find that even though you entered the forest to have a leisurely walk, you are doing something else.'

He called the difference between Kolkata and Fontainebleau 'the smell of the place'. He hypothesised that many companies negatively affected their profit/loss performance because their corporate environment, the smell of their place, was more like Kolkata and less like Fontainebleau. In these companies, the culture disengaged employees rather than energising them. Some leaders create Kolkata environments while others manage to create Fontainebleau environments. (This speech at the World Economic Forum can be seen at www.youtube.com/watch?v=UUddgE8rlOE.)

I am convinced that Dames tried hard to change the 'smell' of Eskom. For lasting cultural change, though, Eskom leadership would do well to ensure that they can answer the above questions in order to analyse and address the 'below-the-surface-of-the-iceberg' part of their culture that matters most. Dames admitted there were weaknesses in the system, but also great managers and employees who had kept their heads down and worked through all the crises. The parallels between Eskom and South Africa are noticeable. Despite all the difficulties, Eskom keeps recovering, which sounds like South Africa to me. We go through difficult times yet we keep on recovering.

||||||||||||||||||||||||||||||||||||||||||||||||||||||||||||||||||||||||||||||||||||||||||||||||||||||||||||

CHAPTER 5

Seamless leader attitude to igniting passion and shifting attitude

WITH
- *Sipho Nkosi*
- *Chris Griffith*

Some time back I shared a couple of tweets from this passage by my father, Louis Groenewald, and received more re-tweets than ever before: 'Passion is a powerful language. Passion for a cause crosses cultural and language barriers. It is felt, rather than mentally understood. Passion feels authentic. It sends out honest vibes. It can be quiet and vibrant and at other times it can be overwhelming and dominant. Passion can also be the most destructive force on earth driving evil motives. Passion is a catching thing! It can be seen in our eyes and body language. Our passion for excellence as leaders has the tendency to cross almost impossible boundaries of cultures and philosophies. Passion is a universal language. The greatest passion is that of unconditional love, often manifested by mothers and leaders committed to universal values.'

Unfortunately, I find leaders are less passionate now about what they do than they were in the distant or even recent past. And the same can be said of employees in general, fortunately with exceptions here and there. Simple passion for one's job seems to be disappearing quickly in the modern workplace, and as this happens the passion for excellence is also severely impacted in a negative way. And of course there is a strong correlation between a leader's passion for the job and that of the employee.

There may be many reasons for this decline in passion. People are working much longer hours than their parents did, with concomitant threats to family ties and increases in stress-related illnesses. Against this backdrop, in today's fast-paced, ever-moving environment, where pressure increases daily, leaders have to be on top of their game like never before – and I would hasten to add that they had better possess bundles of passion if they are going to succeed. But it is difficult to be on top of their game when the facts about the situation they lead seem to fluctuate and change at the blink of an eye. In today's world everything affects everything: the well-known domino effect drives the socio-political, economic and technological environment. Many leaders struggle to gain sufficient insight into their environment to see how dynamic changes around them impact the facts of their own situation.

The environment in which leaders lead seems to be bombarded by all sorts of obstacles, challenges and the negative perceptions of their followers. These too seem to change consistently, and while this is nothing new, the pace and severity seems to continually increase. This clearly has an impact on people's attitudes, and thus a direct correlation with performance – once again because of the dynamic composition of our modern, connected society.

On the positive side, as challenges and obstacles arise, so do innumerable opportunities, options and possibilities. This is the nature of life: those who lose sight of this fact and allow themselves to be consumed only by challenges are on a losing streak.

These distractions make it very difficult for most leaders and their team members to keep a focused eye on strategy and vision. Trying to get a handle on the changing facts and deal with the never-ending challenges, they are easily diverted from what they agreed on. As performance is negatively affected, they panic and seek answers or even quick fixes by unnecessarily changing direction and relevant structures, implementing new systems and procedures in a desperate attempt to impact performance indicators and accommodate or correct the course. And then their organisation moves towards becoming a compliance institution rather than a value-adding institution. This is a dangerous place to be.

Under this mounting pressure leaders neglect to calmly, consistently and systematically follow up, evaluate and measure the right priorities pertaining to the plan and vision. Or, they do far too much of this, because of a compliance culture. The emphasis becomes one of measuring or evaluating for the sake of doing it or to simply enforce compliance, rather than doing it in areas that add most value or that are core to the business. They lose the confidence to adjust when needed and, more often than in the past, act tough inappropriately, out of frustration. They stop trusting and listening, and instruct instead, sending a message of panic and spreading the feeling of distrust and even fear across the organisation. And so the spiral continues. It does not slow down to give them a chance to breathe. In fact it just continues to pick up pace and thrust new and different challenges at them, or the same ones in different guises.

What to do about this? As always, the answer is simple but difficult, yet it remains the answer nevertheless. A leader must implement a process, system or way of always remaining in tune with the following:

1. The changing facts of their relevant responsibility – not only as they see them, but as their team sees them. They have to keep listening.
2. The constraints, obstacles and challenges of their relevant responsibility, together with the negative perceptions their people may have at any given moment. Why? Because these impact directly on their attitude, which has a direct correlation with their performance. Again, they must not be viewed from the leader's angle alone: the team must always be part of identifying and addressing them.
3. The positive opportunities, options and strengths at their disposal, together with the positive perceptions that exist. Also, for reasons of attitude, to remain sane and positively focused on solutions and even ways to miraculously leapfrog the pressured environment into proactive space where profitable movement is achievable.
4. Exactly where they are leading their people to. Destiny must be on every agenda and always top of mind.
5. The clear and relevant plan or strategy that will take them there and continually raise the believability levels of followers that they can get there.
6. The relevant resources and structures needed to follow the plan towards the destiny. If this is not done structures will get out of

hand, irrelevant and expensive, consuming unnecessary energy that should be expended in other areas.

7. The above six points need to be evaluated regularly together with the leader's team, in accordance with the pace of change of their environment.

8. Only when leaders feel on top of the seven points above may they adjust where relevant and even act tough where the situation requires it.

9. Finally, they need to continually focus and re-focus the team and the organisation on the vision, the destiny of where they are moving to.

Once again the universal Destiny Chain process discussed in chapter 3 comes to the rescue. As I have assisted leaders to make this crucial nine-step process a habit, part of their culture, to institutionalise it at all levels of their organisation, I have seen how the timing of when to refresh, revisit or tap back into it has changed. A team may, for example, start by revisiting the process every year or six months, but soon realise that the pace of their changing environment requires a more regular approach. They are forced to stay on top of every point every month, week or even day.

This is the reality under which leaders operate these days. There is no way of escaping it. If leaders do not master these nine steps they will become crisis managers who feel out of control and lose their passion – and when leaders lose their passion, their people lose it too, which can only move one way fast ... and that is the nowhere of failure.

Feeding the instinct to possess and belong

Some are passionate about life and what they do. Some are passionate about their jobs. Some refuse to acknowledge that it is possible to really enjoy their jobs and may flood us with a multitude of reasons why they could not possibly enjoy what they do. Leaders and human resource managers sometimes want to tear their hair out when it comes to creating a workplace that is enjoyable as well as an environment for generating excellence towards the organisation's full potential.

Seamless leaders believe that a passion for what you do more often than not results in a passion to perform, which is one of the most valuable attributes and an imperative for movement towards full potential. A person with a passion to perform is far more likely to prepare, endure, study, learn, find solutions, ignite enthusiasm in others, serve the client and move barriers to full potential.

In the corporate environment it is probably not realistic to expect all employees to be as passionate in their work as some of the bosses and owners. But it is realistic to expect positive results as we follow an intelligent process of cultivating enjoyment and passion in their environment. Many organisations have proven this to be the case. Let's look at some of the guiding principles involved.

As mentioned in chapter one, every human being has an instinct to *possess* and to *belong.* An effective way to form a picture of who and what we are is to examine closely our perceptions of what we feel we possess, where we feel we belong, what we want to possess and where we want to belong.

When we put this portfolio of perceptions together we will have a pretty good idea of our own self-image. And our attitude towards life and work is determined by our self-image, which can be a very complicated and mixed-up set of perceptions of belonging and ownership.

In our quest for better understanding of passion for full potential, we must come to a realisation that no matter what we do, it will always impact on another person's sense of belonging. If you carefully examine your organisation's programme of training and policies you may well find that much of it is intended to generate a clearer feeling of belonging, ownership and excellence amongst staff members. If this is not the case, then you may need to take another look at your approach.

What does 'belonging' mean? As is the case with all of our natural instincts, the instinct to belong is inherent in all human beings. It manifests in multiple ways from the day we are born. Children manifest an intense passion to belong with their mother, and then parents and family. As they grow up, that instinct develops in different ways depending on culture and environmental factors. They may incline towards families, gangs, sport teams, school associations, TV audiences, universities, marriage, own family, political parties, professional groupings, secret societies, etc.

To be alive is to belong. Often such feelings of belonging may have very powerful negative connotations. For example, an abused child may feel that they 'belong' to some kind of category of worthlessness. Whether we have a 'can do' attitude or suffer from the 'cannot do syndrome', it is all about where we feel we belong.

Our attitude towards our environment and associations changes as our sense of belonging matures and then we tend to adjust our passions, often disabling loyalty to unnecessary forms of belonging.

Belonging associated only with physical possessions tends to be intensely selfish. It focuses on self-preservation and self-indulgence. On the other hand, value-driven belonging tends to breed love and respect for others, a hopeful and positive attitude towards life and other people, a victory over fears and doubts, and the cultivation of a seamless leader attitude to life in general.

The instinct to belong manifests in all our feelings, attitudes and loyalties. Very often our sense of 'belonging' or 'not belonging' may generate happiness on the one hand or a long list of social and physical illnesses on the other.

We 'belong' emotionally as well as mentally. Sometimes feelings of belonging are not reasonable or logical or even morally justifiable, but they feel very, very real to the person who is caught up in such feelings. Outsiders will look at street gangs and wonder what on earth is so attractive that draws our youth into such excesses. The gang member may possess different feelings. He or she may feel 'wanted', 'protected', and 'of value'.

One of the major causes of disagreement, dislike of others, and a lack of unity and common purpose amongst people is due to the lack of understanding of the differences between emotional and mental perspectives. I have been involved in hundreds of counselling and coaching exercises that on occasion resulted in dramatic changes in attitude and unity when people were taught to recognise the need to address emotional as well as mental perceptions.

No matter what our mental logic tells us, if we do not feel emotionally secure, we will not belong. We often speak of the major role that 'attitude' plays in human relationships. It is like trying on various sets of spectacles. Negative outlook spectacles provide negative realities to the person wearing them. Our sense of belonging is determined by what spectacles we have on, or what our outlook on life or a specific situation is.

Belonging takes on many different forms. The ability of humankind, with its legacy of instinctive attributes to think, feel and conceptualise is almost unlimited. That is why humankind is constantly devising different forms of belonging in order to feel good, do good or be good. Such forms may differ dramatically, which is why we have multiple forms of associations, affiliations and of course a boom in social media platforms.

Even the person who withdraws from society in some way or other has adopted a form of 'belonging'. He or she may feel mentally or emotionally 'at home' in his or her own world. If we do not actively seek out positive belongings we may automatically default to negative belongings.

Ultimately the perception of followers of whether or not they belong affects their levels of passion for what they do. Seamless leaders see themselves as mentors with the responsibility to cultivate a desire in others to belong, feel at home, and 'possess' attributes that move barriers to full potential. They therefore create an environment where followers feel they belong both emotionally and mentally, because they possess (own) the same values, goals and results.

Building feelings of belonging and possessing happens to be one of the weakest skills of average leaders out there. The steps in shifting and managing attitude by creating a sense of belonging and possessing are as follows:

1. Understand the hard facts.
2. Openly, honestly and boldly identify and confront the negative perceptions of individuals.
3. Take individuals on a journey of exploring possible positives and even opportunities that the situation presents.
4. Help them see some bigger picture, a vision (organisational or personal) that gives context to the current situation.
5. Plot solutions, directions, actions.

6. Ensure relevant structures and resources are there to make the directions work.
7. Ensure follow-through, evaluation, assessment of decided actions in order to adjust and do the necessary to achieve plans.

Sipho Nkosi – CEO Exxaro

|||||||||||||||||||||||||||||||||||||||||||||||||||||||||||||||||||||||||||||||||||||||||||||||||||||||||||||||||||||||||||||||||||||||||||||||||||

Seamless Leader Principles:

1. Look out for Nkosi's principles of increasing motivation by creating a culture of belonging and possessing.
2. Try to identify more signs of a seamless leader attitude. There are many to pick from, including openness and humility.

|||||||||||||||||||||||||||||||||||||||||||||||||||||||||||||||||||||||||||||||||||||||||||||||||||||||||||||||||||||||||||||||||||||||||||||||||||

Sipho Nkosi is originally from KwaZulu-Natal, where he grew up in the area of Vryheid. 'I never aspired to take a leadership position because the environment I grew up in was always an environment of compliance and what was known became normal. I saw myself, for instance, as a clerk at a court, or as a teacher, which was known and available.' Experiences such as the association with a young white friend by the name of Pieter contributed to this kind of attitude. At a very young age Pieter would sleep over at Nkosi's house, eat and play there. But then they started going to school, in totally different locations. Suddenly, during holidays Pieter would refuse to enter their house because he was taught that black people's houses were full of germs. He also indicated to Nkosi not to bother studying as he (Pieter) would always be his boss anyway. Such experiences did not fuel Nkosi's self-belief and ambition at the time.

Fortunately other experiences countered these negative influences. His father pushed the children to make studies a priority by telling them: 'I will do whatever it takes to get you to study whatever it is you have to study.' His brother was the first matriculant in their family and went on to study law at the University of Zululand.

So Nkosi had a choice: Listen to the negative voices around him, or heed the positive influences. Because he decided on the latter, he rose above his circumstances and can today serve as one of relatively few examples of people who overcame the odds and bucked the trend against the system.

He completed a BCom, also at the University of Zululand, after which he went to Ford Motor Company for five years, initially as a graduate trainee and then as a market analyst. But his resolve and desire to move forward were tested. He was retrenched, a huge challenge to his self-esteem, as many in the community looked up to this young BCom graduate from Natal. Although it was difficult to sit down with his parents and explain the situation, his view is: 'It's those things that shaped you and made you a better person.'

As destiny would have it he could not find a job for several months. During this period an earlier application to do an MBA at the University of Massachusetts in the USA, which he had forgotten about, was accepted. The decision to do this full-time was probably made easier because he was un-employed. Of this experience he says: 'I truly believe that every experience that you encounter, or any activity that you get involved in, at some time pays off; the lessons in life – you never know where they lead you. If you allow certain things to happen, you get 'taken' to a particular spot where you should have energy and drive and ambition to do that.' He started de-veloping what many refer to as a 'can do' attitude: 'In terms of saying, no, this I can't do because I lack certain skills, that was not part of my life.'

Upon his return from the USA he started at Anglo American's coal divi-sion, where he spent five years in marketing. The business, industry and his own career took a few turns, and eventually, when Anglo American and BHP Billiton decided to sell some coal assets, Nkosi was encouraged by former colleagues to put a team together, which he did. They looked for funding, bid for the asset and got it.

The vision for Exxaro was born when Nkosi indicated to his team that he wanted the organisation to achieve the vision of becoming a $20-billion market cap business. They went away and crunched the numbers, only to return with a strong case that it could only be achieved by 2019. He then suggested 2020, and everyone agreed; there was full buy-in. Today, every time someone suggests a strategy or project, the question back to them is: 'How will this assist us to get to $20 billion by 2020?'

Under Nkosi's leadership they seem to have achieved much. Not only is there unity around a direction by way of a clear vision that at least most employees follow passionately, but the strategy seems to be clear to everyone. Nkosi knows this because of the kind of questions general staff confront him with, such as concerns around why Exxaro aims to enter the PGM (Platinum Group Metals) market. He is then required to explain the reasoning in greater detail.

Nkosi also feels they have managed to 'encourage employees to feel that they belong to the organisation – 9 600 employees all over who all believe in the system, that the benefits they have seen accrue to them as well'. They created a scheme that has already paid R1 billion to employees outside management – from the cleaner upwards, everyone walked away with R135 000.

Employees are now starting to follow the share price with enthusiasm, because it is their organisation. Nkosi explains further: 'Last year the share price went down because we had made an announcement that we were buying some asset in Australia and the market didn't take that well. The phone calls I was getting from people I don't even know, staff, unions, saying this bad management decision must come to an end. Everyone looked at me and wondered how I could make this decision.'

Nkosi also believes they have brought stability into the organisation as far as leadership is concerned. In his view, 'Everyone knows that for this organisation to be successful, we've got to be flexible, we've got to understand that change is happening every three or six months because we live in an environment that is dynamic and changing, and secondly, we are part of the developing world which is really driving growth. Our business is driven by the Chinas and the Indias, not the Europes and the Americas. So everyone in this organisation understands that we can make an announcement next week that changes the face of the organisation.'

The challenges ahead are clear. Firstly, to make sure they identify and secure the projects that will take them to their 2020 vision. Secondly, 'developing the skill and leaders to do that. Without the people, without the leaders the vision will not happen.' And thirdly, Nkosi believes they need to ensure that the next leader will not easily deviate from the vision. In a sense they need to institutionalise the vision, and he is confident that a next leader will not change it due to the broad buy-in from all stakeholders.

Those around Nkosi seem to view him as a modest and empowering leader, giving his team members space to co-lead. He is willing to learn and accepts that he does not have all the answers, though he knows where he wants to go. He knows he has the final say, yet he is often overruled in meetings by his team. As a CEO he is as approachable as they come. Recently the organisation decided to celebrate the achievement of no fatalities for a year. A fairly junior employee walked into his office and challenged the decision for head office to spend more than the operations on the celebration, since they were not at the coal face, and continually promoted frugal spending. It made sense to Nkosi and he discussed this with his Exco. They changed it.

This is the man who, together with his team and all employees, seems to be bucking the trend in the mining industry, as he did in his own life.

Chris Griffith – CEO Amplats

IIIIIIIIIIIIIIIIIIIIIIIIIIIIIIIIIIIIIIIIIIIIIIIIIIIIIIIIIIIIIIIIIIIIIIIIIIIIIIIIIIIIIIIIIIIIIIIIIIIIIIIIIIIIIIIIIIIIIIIIIIIIIIIIIIIIIIIIIIIIIIIIIIIIIIIIIIIIIIIIIIIIIIIIIIIIIIIIIIIIIIIIIII

Seamless Leader Principles:
1. Look out for Griffith's ideas on moving people's attitude during very difficult times.
2. Try to identify more signs of a seamless leader attitude. There are many to pick from, including:
   ❏ Openness and honesty
   ❏ Motivation in process vs motivation in vision
   ❏ Continually focusing on values.

IIIIIIIIIIIIIIIIIIIIIIIIIIIIIIIIIIIIIIIIIIIIIIIIIIIIIIIIIIIIIIIIIIIIIIIIIIIIIIIIIIIIIIIIIIIIIIIIIIIIIIIIIIIIIIIIIIIIIIIIIIIIIIIIIIIIIIIIIIIIIIIIIIIIIIIIIIIIIIIIIIIIIIIIIIIIIIIIIIIIIIIIIII

Chris Griffith, CEO of Amplats, the largest platinum producer in the world, started his career in that industry in 1990, at the most junior level, and worked his way through the ranks [of the mining industry] to where he finds himself today. And where does he find himself? It is without doubt his greatest leadership challenge ever, at the head of an organisation that has been troubled with countless obstacles, some of which include violent labour unrest on the back of the Marikana tragedy; a market that is over-supplied; the price for platinum remaining flat with a demand that has still not recovered to pre-crisis levels; difficulties in Europe; cost escalations that are 5–10 per cent above mining inflation; and the first loss in the history of the company in 2012. Griffith returned [to the platinum industry] to oversee the final stages of a platinum review that Anglo American had commissioned in the early part of 2012. The purpose was to 'completely review the status of the platinum industry and company, to understand what needed to be done in the business,' he explains.

He clearly has leadership instincts and ability, and will need every part of it. Within 10 years of starting his career in 1990 he became the youngest

General Manager in the group, overseeing 10 000 people at the organisation's flagship operation. According to him, what prepared him most for the current leadership challenge is: 'First of all I have done the hard work. I have come up through the ranks, which has prepared me not only in terms of knowledge about my industry, but I have done work at all levels of the organisation and have the ability to connect on all those levels.' He further realises it is a people's business and his life experiences have taught him to work with people. Griffith believes his education, good mentorship and a healthy family support structure prepared him – and, he adds: 'I worked my backside off throughout my career. I worked harder than anyone else around me. I spent more time with the people than anyone else around me. It was my own personal desire to succeed and be better.'

He has seen the cycles of good and bad times and is familiar with challenges that the platinum industry poses, but by his own admission what he now faces falls in a different league: 'I know the industry. I know the kind of challenges it throws up, I think none as big as we have now, though.' According to Griffith, even during difficult times in the platinum industry 'it was always around growth, the story was growth'. This time it is different.

Before taking on the current and relatively new challenge, he was the successful CEO of Kumba, which was a totally different leadership experience. While Kumba had its challenges, they happened against the backdrop of positive movement – a positive mood, positive contribution to stakeholders, positive growth, positive financial results and much more. The Amplats leadership experience is and will be in total contrast, because the agenda is driven by a need for contracting and downscaling before returning back to a more positive space of movement seen by growth and profitability. The platinum review was clear in its recommendations and this meant tough decisions had to and still have to be made. The market is over-supplied and as the largest platinum producer Amplats must take volume out of the market. Griffith explains: 'We had loss-making operations that were clearly the first operations that we needed to shut down or reconfigure, to make the remaining operations more profitable.' While this takes place, proposals have been delivered to government, labour and other stakeholders, which are now at the centre of discussions and consultations on alternatives to contraction and ways to better offset necessary steps. In Griffith's words, 'So that's going to be the very difficult leadership journey that first needs to be taken before we can consolidate the company again and reposition it for future growth. This is the phase we are going through now.' It is a very difficult process and period for every individual in the organisation, for management, government, unions and in fact, for all stakeholders.

Such an unsure environment is simply not conducive to positivity and motivated staff, which in today's competitive and ever-changing environment happens to be crucial for needed and expected performance. To add to this, Griffith says: 'It is part of human nature, business nature, to want to grow, contribute, employ, and share more with communities and society.' Supposing he is correct in this assertion, it means they are employing 60 000 people in an environment where what currently happens and needs to happen is in fact contrary to human and business nature. It can't get much worse than this. Fortunately, from such 'desperate' situations arise the greatest opportunities and the development of invaluable attributes and character.

How does one motivate 'unsure' people? Because most leaders don't appreciate the depth and magnitude of such a problem – a situation against human and business nature – they take so much longer to get through the difficult period. Griffith realises that in instances like these, probably the best a leader can do is add to their already powerful and motivating vision the communication and application of clear process – how exactly we will deal with the situation. The vision must remain, but it will probably shift to the background; most employees will become somewhat blind and deaf to it and look for clarity and honesty of process, no matter how difficult. So, 'motivation in process' takes preference to 'motivation in vision'. Though motivation in process is not as powerful and effective as motivation in vision, this is the nature of an unnatural situation – you have to move through the negative space, mostly governed by process, with vision in the background, before you can authentically arrive in the positive space where vision governs, with process in the background. Griffith realises there is no room for pretending here. This is true for the company's actual journey towards healthy return on investment as well as the attitudinal shift every individual needs to make.

The fact about a leadership challenge like this is that leaders all the way down the structure must be better than ever at managing and 'moving' attitudes of people, by following the universal Destiny Chain process to build feelings of belonging and ownership. This sounds simple, and it is. However, it is difficult and takes confidence to actually do. If every leader, or at least key leaders, can follow such a process confidently and effectively the period of uncertainty and resultant de-motivation will be shortened. And this is what Griffith hopes to achieve. He suggests dealing with the situation requires the following: 'First of all you have to try and limit the time that people are unsure. Do all the difficult things as quickly as possible. Then you have to be open with people. The worst possible thing is to not communicate. This is the time to talk to your people and to share the values. This is important, because people are not misinformed. They can read the signs and it does not have to be in newspapers.' He acknowledges that in his present case it is a slower and protracted process, so limiting the unsure period is difficult to do.

The leader of one of the Amplats operations that may be closed down sent this message to me, which illustrates a mature attitude: 'My operation is affected. There is no certainty in terms of my future. No guarantees. We will see. But I will stay here and support the company to the last day of my operation's winding down process into care and maintenance.' With such an attitude they can make it through deep waters.

Even though this is clearly a very difficult period, Griffith says, 'We are trying to send a message that, unlike the opinion by some that it is impossible to do business in South Africa, it is not impossible to do business here. South Africa is actually a good place to do business. There are processes.'

Q&A

Q: Leaders work hard at creating values-driven organisations, promoting a set of values, yet in some cases it seems at the drop of a hat employees still decide to strike, often violently. Do all these values and cultural improvement initiatives actually work?

Griffith: It is like me saying I should not teach my children values because one day they might fall out the bus, go for the wrong friends and do the wrong things. I think the more you engrain culture and learning, eventually that will prevail. Does that mean you will never have a setback? And that is why most people turn out okay and most people have setbacks along the road. I think learning values, culture and leadership from your parents and from society is important. So, is all this work a waste of time? I certainly don't believe so. Does it prevent you from ever experiencing some of these setbacks? No it doesn't because in this case it is not only our culture that's prevailing. There are other cultures out there. Can we turn everything around at work? Heaven help us if we ever get to a position where we say this does not help. In doing this, does it mean a strike may be less violent, or that its duration will be shorter and less intense, or that after a strike you will get back quicker to where people do trust each other? I don't know the answers, but I am absolutely convinced in my mind that you have to do the right things. Keep on doing them and eventually you get to a higher place. Look at the improvement of our safety record for example. It has improved vastly, because we are instilling a value of caring that people are starting to feel.

Q: You have been in a pressure cooker in your first six months on the job. What are some leadership lessons you have learned?

Griffith: I think when things go well you are pretty much left alone. Of course you buy your freedom. In this kind of environment I continue to learn that you need to engage more and more. Often we take too much of a legalistic approach to dealing with these kinds of issues when more engagement is what's necessary. The changing face of business in South Africa and perhaps worldwide needs leaders to become comfortable with spending more time outside the business to engage other stakeholders. There are just so many more stakeholders nowadays that have an effect on your business.

Q: And what is your leadership philosophy?

Griffith: My leadership philosophy/approach is based on two main focus areas: 1) Delivery on your promise (this creates trust); and 2) 'How you do it' is as important as 'what you achieve' – that is, sustainability maximisation must have the same focus as profit maximisation. It is in the area of 'how you do it' that my leadership focus fits in. Firstly it's about the team and creating the collective ability of the team to deliver. Allowing myself and encouraging others to be passionate, courageous and tenacious in the way they go about their work and to be caring and values driven in the manner in which they do this. Lastly, 'make a difference'.

||||||||||||||||||||||||||||||||||||||||||||||||||||||||||||||||||||||||||||||||||||||||||||||||||||

CHAPTER 6

Seamless leader attitude to consistent performance

WITH
- ❏ *Gill Marcus*
- ❏ *Greg Bell*

We sometimes speak of someone who is on a winning streak or performing exceptionally well on a consistent basis in sports as being 'in the zone'. In other words, their level of performance is consistently higher than that of their rivals, because they somehow manage to be sharper, more focused and disciplined when it matters most. Often winning is not so much about the person or team with the best skills as about who has the ability to access that zone or get close to it as often as possible. Therefore, what matters most in winning at the highest levels is understanding what it takes to get closer to the zone, assuming that great skills are a given. Ingredients may include extraordinary desire, extraordinary discipline, extraordinary focus, extraordinary passion and energy.

For seamless leaders it is about getting close to or inside that seamless leadership zone as often as possible. It is much harder to be in the seamless leadership zone when you are in the spotlight every day – not infrequently like a tennis or boxing star. A seamless leader who manages to enter the leadership zone or at least come close performs on a much higher level and tends to pull the organisation or responsible area into the zone with him. The extraordinary ingredients above will certainly help. In addition, though, a principle that brings seamless leaders closer to their seamless leadership zone is: *passion and caring for their people, while not being over-sensitive to what they and others think of them.*

Some leaders really care about their people, but they also care so much about what their people think of them (wanting to be liked and respected) that they shy away from doing the tough and difficult things like reprimanding, confronting challenges, airing their views no matter how controversial and making decisions that are unpopular but right. This is not seamless leadership.

On the other hand, some leaders actually don't care what their people think of them and can do what needs to be done no matter what, which is strength to some degree and results in fearless and decisive leadership. Leaders like these can be very powerful and even successful on the surface, but insensitivity – when they don't care about their people – will more often than not eventually contribute towards their downfall. Their fearlessness may be built on some selfish and even shaky foundation. This too is not seamless leadership.

To find the balance between passion and real caring for our people while honestly not caring what they think of us is difficult to do. Many achieve this partially, either the one or the other, or they succeed in the one area and partially in the other. Very few manage to live both parts of this principle consistently. Seamless leaders get this right more often than not, because their seamless leader attitude and the core purpose of life dominate who they are. There is no need or even time to be driven by the need to be liked or approved of.

Applying this principle in full does not automatically mean you are moving your people and organisation in the right direction. However, more often than not, chances are that seamless leaders are leading people down the right path because they listen to them, involve, empower and respect them, look after them and express appreciation regularly. They also manage to confront individuals when they don't perform, with the right motive to help them and the organisation confront barriers to full potential. In other words they are able to do the right though unpopular and difficult thing for the organisation, with an underlying motive of balancing the benefits for the organisation with those of its people, in the long run. They are assertive and seldom aggressive.

What helped rugby icon Francois Pienaar move closer towards

applying this principle was when he realised the following, in his own words: 'I learnt early in my career that 50 per cent of people like you and 50 per cent don't. That's just nature. It does not matter what you do, some would brand certain actions as visionary while others would drag one down.' He further explained that once he made up his mind that no matter what he did not everyone would appreciate it, he almost felt liberated.

To always be concerned about what followers, peers or your boss think of you is a heavy burden to carry. We all suffer from this syndrome, but the further you move away from being driven by this motive, the more powerful and free you become.

There are leaders who enter into their leadership zone by applying this same principle with a different emphasis – that of passion for their goal overriding any element of self-consciousness. Then there are those leaders who will stop at nothing to achieve their goal (often P&L leaders), who are obsessed with the goal to the exclusion of the people they lead. When these 'stop-at-nothing' leaders tap into a goal and own it with their mind (how they will get there) and heart (passion), chances are they are close to or may even be in a leadership zone. However, those who really want to be a seamless leader, remaining in or close to the exclusive seamless leadership zone that respects the core purpose of life, need to also start genuinely caring about their people – equipping them with the necessary knowledge and understanding by thrusting situations and experiences on them; teaching them the value and skills of effective relationship management; affording them the space to make decisions as forward thinkers; teaching them how to overcome challenges and obstacles, personal and business, and then creating movement towards full potential. In short, offer them the opportunity to build lasting characters by engaging SiPCOM.

How does your leader stack up? How do you stack up? If we asked the people you are responsible for what their perception of you was, what would they say? Are you in your seamless leadership zone, or part zone or even the no zone?

Destiny Chain and consistent movement

Seamless leaders consciously or even subconsciously use the Destiny Chain process (see chapter 3) to be in or close to the zone in order to create consistent movement. I have used this situational and attitudinal positioning process successfully hundreds of times in the past. Yet it remains an invigorating experience to feel the change in attitude of the participants in the process.

The Destiny Chain is about successfully activating and managing the universal law of movement: 'All movement is *process* governed by integration of *motivation, direction and structure*'. The process ensures the leader becomes more conscious and active in three areas:

1. **Understanding the context of the situation that needs to move, while shifting attitude from negative to positive.** Understanding the facts of the relevant area involves two perspectives: a) from a negative perceptions and constraints point of view – e.g. what prevents movement? – where the process emphasises even more honesty and boldness so that all constraints can surface; and b) from a more positive perceptions and opportunities point of view – e.g. what positive perceptions, strengths, opportunities do we have to leverage the current situation? – where the process also shifts attitude from negative to more positive.

2. **Entrenching movement dynamics.** Applying the law of movement involves a) *creating motivation*: uniting the team around positive aspirations and ensuring these align with aspirations, vision, values from the top; b) *strengthening direction*: embracing more passionately current plans and actions that work, and then adding more where there are gaps; c) *aligning structure*: matching resources to the directions to ensure structures support directions and motivations.

3. **Managing movement dynamics.** There are four areas of focus here: a) Evaluate areas 1 and 2 regularly, because change is constant; b) Adjust where necessary, again, because change is constant; c) Act tough or do the difficult thing where necessary when people don't follow through; d) Always refocus on aspirations (motivation), directions and structures to keep motivation alive.

The process requires a high level of honesty in identifying facts and perceived and real obstacles and barriers to progress, which can often be very painful and emotional and also confrontational. The seamless leader exhibits a fearless attitude of openness and courage in encouraging people to be completely honest and open about their feelings. As the process unfolds, the feelings of those involved become focused on the positive aspects of their situation. This results in a tangible boost in unity and mutual respect amongst the people involved, be it a leader with one follower or a leader with a team.

Universal principles of movement

At the core of positive movement of change and growth is the embracing of a seamless attitude that motivates us to move barriers to full potential. I have seen some really tough and apparently inflexible people undergo significant changes in attitude if the proper process is followed. The universal attributes to be employed in guiding people towards an attitudinal change and resultant movement for the better could be captured in our principle of being a **ShaRP** leader – Sharing, Respecting and Performing. Seamless leaders are ShaRP leaders, which they need to be in order to successfully implement the Destiny Chain or movement dynamics.

Sharing attitude: The seamless leader adopts a frank and sharing attitude. Resist the inclination to revert to a 'telling' style, but listen and sincerely encourage open discussion of the facts and concerns. During the process, if participants share their knowledge rather than resorting to personal accusations, responses will generate a climate of sharing.

Sharing hard-won knowledge and wisdom is not simply a case of 'telling' others. It is generally recognised that the person receiving knowledge needs to go through a mental as well as emotional process of taking ownership of that knowledge or skill. Seamless leaders know this and therefore commit themselves to tested processes that guide others to take ownership. Often mistakes will be made, and this may be a necessary part of the convincing process. Certainly encouragement of free expression can help significantly in measuring the level and degree of ownership taken.

Respecting attitude: The seamless leader pays considerable attention to treating others with respect. Respect is demonstrated in various ways, including asking pertinent questions and listening carefully to the responses. Followers will develop newfound respect for each other as well as for their senior leader present. During the process the group will develop an increased desire to live up to the authority and imperatives of their positions of core responsibilities.

Performing attitude: The process does not stop at sharing and respecting, but demands passionate participation in creating, formulating and therefore owning actions that generate a measurable increase in movement or performance. Somehow leaders' imperative to perform adds immeasurably to the first two attributes of sharing and respecting. Without a passion to perform by creating movement, a sharing and respecting person is simply a nice guy or lady. We need to perform while we share what we can offer and also respect all our stakeholders. It is especially important in the multicultural and diverse social make-up of our country that we encourage and develop leaders who share, respect and perform (create movement).

Seamless leaders who demonstrate ShaRP leadership when implementing the Destiny Chain process bring to life universal principles like: 'What human beings create they support' and 'Level of unity = level of performance'. In other words, as important as it is for leaders and their teams to align with what comes from above, they also need to feel part of the creation of their own aspirations (motivators), directions and structures.

What human beings create they support and even love

US entrepreneur James Ritchie – a very successful leader who retired in his early thirties after having successfully built over 20 different businesses – shared this principle with me. The principle is: 'We support what we create,' which was said by one of a number of very bright and motivated people who were spending a day committed to creating something for the benefit of others, knowing that not a penny's worth of personal financial reward would accrue to anyone present. Ritchie explained:

The nine people in the room had come together with some predetermined thoughts as to how the meeting ought to proceed and the 'obvious' conclusions that ought to be reached. Several of the people had never met each other before and some were of different faith than the majority of us. It was interesting observing and participating in the debate that ensued over the first few hours where the different 'factions' found themselves supporting that which they had created in preparation for this scheduled meeting. As each of us defended our cause and creation it became apparent that we were in for some tougher sledding than we had anticipated because so many in the room had already invested so much time in the creative genesis of the project.

Gradually, synergy began to happen! Why? I believe it was because everyone in the room began to jointly 'recreate' a bigger and better 'mousetrap' and as each made contributions to the new creation, support began to grow for the new, better looking and better designed program ... the more input each made to help *create*, the more they *supported* it.

An example would be how amazing it is when a mother looks upon her new-born child, many of whom are less than beauty queen material when first born, but notice how the matriarchal creator of each of these urchins unconditionally loves, cuddles and protects and totally supports! Amazing – but it fits the theme of this lesson. We support (and usually love) what we create!

We have all come to this earth to create; new life, healthy body, financial independence, happy family, terrific marriage, great business or career – and in the process of creation we do everything to support and defend and be loyal to those creations. When we fail to create but only consume or take from others we lose all the joy and power that is reserved for the creators.

That's what is happening to America. We are fast losing the creators and becoming instead a land of moochers, takers and entitlement people and as such we are losing our moral backbone and our creating mentality. We must be careful even in our families and typically strong conservative communities where much of that history of creation is being replaced with a 'gimme' mentality or 'I deserve it' or even 'I want it but not enough to go work for it'. We are on a slippery slope and the incline is getting steeper and the possibility of all of us ending up on the bottom end of that pile of spoiled rubbish is scary. It must not happen but it could – and will – if the creators stop creating and loving what they have created.

We support what we create. Love the principle and may it never change!

How successful are you as a leader at involving your people in creating and by implication multiplying creators? How relevant are these comments in our broader South African socio-political and economic landscape? Are we developing creators? Are we instilling a culture of rewarding creators, or are we entrenching a culture of entitlement, a 'gimme' or 'I deserve it' mentality?

Gill Marcus – former Governor of the Reserve Bank

Seamless Leadership Principles:

1. Look out for Marcus's commitment to purpose and the goal. One gets the impression she passionately cares about the goal and the people.

2. Also notice her comments on sense of purpose and decision making.

3. Try to identify more seamless leadership attributes and signs of a seamless leadership attitude. There are many to pick from, including:
   - ❏ Life is a challenge of 'to be or to have'
   - ❏ As a leader it is not only about what is right for you but what is right for the greater good
   - ❏ It is about understanding yourself, the greater good and then the 'office' or position that is thrust upon you
   - ❏ Consultation is a process where, when possible, the different parties should be in the same room
   - ❏ Decision making is about the quality of the information and the quality of the people around and then the rigour with which you all examine the data.

Gill Marcus never had leadership ambitions. If someone addressed her as a leader she would probably look behind her. She says: 'I don't see myself in that role. I never saw myself with the ambition to be a leader. I don't see that now.' She simply sees leadership as 'an honour bestowed on someone because people want to hear what you have to say, because you reflect, for them, what's important'.

For Marcus it has also been a quest of 'What matters to me?' What has been important to her is what kind of society we live in; what kind of values we have; who we are. She believes it is also a challenge of 'to be or to have'. For her personally 'to be' is more important: material wealth, position and authority 'has never been a part of what I see as important'.

Marcus has never applied for a job in her life. In her teenage years she joined the ANC. From there on, life was about what she could do to match her desire to make South Africa a better place. With whatever came her way she did her best and was asked to do more and more. In essence it has been like a symbiotic relationship of adding value by shaping situations and responsibilities, while these very situations shaped her views in return.

Remaining true to her values and purpose was always a given, but on her journey more started to matter. 'When you are exercising your role or responsibility you have to take more into account,' she explains. This 'more' to her is 'the greater good'. So, as a leader it is not only about what is right for you but what is right for the greater good: 'It [the role] can't be against your values, but it's not about yourself and when you are exercising judgement it is about the greater good.'

According to Marcus, this mindset lifts the leader onto another level, where, 'It is not about how I feel today; this is secondary. I could be feeling totally lousy today but if this is what I have to do then this is what must be done.'

It seems that it is therefore about understanding yourself, the greater good, and then the 'office' or position that is thrust upon you. She says: 'The question is to draw the distinction between what is the authority of the office and what is your personal authority, because office has huge authority.' Marcus believes the leader's personal conduct can add to the office or detract from it, and 'Your best combination is when you can combine your personal leadership and authority with the authority of the office, because then you can use that combination to effectively achieve what needs to be done.'

Every day is a great adventure for Marcus and she loves waking up to a new day, needing only four hours' sleep. With the world in its current state it can however be a challenge to sleep well, never mind waking up. She and her team try and understand the current global turmoil by asking questions like: What are we seeing? How are we seeing it? What are the implications? What is our responsibility to do, 'so that we can minimise the impact of an imploding world, because that's what's happening?'

Against the backdrop of an imploding world I came away from the leadership conversation feeling confident that Marcus and her team have the clearest picture possible of our economic situation in South Africa. This is why.

While the Reserve Bank is an independent organisation of roughly 2 200 employees with seven branches across South Africa, it functions like an integrated stakeholder of a society that is part and parcel of it. The independence, according to Marcus, stretches as far as 'exercising our constitutional responsibility without fear or favour'.

We know that every two months Marcus's team report to the country about what they think are the risks to the inflation outlook; what the outlook of the economy as a whole is; and their resultant decision as regards interest rates. They try to be as accessible as possible and their degree of engagement of different stakeholders within our society is extensive. They hold national and regional monetary policy forums where anyone may attend; they meet economists and analysts six times a year to discuss what they see; they regularly meet with different sectors of the economy; meet all political parties, and so on. Marcus also highlights 'we are in many instances the only African country that is a participant in our own right in many of the international forums, like the G20, G24, BIS, etc. We have a voice internationally and try to influence decisions about the world we believe we need to live in.'

Marcus herself may be unique in that she has been in parliament, government and the private sector, which includes chairing the ABSA board.

All of the above, and more, enhance confidence in decision making. When Marcus is comfortable that she has sufficient information she takes a decision. As a consultative leader she views consultation as a process where, when possible, the different parties should be in the same room so that they can bounce their views off one another. In this way it is not only consultation between the leader and individual parties; everyone's views will be aired and influenced one way or the other. This approach improves the chances of arriving at a collective agreement. Of course, mature individuals who are knowledgeable yet willing to listen and even shift from their original positions are needed, for the greater good.

Marcus expands regarding decision making: 'I think there are different levels of decision making. There are decisions about organisational day-to-day issues that must be decided on, and then there is decision making around for example the monetary policy stance.' In the case of the latter they don't simply make the decision when they meet as a committee every two months. They build up to that decision every day. So, when the time comes they pull all the preparation together, evaluate and decide. Marcus comments: 'I would say it is the quality of the information and the quality of the people around and then the rigour with which you all examine the data and discuss what needs to be done. You want people with strong and thoughtful views, and I believe we have them here.'

In my view Marcus is passionate, intelligent, purpose driven, humble, human, engaging, approachable, fearless, a big picture thinker and authentic. Her weakness may be that she does not necessarily enjoy being a public figure. Then again, this could very well be a strength.

Greg Bell – former Lt Governor of Utah State, USA

Seamless Leadership Principles:
1. Look out for the clarity of vision and direction, sense of ownership and big picture thinking
2. Try to identify more seamless leadership attributes and signs of a seamless leadership attitude in this piece. There are many to pick from.

Utah State in the USA used to have a reputation as a 'fly-over State' between the East and West Coast. Utah was seen as conservative, with strict liquor laws and a weak economy in the 1970s and 1980s. A lot of talent was exported to other States as not all professions could be absorbed into its economy. In general Utah's citizens were involved in industries like real estate, building, land speculation, services, retail, mining, manufacturing, insurance and 'things you could do as an individual', explained Lt Governor Bell when I sat down with him on my 2012 visit to the USA.

Federal government owns 65–70 per cent of Utah land, so land is limited, and they don't receive any revenue from it. They have managed to negotiate some drilling and mining permits, but the Obama Administration have clamped down on that. There was also the Mormon versus non-Mormon ratio, which has changed significantly and seems to have faded into the background a lot. And of course this State with a 2.8-million population is dominant Republican.

In the 1990s they started establishing the Utah Brand, when companies like Word Perfect, Novel and others emerged. The Winter Olympics also contributed hugely to this repositioning process. Bell comments: 'It just blew the doors open. In a lot of ways it turned a key.' Being about six months after the 9/11 event meant it was a real target for terrorist activities. According to Bell, 'the stakes were huge'. Of course there was the scandal around the Olympic preparations that Mitt Romney fortunately rectified.

At the time, under the leadership of Governor Gary R Herbert and Lt Governor Greg Bell, the State was very clear about its three- to four-year-old vision: 'Utah will lead the nation as the best performing economy and be recognised as a premier global business destination' – a simple, clear and even measurable vision that everyone seems to drive.

Bell, a lawyer by profession, landed in politics quite by accident. He got involved in more than one successful community project as the appointed spokesperson. The community noticed him, which led to being elected onto the City Council. He was then asked to run for Mayor after their representative in the legislature decided not to run again. While serving there for eight years he experienced a lot and learned some simple leadership lessons. He had a colleague who always came to him with the relevant problems, but invariably followed the announcement of the problem with a possible solution. Bell started adopting this principle and even today he tries not to go to the Governor with a problem only but also with alternatives, possible solutions. This may sound like common sense, but as we know, common sense is not always common practice.

As Mayor he became involved in regional planning, and was appointed the chair of Envision Utah, an internationally recognised long-term non-profit planning organisation. Through collaborative community planning they found that when the planning horizon is far enough out, everyone will participate – realtors and developers, environmentalists, preservationists, all relevant parties. If any planning forum expects interested parties to engage in the short term and a rushed fashion as opposed to a 40-year timeline, for example, 'they will fight', explains Bell.

Leaders who therefore have a clear long-term vision and plan will find more time to collaborate and include all stakeholders. Bell elaborates: 'People understand that if you're not at the lunch you are on the menu. So they show up. If you say you are doing a transportation plan, the truckers are there, the railroads are there, the environmentalists are there. They realise that once these things are theoretical on someone's map, that's when you have to be there, because thereafter it is just a fight about when, how much and exactly where. But the idea of the road is done, and if you didn't come to the early hearings you are just too late.'

From his activities as Mayor, Bell was noticed once again and moved to the legislature for two terms; Herbert became Governor and picked Bell as his Lt Governor.

As a public leader he is very aware of the fact that he has a 'brand', as does Utah State, and as such he wants it to represent unquestioned integrity, high ethics, very collaborative and politically principled. He and the Governor strive to be 'conservative in principle, moderate in tone, inclusive in process', which he also sees as part of his brand.

After visiting with Lt Governor Bell I also sat down with Spencer Eccles, a successful businessman in his own right who was heavily involved in the Winter Olympics. He drives business, tourism, film and other areas for the Governor's office. Eccles' division also recruits companies to the State or assists them to expand by making it as simple as possible to open and run a business in Utah – a stable and vibrant environment, predictable, no crazy legislation and regulation, healthy tax environment (one of the lowest with a flat rate), low power costs, educated and productive workforce. As Eccles stated: 'The goal is always to make things easier for business. Are we doing it perfectly yet? The answer is no. But I think we are probably better than anyone in the nation.'

They went through a full regulatory review and identified approximately 2 000 regulations that impact business. Eccles explains that 'in the last legislative session we either eliminated or modified over 350 business regulations'. As a result the USA Business Chamber expressed interest in how they did this. The recruitment programme, from 2009 when the economic downturn took off, in public-private partnership initiated about 4 200 jobs, which improved to almost 10 000 in 2012 alone, most of these being high-paid jobs. Eccles attributes this kind of growth and environment to the long-term leadership of the State.

One of the first things he did when I met him was to pull out of his pocket a laminated card with the vision and four key objectives on the one side and 'ten reasons to do business in Utah' printed on the other. Everyone in 'Team Utah' carries this with them, including the Governor! Eccles even carries extra cards to hand out at meetings. There was an immediate sense of order, clarity, unity and commitment to the vision and objectives of this State. They realise that their State is small in terms of population and they therefore have to be on top of their game, be nimble and do things differently.

Eccles then handed me another pocket-size laminated card with a heading: 'Utah is four cornerstones strong', under which is written the vision, followed by a summary of the four cornerstones – education, jobs, energy and self-determination. On the other side of the card is listed 'Utah Accolades', which clearly confirmed they are achieving their vision: '#1 Best State for Business & Career; #1 Best Managed State; #1 State for Economic Outlook'; and several others.

I was impressed and immediately sensed an atmosphere of great leadership. I felt that I could walk out with the two cards and a clear sense of where this State is going, how it is led, confident about the future, amidst very uncertain economic times. Seeing another accolade of being '#1 Most Fiscally Fit State' added to the feeling of confidence.

A few days after my visit the South African Ambassador was due to visit Utah State leaders. There was much to discuss as exports from Utah to South Africa had increased by 825 per cent over the past year, with about 50 per cent in the commodity arena.

With leaders like Bell, Eccles and others at the helm of Utah State, complemented by their 'team mentality', I got the impression that the sky was the limit. South African businesses that are contemplating a 'home' in the USA would do well to consider the State of Utah, because as we know, when all is said and done, everything rises and falls with good or bad leadership. Utah seems to be on the rise because of great leadership.

||||||||||||||||||||||||||||||||||||||||||||||||||||||||||||||||||||||||||||||||||||||||||||||||||||||

CHAPTER 7

Seamless leader attitude to multiplying leaders for real impact

WITH
❑ *Mike Brown*
❑ *Zunaid Bulbulia*

As mentioned in chapter 2, seamless leadership is about multiplying. To be more specific, it is about multiplying leaders with a seamless leader attitude, because then one is assured of making a lasting impact on the bigger picture. To achieve this one must develop confidence in the macro and micro processes or system of developing and multiplying leaders, especially when one desires to multiply seamless leaders.

Seamless leadership development takes courage, commitment, patience and vision. The result, however, is leaders with the attitude and confidence to lead in whatever culture they work in, and even to change the environment around them, if this is necessary to achieve full potential. They will lead effectively beyond expectation and beyond their responsible boundaries. This is the aim of this book – to spark the desire to multiply seamless leaders that will result in movement of society towards its full potential.

From a broader societal perspective, a real impact will be made when the role and purpose of the family unit is understood and supported fully; when the education system catches the vision of not only focusing on knowledge and skills transfer but also stimulating seamless leadership; and when the workplace catches the vision that the mark of a true leader is a passion for multiplying seamless leaders.

The family is the first school of leadership and multiplier of a seamless leader attitude as it sets the foundation on which other societal leadership development structures will be built. Then follows the school environment, where the prospective young leader is tested in the real world and moulded further. After school follows the tertiary learning environment, and then, finally, the real world of adulthood and work where seamless leaders are rewarded handsomely – not necessarily financially, but through making a difference in several ways – as parents to children, managers to employees, civic leaders to society, ordinary citizens to fellow citizens, and so on.

Throughout the entire process the family remains the golden thread, hopefully the stabilising factor on this seamless leader journey. Most of us return to some sort of family every day, or, when we are younger, during holidays.

Thoughts on the family

Todd Christofferson, a spiritual leader based in the USA, recently made the following bold comments during a global satellite conference:

> The societies in which many of us live have for more than a generation failed to foster moral discipline. They have taught that truth is relative and that everyone decides for himself or herself what is right. Concepts such as sin and wrong have been condemned as 'value judgments'. As a consequence, self-discipline has eroded and societies are left to try to maintain order and civility by compulsion. The lack of internal control by individuals breeds external control by governments. One columnist observed that 'gentlemanly behaviour (for example) once protected women from coarse behaviour. Today, we expect sexual harassment laws to restrain coarse behaviour...' Policemen and laws can never replace customs, traditions and moral values as a means of regulating human behaviour. At best, the police and criminal justice system are the last desperate line of defence for a civilized society. Our increased reliance on laws to regulate behaviour is a measure of how uncivilized we've become.

How relevant are these comments in our society? If this observation is accurate it means society at large is moving away from the seamless destiny designed to help people achieve their full potential.

One prominent example that comes to mind is South Africa's crime epidemic, which most citizens expect should be curbed by law enforcement structures. But, if the above comments are remotely true then perhaps the South African society is not as civilised as it believes, because it is gambling with the future of its children by depending too heavily on this 'last desperate line of defence'.

What is society to do? What should be expected from society at large and its politicians, or in fact all leaders? Remember, society is depending too heavily on its law enforcement agencies and government structures that legislate. And how would you rate the performance of the 'last line of defence'? Are they at least turning the tide of violent and hate crimes, corruption, dishonesty, selfishness, and other illnesses in society that stem directly from a terminally ill or deficient moral compass? The answer is obvious.

We have to find a way of urgently and effectively addressing that precise part of society where moral compasses are shaped. We cannot afford to get this one wrong, especially for the sake of future generations. What should we do differently so that we can experience different results, rather than continue debating and doing the same things over and over and over while expecting different results, which of course indicates a form of insanity?

Moral discipline and the foundation for seamless leadership are learned at home, in the family. This is the first school of morals, discipline and – as a natural consequence – seamless leadership, because seamless leaders possess a sound moral compass that they confidently follow. The family is where virtue and seamless leadership principles are and always will be implanted into the rising generation. This is that exact point, the most important unit and educational institution, where we have to focus as a society. In other words, we should vigorously shift our energy to ensuring successful families, even before we have these endless debates about trying to create effective schools and education systems, though such debates are important. If we do not do this now we will be forever dependent on laws for changing self-destructive behaviour, and those that enact them. In short, we will become increasingly uncivilised as we allow the pool of morally undisciplined and deficient leaders to rise through our debilitating social structures.

Christofferson ended his speech as follows:

> We cannot presume that the future will resemble the past – that things and patterns we have relied upon economically, politically, socially will remain as they have been. Perhaps our moral discipline, if we will cultivate it, will have an influence for good and inspire others to pursue the same course. We may thereby have an impact on future trends and events. At a minimum, moral discipline will be of immense help to us as we deal with whatever stresses and challenges may come in a disintegrating society.

But first, let us change the trend of leaving the family unit to tread water in a rising pool of negative influences that threaten to weaken or even destroy the very institution that should ensure we reach our seamless potential as a morally sound nation, with seamless leaders. Let us go back to the beginning and strengthen the family, for if we don't, the end, a disintegrated society, will stifle our nation's exceptional potential sooner rather than later.

Thoughts on critical life skills for the next generation – the school years

Following on from the foundation set in the family, I have thought long and hard about the critical social skills young people need to develop at school level in order to awaken a seamless leader attitude for today's workplace. The following list is not all-inclusive, though it is top of mind and mostly describes what institutions should aim towards when teaching young people. If aspirant leaders can start consciously working on at least these points today they will do themselves and society a great favour in the future.

'Healthy' patience: Young people of today want two cars, their own home, flat-screen TV, status, wealth and so on much sooner than their parents ever dreamed of acquiring these things. It is exciting to meet executives in large organisations who are in their mid-thirties to early forties who in some cases are already wondering where to from there. While such achievements at an early age are commendable, they are also the exception. Ultimately age is not the determining factor, but life experiences, maturity, and the ability to make wise decisions. One cannot escape the time ingredient in this recipe called experience. Young individuals must just guard against becoming so patient that life passes them by. Healthy patience should not be confused with apathy.

Discipline to be consistent: This goes hand in hand with point one. Research shows time and time again that real success comes after effort, perseverance and time, as illustrated in Malcolm Gladwell's *Outliers,* which explains that no obviously successful person or even music band ever achieved their goal before investing at least 10 000 hours or ten years. Young people must find what they love and are most talented at, dream, set goals and keep at it. In other words, become forward thinkers and movement specialists. Some may argue that they will change careers several times in their lifetime. While this may happen, they must stay alert and be careful that it does not counteract consistency.

Clarity about values: The world is changing at a rapid pace. More than ever, the next generation not only need intelligence to handle complexity, or the emotional intelligence to deal with relationships, they also need to be able to make the right moral decisions under pressure and open scrutiny. They need to have a good sense of what is right and what is wrong. For example, they should learn at a young age that family, health and reputation are valuable and not discover this after achieving 'success' and having to celebrate it alone, in ill health or behind bars.

Early interest in leadership: The challenge in today's society is to prepare through formal studies to become confident at some technical skill – medicine, law, business, engineering, teaching, etc. Ironically, as youngsters enter the workplace, if they are very good at what they do they are promoted away from their technical competence and need to start managing and leading people. This becomes their most important skill for most of their career. The sooner they become interested in leadership and study and practise it, the better off they will be. Also, as youngsters become aware of leadership early on, society stands a better chance of catching seamless leaders while young.

Ability to simplify: The more the world attempts to simplify things and become more sophisticated, through for example technology, the more the opposite happens – life becomes more complex. Leonardo da Vinci said: 'Simplicity is the ultimate sophistication.' The future generation must hold on to this truth. The ultimate sign of intelligence is the ability to simplify. Decisions cannot be made in complexity. They must not be fooled by the temptation to impress through complex talk. Great leaders are able to simplify and they need this skill in today's workplace. The reason they should study for a good qualification is to gain an understanding of complex subjects and the ability to simplify this knowledge for productive use – to create movement and confront barriers to full potential.

Broader view about life, people, and society: In South Africa specifically this includes a view that human beings are equal; that no race is better than another; that underneath our skins we all have more in common than not, in terms of our aspirations and the five universal commonalities. But, perhaps the paradox is that every human being is also different, unique and complex. Our next generation should broaden their horizon. Travelling is often a great way of doing this. We live in a global village; so much is interconnected. They must learn to see and understand the world as one huge interconnected entity, driven and affected by simple social, political, economic and universal dynamics.

Over and above this, they need to start understanding the bigger universal picture, the core purpose of life.

Learn to work hard, but clever: The next generation must learn that they cannot achieve without consistent hard work (see chapter 6 on consistency). But, they must also learn to do so in a clever way – without sacrificing important relationships, their reputation, their health and their value system. Hard work only sometimes equates to long hours, not always. To find this balance is harder than ever before. However, they should never stop trying, because then they will most certainly lose the battle overnight.

Become a skilful confronter: A clear weakness in society, up to the highest echelons of organisations, is the ability to confront others in a skilful way without contention (argument or quarrel). There are ways of doing this effectively and any leader should learn the skill of having effective courageous conversations (see chapter 12).

Humility: Our young people must not let 20 years pass before realising that humility is strength and leads to lasting success and legacy, while arrogance and pride are weaknesses that eventually lead to failure. All research of substance points out that those individuals of substance have humility; they are teachable; they realise that they are where they are not only because of themselves but because of the efforts of others. With humility goes an attitude of gratitude. Appreciate people, small things and life in general.

Multiplying seamless leaders in the workplace – the Leadership Impact Model (LIM)

To ensure the legacy of an organisation and society one must consciously multiply seamless leaders. It is a strategic imperative. A seamless leader moves through at least four stages before making a real impact in leaving a lasting legacy.

Stage 1: Understanding and acceptance. This stage – long before handing over – involves gaining knowledge and understanding about the situation or experience that has been thrust upon you, including structure, people, environment, drivers of the organisation, culture, product or service, target market, etc. Doing this helps you to gain a level of acceptance from all stakeholders, while realising that this cannot be claimed but has to be earned over time. Showing followers that you are trying hard to understand assists with this. Eventually all or most of the stakeholders accept that the seamless leader understands what is going on.

This is often the most difficult stage and some leaders move on to new challenges before successful completion. A seamless leader mostly continues and pushes through to stage 2.

It is during stage 1 that the seamless leader mostly observes, engages, asks questions, listens and does whatever is necessary to understand the entire situation. Of course this does not mean that no decisions are made at all. It simply means your overall modus operandi is one of understanding.

Several factors impact on the length of time that a seamless leader takes to successfully complete this stage of understanding – the current condition of the situation, credibility of the leader based on past performance, internal appointment vs external appointment, technical knowledge of the specific industry, political dynamics of the environment, and so on.

Stage 2a: Credible management for consistent performance. For the seamless leader the purpose of this stage is to leverage off your understanding and acceptance, where you now have a certain measure of credibility, towards maximum impact. This can be done as a manager or as a leader, or both. The seamless leader chooses the latter option.

Credible management means understanding what structures should be in place and consistently functioning in order for the situation (company, division, branch or department) to run like a well-oiled machine. This includes crucial meetings that serve the organisation's direction and strategy, relevant systems, procedures, reports, etc. This stage supports the age-old principle of managing things and leading people, the latter happening in stage 2b.

In larger organisations a manager can manage during stage 2 and achieve consistent performance. While this is acceptable because there is performance and stakeholders are obviously comfortable, remaining in this area of stage 2 is not an option: a seamless leader knows the importance of moving on to the critical stage 3. The truth is that an ordinary leader can easily get stuck in stage 2a because the organisation tastes success; recognition by shareholders and the market place starts pouring in; large bonuses are paid, and so on. Falling into this trap results in a drift towards arrogance instead of entering stages 3 and 4 where the legacy of success is actually cemented.

Stage 2b: Credible leadership for consistent performance. In order to move to stage 3 the seamless leader first leads for consistent performance in order to gain credibility as a leader and not a manager only. This is where the foundation for success in stage 3 is set, because it allows future leaders to model their seamless leadership behaviour as they move into stage 3 to more actively multiply seamless leaders. Leaders who remain in stage 2a will transfer managerial skills only and this is not sustainable in the long term.

As a seamless leader in the making, before you lead consciously you have already answered certain questions with confidence and clarity: **What is my leadership philosophy – how do I lead? Should I be asked to lead in two totally different environments, what universal leadership principles would I implement that are not necessarily industry-based?** Asking these questions enables you to add your own personality to this universal leadership philosophy. How do you do this? Ask the following question: **How do I practically implement the seamless leadership philosophy?** By way of example, part of seamless leadership is to care for one's people. The practical implementation of one seamless leader may be to hold one-on-one sessions with each direct report on a regular basis to remain attuned to their needs, personal and professional. Another seamless leader may add to this a system of remembering people's birthdays and using this as a way to make personal contact.

Finally, the seamless leader can also answer this question: **What are my personal strengths and weaknesses as regards the seamless leadership philosophy and practical implementation model?** Knowing the answer to this question assists you to become more focused on your personal development. Remember, seamless leaders are not perfect.

It is frightening to discover how few senior leaders have ever taken the time to answer the above questions. Most remain and even retire in stage 2b, which does not ensure leadership multiplication, as achieving the noble task of truly multiplying leaders takes intense conscious effort and focus. What distinguishes seamless leaders is becoming as passionate about multiplying more seamless leaders as they are about achieving their goal.

Stage 3: Leadership multiplication for legacy. This is a powerful stage as the seamless leader starts focusing on consciously developing seamless leaders:

- ❏ Empowering them with knowledge by thrusting challenging situations and experiences at them.
- ❏ Engaging them in deeper discussions about the purpose of life.
- ❏ Teaching them the universal principles that govern and maximise

decision making, movement and confronting of barriers to full potential.

❏ Actively holding personal leadership conversations with reports. In other words, do not only hold them accountable for functional performance but also for how they lead and eventually for what they do to multiply leaders under them.

❏ Ask your reports to answer the questions mentioned earlier, for themselves.

❏ Involve your reports in decision making.

❏ Consciously mould your reports to become even better than you.

❏ Employ individuals who will challenge you rather than bow to your greatness.

All the while, as a seamless leader you ensure management structures continue functioning consistently (stage 2a) and do not deviate from leading consciously according to your seamless leadership philosophy and practical model (stage 2b).

I believe that where the reins of a business are handed to an outsider, rather than an internal candidate, it usually reflects negatively on the leader handing over: it is proof that you failed in grooming potential successors and so failed in stage 3. Questions to ask in such instances are: **Why is there no one internally good enough to take over? How could the leader manage this organisation or division for however many years without grooming several potential successors?**

There is a school of thought that the time to consider bringing in an outsider is when the organisation is in turmoil or perhaps huge change needs to take place, and perhaps there are other good reasons as well. But, I still maintain that if a leader moves through stage 3 successfully there will almost always be several individuals ready to take over.

Stage 4: Successful handover. This is the exit stage. Because the seamless leader has moved through the above three stages, this stage mostly becomes a natural next step. There will be a successor who is ready to take over; the leader will feel ready for another challenge from life.

Good examples of leaders who seem to have demonstrated seamless leader characteristics by implementing the LIM effectively are Tom

Boardman at Nedbank, together with Mike Brown; Paul Harris at First Rand Group; Mark Lamberti at Massmart; and Raymond Ackerman at Pick n Pay.

Some leaders get stuck in stage 2 somewhere and hesitate or even refuse to exit, which could be detrimental to the organisation – or the country, depending on who the leader is. It takes great maturity to positively and consciously set one's sights on stage 4. In fact, it requires a seamless leader attitude from someone who senses the bigger, universal picture.

Mike Brown – CEO Nedbank

IIIIIIIIIIIIIIIIIIIIIIIIIIIIIIIIIIIIIIIIIIIIIIIIIIIIIIIIIIIIIIIIIIIIIIIIIIIIIIIIIIIIIIIIIIIIIIIIIIIIIIIIIIIIIIIIIIIIIIIIIIIIIIIIIIIIIIIIIIIIIIIIIIIIIII

Seamless Leadership Principles:

1. Look out for how successfully the Leadership Impact Model seems to have been implemented inside Nedbank.

2. Identify where Brown demonstrates a seamless leader attitude.

3. Try to identify more seamless leader principles.

IIIIIIIIIIIIIIIIIIIIIIIIIIIIIIIIIIIIIIIIIIIIIIIIIIIIIIIIIIIIIIIIIIIIIIIIIIIIIIIIIIIIIIIIIIIIIIIIIIIIIIIIIIIIIIIIIIIIIIIIIIIIIIIIIIIIIIIIIIIIIIIIIIIIIII

Mike Brown, CEO of Nedbank, comes from a family of bankers. His father, grandfather and an uncle were bankers. His entrance into banking, though fairly coincidental, was probably inevitable.

He qualified as a chartered accountant and, like so many CAs, joined Deloitte & Touche to do his articles. He was placed in the financial services division, to eventually audit banks, which resulted in a job offer from NBS bank in the early 1990s. He stayed with NBS until today, though of course NBS has changed through several acquisitions along the way.

Brown learnt from his father that 'one only gets one chance at today', meaning one has to do one's best every moment of every day. He was also taught 'to appreciate opportunities that come one's way in life'. Unlike his father, who wanted to become a doctor but became a banker instead because of financial constraints, Brown had the opportunity to do what he really wanted to. He has a great appreciation for this.

Pivotal to his leadership development was being placed in leadership positions relatively early on in his career. Exceptional academic achievements certainly bolstered these early opportunities and, at about the age of 30, he was appointed MD of BoE Corporate. The next youngest person on his executive team was over 40. He had to learn quickly how to interact with people and manage relationships because technical and functional knowledge just wasn't adequate any more.

Brown has therefore led older colleagues most of his life and is currently one of the youngest people on the Nedbank Executive.

His leadership abilities were no doubt accelerated by experiencing three mergers along the way – NBS/Boland; BoE/NBS Boland; and finally the merging with Nedbank. Inside this new Nedbank, Brown managed the Property and Asset Finance Division that formed part of a four-way merger with businesses from BoE, Nedbank, NIB and Cape of Good Hope.

These invaluable experiences taught him not only about the complex technical aspects of merging banks, but also the traps leaders can step into during such a process. The following are key lessons learnt: You cannot over-communicate; you must have the right leaders in place with the right attitude as quickly as possible; if the strategy is compelling, notwithstanding the challenges, people will buy in to a better future; and think of the journey as a once-in-a-lifetime learning experience. Possible traps include too much focus on the spreadsheets and not enough on the people (clients and staff); too many consultants; and becoming too internally focused.

Also significant about Nedbank's leader was his part in an exemplary handover from one CEO to the next. Nedbank announced Tom Boardman's retirement date and Brown as his internal replacement, almost a year before, in the middle of a recession. The announcement did not affect the share price in the least. However, the internal dynamics of having both an outgoing and an incoming CEO for almost a year had to be managed in a mature manner. What made this possible was the good relationship between Boardman and Brown, and their emotional maturity to understand that it was a healthy process.

Brown said that not for one minute did he want to rush into the position sooner than planned, because it would not be beneficial for anyone. He also set aside two months of this period to attend a course at Harvard, using some of this handover period for personal leadership development and enrichment.

About two months before Boardman left they sat down and crafted a detailed plan on how he would say farewell to Nedbank and how Nedbank would thank him for a job well done. This required extensive communication, road shows, facilitated conversations and exercises with the Exco team, and much more.

Even though Boardman is in many ways a legend due to his remarkable rescue of Nedbank, Brown has never felt a need to move from under his shadow. The reason for this is that everyone, including Boardman, would be the first to admit that the rescue was a team effort.

What the organisation got with Brown was absolute continuity, thus placing the team and Nedbank before any personal ambitions and egos. In my view this is proof of a healthy handover, healthy organisational culture and the advantage of an internal successor.

For the first period of his tenure, the investment community often wanted to know what new direction Brown would take the bank into. Yet, he and several of the team members had worked alongside Boardman for several years, jointly carving out the bank's strategy, so why the need for sudden change?

The strategy of the bank would simply evolve under the leadership of the Executive team. Brown believes an important part of the CEO's job is to be ambitious for the company, not yourself.

A key challenge Brown and other banking leaders face moving into the future is to lead in an environment of regulatory and economic uncertainty, and to balance short-term performance with long-term investment – focusing on capital and liquidity, yet growing and building sustainability for the long term.

For Nedbank the future holds a challenge of how to grow business in Africa, while continuing its constant journey of aligning current and desired values inside Nedbank, to create a culture that is 'facilitative of their organisation being more agile, mobile and competitive'.

In a recent meeting Brown explained to me: 'The Nedbank of today is a significantly better organisation in all spheres than it was a couple of years ago, whether you look at it from a shareholder's performance lens, a staff engagement and values journey lens, a client lens, a regulatory lens or what we do in the community.' Their vision to become Africa's most admired bank with sustainable long-term success is built around these five components – shareholders, staff, clients, regulators and communities.

Now that Brown has been in the hot seat for several years, what has he learnt, discovered or been surprised at? Not much, in fact. He had significant experience and exposure to banking in general and Nedbank in particular. He had exposure to various parts of the operations, had been the CFO for five to six years and the transition from the previous CEO to him was seamless and exemplary to say the least. So there were no real surprises. However, if asked, he would advise a young or newly appointed CEO as follows: 'First of all you have to be clear as to the role of the CEO of any organisation – and the way I see it and what we are trying to build here is an organisation that is vision-led and values-driven. One of the key roles of the CEO is therefore to be owner and custodian of the vision. You can't do that on your own, but by the time it is crafted you have to be the one that is out there championing that to internal and external stakeholders.'

As Brown sees it, another critical function of the CEO is to focus on creating a 'values driven' culture and organisation. What has in a way surprised him is 'the role-modelling that happens in an organisation off the behaviours of the leadership group'. Crucial to the journey are the values that the leadership team truly live by and the behaviours that they portray. These are modelled or imitated by the rest of the staff.

Yet another crucial role of a CEO is to make sure you have the right people in your team and that they are on the right seats. Brown believes that with a clear vision, the right values and the right people in the right seats on the bus, you would probably be in good shape.

Nedbank is known for its strong emphasis on values, a journey that resumed almost eight years ago, and that internally is branded as 'leading for deep green'. Brown explains: 'It started with the executive team going through a particular process around leadership, understanding your influence on others, personal mastery, a very defined leadership and culture values journey for the leadership team of the organisation.' They have now been successful in cascading that further down the organisation to thousands of staff.

Measurement, monitoring and tracking is very important in any organisation, according to Brown. And this is a universal truth that all great leaders understand. Brown says: 'If you set the aspiration of being vision led and values driven and you push the 'leading for deep green' journey, you have to figure out how to measure, monitor and track or evaluate progress.' They came across a specific survey that they have been using consistently for the last five to six years as a measurement system to track their journey around culture and values, 'with the outputs being things like values matches and an entropy score in the form of a percentage point,' explains Brown. Their latest measurement came in as world class, which is a great achievement.

The remuneration of leaders is linked to their ability to improve values matches and cultural entropy, as part of their performance appraisals.

Other ways of measuring the health of their internal culture also confirm the suggested improvement, again giving them different lenses through which to measure culture improvement. Brown says further: 'We also measure how many staff are lost to competitors versus how many new hires are coming from competitors and are you a net gainer or loser in the talent pool.' Over the last couple of years they have been a net gainer. And finally, they have employees that they have lost but who came back, many of them ascribing their return to the positive culture of Nedbank.

Not all organisations focus so intensely on creating a values-driven organisation, perhaps because deep down they just don't believe it will have a significant impact on their ultimate performance. Brown is sure that their values focus has impacted performance: 'It is probably impossible to make the connection scientifically, but certainly I have no doubt that the culture and values journey has played a big part in us retaining people in our organisation, attracting talent – and the outcome of all of that has actually been pretty good performance.'

As CEO of Nedbank and a leader in the current dynamic, fast-paced, constantly moving business and socio-political environment, Brown sees the current environment as an opportunity: 'The world is in a very difficult place right now, economically, with lots of challenges everywhere. I suppose leaders have to find the opportunities for their businesses within those challenges, and focus your people and leadership team on things they can control and make a difference to. What fascinates me is that there is always so much you can do in business, irrespective of what the outside environment is.'

Brown ultimately believes: 'At the end of the day, it does not matter what you are paid unless you enjoy coming to work every single day, which means you enjoy what you do, you enjoy who you do it with, you enjoy how you are treated. All those things that have to do with what it feels like around here, which is all about values, behaviour and culture – if this is not right it is not going to work for you.'

Zunaid Bulbulia – CEO MTN South Africa

Seamless Leadership Principles:
1. Note Bulbulia's seamless attitude towards competition.
2. Note the principle of becoming more consciously aware that one shifts from being a technical expert to being a leader.
3. Note Bulbulia's emphasis on movement.
4. Try to identify more seamless leader principles.

'Thank you, Alan Knott-Craig!' may be a strange statement coming from the CEO of MTN South Africa, but these were the exact sentiments shared by Zunaid Bulbulia as I sat with him discussing leadership and the opportunities and challenges facing him while filling that office.

This particular statement came on the back of my question of what Knott-Craig and Cell C have brought to the South African mobile telecoms market. Bulbulia shared that he has great respect for his competitor because he is such an experienced campaigner in their industry. Bulbulia and his team have had to make sure they are working harder and with greater focus than ever before: 'We're learning to make decisions quicker, we're learning to be more market aware, and we're learning to not take them for granted. Alan knows the industry – he's not a guy that parachuted in here and doesn't know anything about South Africa. The unintended consequence for Alan is that he's made us, and Shameel Joosub at Vodacom, even more determined to be successful ... and he's made me more match fit.'

This is the invaluable contribution that competition offers the market place and consumers.

Zunaid Bulbulia is one of only two who remain of the original group of seven who were there at the birth of our familiar yellow telecommunications company, MTN. He has devoted 19 years to assisting it to move from a start-up to a small company of 200 to 300 staff members and 50 000 customers, which today is a multinational player whose reach extends into 19 different countries in Africa, Europe, and the Middle East and now employs well over 17 000 staff members, supplying services to over 189 million customers.

But who is he and where did it all begin for him? 'I grew up on 14th street, which is the old Pageview area of Johannesburg, running my father's shoe store which was also the beginning of my leadership career. I would often have to run the business because my dad would be involved in many other things, he travelled quite a bit, he was a seasoned traveller and loved seeing the world and doing all kinds of things – which is why I was actually born in Canada. My parents just happened to be there when I was born, but I have lived in South Africa all my life.'

He would later go on to study accounting and qualify as a charted accountant, having completed his articles with the then highly regarded Arthur Anderson.

This upbringing seems to have set the stage for his journey with and throughout MTN. After joining them in 1994, he spent the next 19 years meandering all over MTN – from marketing, sales, and distribution to managing a customer care call centre for about five years and even doing mergers and acquisitions. He adds: 'I've had a very good cross-section of experiences that I would probably not have got in a company that was not growing like MTN was, and MTN, because it was growing so quickly, had more opportunities than they had people that they trusted.'

And this journey no doubt naturally prepared Bulbulia as a leader and positioned him well for his role as Chief Executive of MTN South Africa.

Many leaders, but not all, undergo a natural process of shifting from seeing themselves as a technical, functional person to becoming a leader by profession. Let me explain. Years ago, I quoted Liberty CEO Roy Anderson in *The CEO Leadership Handbook*, and he asked for a copy of the book. He explained why: 'Years ago I realised I'm not a Chartered Accountant any more, I'm a leader, that's my profession.' Anderson had made a conscious shift in his mind: if someone from his distant past asked what he does or what he had become he would have told them that he was a leader, not a CA.

Often top executives don't make this conscious shift and still see themselves as specialists in their area of vocational studies. They may barely use these technical skills but remain devoted to the notion that they are still those people. As a result, many do not improve their leadership skills actively enough.

When top leaders are questioned regarding this, most have to admit that their day-to-day functioning requires maybe 10 per cent specialist, technical knowledge while the remainder of what they are needed to do requires a 90 per cent leadership skill set to be employed.

Bulbulia's journey seemed slightly different. Although he first became a CA he never really functioned as one and it almost seems he never made that conscious shift in his mind. When asked whether he describes himself as a leader he responded: 'I think if the definition of leadership is I display a passion for providing clarity based on insight when clarity is being sought, then I would say that is a definition of me and if that also defines a leader, then I'm a leader, yes.'

And of course he is a leader, because to create movement effectively leaders need to provide their followers with a clear, concise strategy that is going to lead them to realise their goals. However, this cannot be done without first simplifying the situation by having a solid hold on all the facts and an understanding of the team's strengths and weaknesses within these facts.

Bulbulia has an interest in and a natural instinct to analyse, scrutinise, and demystify situations where there previously existed vagueness, ignorance and complexity. Not only did he describe his leadership role as needing to provide clarity and insight, but he also seemed to have the courage to take on projects even where he had little or no background or training. No doubt these initiatives moved forward successfully partly because of his natural and then further developed ability to simplify, clarify and give direction. He explains: 'Every time something looked vaguely interesting and they were looking for someone, I put my hand up and said I'm happy to give that a bash. With the result that I did things that had nothing to do with what I had studied at university for the longest time. In fact, even when I became CFO of MTN SA, I did very little accounting, because the accounting strategy had been created and I was focusing more on running the business with Carel and the rest of the guys.

'It's been a journey I can't really explain – it's been the most hands-on learning about how corporates should grow and gain and sustain value. You can't put this in a MBA package I think. It's been a collection of experiences that are priceless for me and priceless for many people that have gone through MTN.'

Bulbulia calls it being a 'go-to guy', which he believes he became because of always volunteering. He says 'go-to guy', we say leader. His continuous leadership journey will no doubt accelerate as he consciously views himself as a leader.

Leading an established business like MTN means you no longer ride that original exciting tidal wave of growth. Structures and systems are in place; growth opportunities are perhaps limited. One understands that they are moving from voice to data, but is it still so interesting and exciting to be at the head of MTN SA?

Bulbulia simplifies and clarifies the question well: 'I've learned to take more than one brand of medication, I guess. So the drug in this organisation has been growth, which is a very destructive drug in that it lulls you into this sense of we can do anything we want; it masks a lot of things that are not working because under the cover of growth you can make many mistakes and you can get away with them. I'm learning to take new drugs. It's fascinating that people have this perception that because the organisation, from a growth point of view, is slowing down in our traditional business of voice, that MTN is not sexy anymore, that MTN has become less of a drug, less of an organisation that makes you want to get up in the morning and come to work with a passion that makes you want to change things.'

MTN is growing data at a double-digit rate. That presents its own challenges. The purchase of an internet service provider provides a new context. And they have started an enterprise focus. Bulbulia feels they are learning the skills necessary to be successful in a saturated market: 'So now we're trying to reduce our costs faster than we're growing our revenue. It's just a whole new set of skills and experiences that we have to learn in order to continue to create value. That in itself is providing me with ample raw material – a new variety of drugs to keep me hooked on this organisation.'

In fact their entire context has changed because they are no longer just a mobile company. They are many different things to many different people. The exciting journey, according to Bulbulia, is one of making the cell phone device the centre of people's universe. Also, 'becoming a service company is now a challenge – we're not a service company, we're a growth company, we sell and move lots of product, but we can become a damn good service company where people say when I think about MTN I think about the most unbelievable service. It's a huge journey,' he explains.

Admittedly this is a huge culture change for MTN, and employees need to get used to this new context. An interesting leadership challenge. In an industry with so few players, where technological changes occur at breakneck speeds, and competition is extremely high, the difference may very well come down to which leader is more 'match fit' and positioned in such a way to understand where to next create movement. This makes for interesting times ahead in this industry, with the ultimate beneficiaries being us the consumers – nothing wrong with that.

Q&A

Q: We know you try to remain physically fit, but how do you remain leadership fit?

ZB: Yes, I try to remain physically fit. I've been cycling for let's say 10 years now. I'm not pro, but I'm a pretty good amateur cyclist. I do the 94.7 in less than three hours, which is quite decent. I've taken to running in the last couple of months. I ran the Comrades for the first time this year, which was a fascinating experience. I'm hoping to do Iron Man next year.

I'm increasingly learning to remain leadership fit by remaining in the now and remaining resourceful; by knowing that by remaining in my present context I can make a difference. The future – sure I can help shape the future – but it's not happening now so I really can't do much about it. The past has happened; there is not much I can do about that either. But remaining resourceful and in the now I can be very very effective in how things may be operating or working currently.

Q: People often try to position leaders as having the same attributes and skills and personality traits and whatever it may be, but actually what they have in common is that they have created movement. So here you are – you have now been asked to move MTN from where it is to something better. Where do you want the business to move to and how happy are you with the movement that's happening at the moment, as a leader?

ZB: There are two areas of movement I want to create in this organisation. There's a need for us to become the number one service company in South Africa, not just in our industry. I want us to become synonymous with service. The sustainable benefit of that goes well beyond just being able to grow revenue faster than you are growing costs. It's about people wanting to do business with MTN and wanting to be a customer of MTN because the experience is so good. I think the multiplier effect it has on your bottom line is phenomenal if you can position yourself and sustain yourself as a top service company. Becoming that company is going to require enormous movement, because I don't believe we're anywhere close to that at this point in time. We are a company that knows how to manage growth which is exponential. So that is the first bit of movement that I want to create – a very real movement to becoming number one in service.

The second is I want us to be able to sustainably grow faster than our competitors along all the key areas of our business, whether that's in revenue, in profit, in market-share, in brand awareness, in social responsibility, across all the key metrics that make a business successful. We've had periods where we've been ahead of them; we've had periods where they've been ahead of us. It's almost been like watching a Formula One race and on every lap someone else takes the lead. I will feel we have created meaningful movement if we are able to sustain over a long period of time consistently beating our competitors across all the key metrics in our business. That's the challenge I've set for myself and for my team – to find the formula and the way of work that results in that movement.

Q: The world has changed, the world is changing – what three skills would you say are necessary for future CEOs of MTN to develop now and in the future to ensure that the movement you are looking for will be sustainable?

ZB: I think being visible is a key element of the skills that will be required. I think we have a very strong element of invisible leadership in MTN, not just in MTN, but in this industry. We've always been just too busy to make the time to be visible, never mind the outside world, but even to our people inside the organisation. So yes, becoming more visible to our people and to our customers. I think accessibility is a key one – again under the mask of growth we've been not seen, not heard, too busy crafting the way forward, managing the growth. And above all I think is probably humility. I think this industry has become arrogant, we've lulled ourselves into believing we are the success story that the JSE says we have become, but which can be taken away from you overnight because something happens from a regulatory point of view or the economy doesn't perform in a certain way. I think humility breeds in you a very strong desire to find ways to continue to be successful. We're not a humble industry and becoming humble will give us the ability to remain grounded in order to know that tomorrow's future is not guaranteed. I know that more now than I knew it six months ago, because things have changed in our industry in the last six months.

||||||||||||||||||||||||||||||||||||||||||||||||||||||||||||||||||||||||||||||||||||||||||||||||||||||||||||||||||

CHAPTER 8

Seamless leader attitude to people performance and motivation

WITH
❏ *Edward Kieswetter*
❏ *Paul Harris*

The work environment has obviously changed a great deal over the last few decades. While most leaders would agree with this statement, not enough have gone out of their way to understand the changes and to adapt their own leadership philosophies accordingly.

I often ask leaders the following question: 'When your employees come to work, how much do you expect them to give while here – 50 per cent, 80 per cent, or 100 per cent?' You may guess that most of them answer that they expect 100 per cent output, commitment and effort from their people.

I then refer to a bank account and make the point that should one want to withdraw R100 out of the account there would have to be at least R100 deposited there first. And perhaps our people are the same: if we want to 'withdraw' 100 per cent energy, commitment, performance out of them we need to make sure that at least 100 per cent energy, commitment, etc is being 'deposited' into them.

A long time ago, during the Industrial Revolution, employers expected their people to also give their all, but this expectation did not necessarily include the cognitive ability of their minds and the passion of their hearts. All the workers were required to bring to work was their 'hands' (simple functional skills) and then they worked like robots. Work was monotonous and physical.

But, as the macro socio-economic landscape changed, so did the working environment. Employers started noticing that their employees had minds and even hearts that followed their hands to work. Of course the business environment became more competitive, employees became more informed and so employers started realising that expecting their employees simply to bring 100 per cent of their hands (skills) to work was no longer sufficient. The business needed 100 per cent of their minds and hearts in order to remain competitive.

Although this is where we are today, up until recently the 100 per cent deposit or investment from an organisation into the employee equated to a salary and benefits only. Today, paying a salary and benefits is not perceived as an adequate deposit and does not add up to 100 per cent as it used to. In addition to salary and benefits, companies have to deposit recognition, stimulation, consistent development, caring, a balanced lifestyle, and so on.

An organisation or leader with the attitude of 'I pay my people a salary and perks so they must give me 100 per cent' is stuck in the past. It is like wanting to withdraw R100 from a bank account into which you have only deposited R50. Seamless leaders realise that the simple truth is if they want their people to bring 100 per cent of their minds, hearts and hands to work then somehow 100 per cent must be invested in all three of these areas.

Few leaders are equally skilled at 'depositing' (developing, caring, inspiring, recognising, motivating, showing appreciation, etc) and 'withdrawing' (holding accountable, insisting on performance, expecting commitment, asking, confronting, measuring, etc). Yet seamless leaders work hard at being excellent at both skills in order to assist their people to perform in today's competitive environment.

Also, organisations often have a 'deposit' or a 'withdrawal' culture and few have a perfect balance. Some are strong on 'withdrawing' (results driven) and weaker on 'depositing' (people development), or the other way around.

I am absolutely convinced that there is a direct correlation between the 'bank balances' of your employees and the bank balance of your business.

I suggest you ask yourself two questions, independent of the level you are on inside your organisation: 1) Where does my natural strength as a leader lie, on the 'deposit' or 'withdrawal' side, or both? 2) Do we have a 'deposit', 'withdrawal' or balanced culture in our organisation?

Seamless leaders realise that they can only give what they have; that one cannot fill a glass from an empty jug. In other words, if, as leaders, our minds are 'empty' we cannot connect with our people's minds. If our hearts are 'empty' the same principle applies. Our duty is therefore to make sure that we consistently develop our own hands, minds and hearts so that there is something to give ('deposit').

This is why so many of the leaders we meet who demonstrate a seamless leader attitude are avid readers. They consistently update themselves with the latest social, political, functional, leadership and other trends and developments out there. They strive to consistently grow in all areas of their lives.

For an organisation to improve its culture on for example the 'deposit' side, it needs to develop the skills of leaders so that they can do the 'depositing'. Leaders must learn to connect with or stimulate employees' hands (coaching employees to improve their technical and business skills), minds (coaching employees to think for themselves, how to be creative, how to evaluate situations effectively, how to solve problems, how to fill the mind with knowledge, how to align with company direction, etc) and hearts (coaching employees to connect with their and the organisation's purpose, values, etc).

If you are in an organisation that has a comprehensive deposit culture you are fortunate; if not, you have to take more responsibility for this yourself.

Deposit and withdraw exercise

To test your 'deposit' skills (people focus: points 1–7 below) and how much you 'deposit' into yourself (personal development: points 8–12 below), rate yourself objectively on a scale of 1 to 10 on the following questions (1 = useless; 10 = perfect):

    1. Are you considerate in your day-to-day interactions?

2. Do you express sincere appreciation to people around you?
3. Do you express interest in others, beyond work activities?
4. Are you happy to see your people and do you take the time to greet them every day where possible?
5. Do you focus on actively developing, growing your people?
6. Do you listen to your people – set aside your own opinion to hear theirs?
7. Do you give clear recognition where it is due?
8. Do you appreciate opportunities of learning when these come your way?
9. Do you remain true to yourself and your values?
10. Do you invest in yourself; actively develop your mind (study, read regularly), heart (emotional, spiritual development) and hands (refine technical knowledge)?
11. Do you proactively ask for feedback about your performance and leadership approach, so that you can continually improve?
12. Do you make time to 'give back', to serve outside work?

To get a feel for your 'withdraw' skills (focus on results) rate the following on a scale of 1 to 10 (1 = useless; 10 = perfect):
1. Do you insist on and promote responsibility and accountability?
2. Do you lead by example by giving the organisation 100 per cent, and can therefore expect the same from your people?
3. When someone does not perform, do you investigate willingness (attitude) and ability – if the cause is a wrong attitude you have a courageous conversation; if the cause is lack of ability you train or put the person in the right seat?
4. Do you create a culture where obstacles to success are openly identified and addressed?
5. Do you go out of your way to find talent?
6. Can you hold courageous conversations when necessary?

Edward Kieswetter – CEO Alexander Forbes

Seamless Leadership Principles:

1. Look out for the Alexander Forbes' culture of deposit and withdrawal.
2. Try to identify more seamless leader principles and signs of a seamless leader attitude. There are many, including an emphasis on values, multiplying leaders and focus on purpose.

Following a leadership conversation with Edward Kieswetter, Group Chief Executive of Alexander Forbes Ltd, we walked through their magnificent building. It is a spectacular edifice that reflects their values and ethos.

What impressed me even more than the building was the way Kieswetter engaged his staff. He greeted them as we walked along. At one point he excused himself for a moment and walked up to a table to politely interrupt a conversation between two individuals, a man and a woman. The man rose to his feet and respectfully shook Kieswetter's hand. Kieswetter then turned to the woman and explained that the gentleman she was talking to was one of their best consultants. I realised this was a business meeting between a consultant and a client. The lady smiled and asked Kieswetter what he did around there. He answered: 'A bit of this and that; a bit of everything.' The gentleman then announced that Kieswetter was their CEO. She was visibly impressed and I have no doubt that if the consultant hadn't clinched the deal at that stage it would have been after that interaction.

On several fronts this experience trumped even the very interesting two-hour conversation.

Kieswetter has been the CEO of Alexander Forbes for some years and movement there has been a natural consequence. I interviewed him just as he became the CEO and wrote the following at that time: 'He stands a very good chance of making a huge success of this challenge. I will give at least three reasons: 1) His sound values-based upbringing and the direct effect on his leadership approach; 2) His ability to understand the direct impact of a leader's actions and example; and 3) Principles in the letter he wrote to all Alexander Forbes staff that was sent out on the first day of the year, just before his official starting date.'

On whether he has been successful he comments: 'With the understanding that success is a journey and not a destination, the journey has been successful. It's been rewarding; it's been harder than what I thought it would be, but it's been extremely rewarding.'

When he took over they were receiving some negative media coverage regarding their involvement in potential litigation arising from historical issues. It was also a difficult time for financial institutions in general. Kieswetter explains: 'I was coming in at a time when the organisation performance was down, when there was disenchantment between the shareholders and the management, we had a flat to erosion of profits for three years, and we were in the media for all the wrong reasons.'

Under his influence the picture changed on at least three levels – leadership alignment, employee culture and of course financial results. About leadership alignment he says: 'To engage leaders is hard work because if you think about it, generally strong people become leaders. They are strong-willed, strong-minded and clear about their leadership philosophy.'

In addition to his on-going engagement and performance reviews with smaller leadership teams, once a year he gathers together the top 100–120 leaders. The last time he did this, after reviewing the strategic plan, three questions were confidentially posed to every attendee: 1) Is the strategic intent that you have clarified and communicated appropriate at this time for the organisation given your circumstances and challenges? They had 96 per cent agreement. 2) Do you believe you have made progress against this intent? There was 95 per cent agreement. 3) Do you believe the challenge you have set out for the next 12–24 months is achievable? There was 88 per cent agreement. Kieswetter says: 'So that's a very high level of alignment, in the strategic choices we've made; in the progress we've made against that, and in the journey ahead.'

On employee culture they decided to build a more engaging workforce and focused on five extensively measured areas:

1. Negotiate with every individual to find work that they enjoy doing. It's not a one-way street – it's a negotiation. Kieswetter believes that 'enjoyment comes from two things: being competent to do it, and being interested in doing it'. So they attempt to put people in the right seats, where they are happier, leverage their talents and abilities, and are more motivated.

2. Make sure that people understand the meaning of their work, the higher purpose of it, the impact that their work has. Again, this emphasises the motive behind actions and increases motivation. Kieswetter comments: 'We introduced the language of why we exist. Park what we do and how we do it – just talk about why we do it.' It is the 'why' behind all actions or required actions that fuels motivation.

3. Define success – what does winning mean? He believes 'too few people know specifically what winning means. One of the things I liked about my SARS job is that I knew what winning meant – R651 billion, broken down by corporate income tax, VAT ... it was very nice, you knew what winning meant.' Knowing what winning means highlights clear direction. There must be a clear, mutually desired destiny, a better future.

4. Give people regular performance feedback. In other words, are you on course as regards the direction of where winning is?

5. Reward and sanction the right behaviour. This of course helps change behaviour towards the desired culture and environment. Kieswetter says: 'So if you didn't do well and I don't tell you, I'm not being fair to you. If you didn't do well and I pay you a bonus I'm giving you mixed messages. If you did do well and I'm treating you the same way as someone else that didn't do well, I'm also confusing the issue. So I don't believe in equal treatment. I believe in fair treatment and fair treatment differentiates based on contribution.'

To bring home financial results – growing the revenue, improving the profitability, improving the efficiency, the margins, managing cash well, and so on – they introduced the notion of the goose and the eggs. Kieswetter says: 'We will measure the leader on two things: the goose is the organisation, our eggs are revenue growth, profitability, cash management, cost management, the hard-core numbers. Our goose is also the quality of our people engagement, the quality of our customer retention service, the quality of our risk management and the quality of our investment projects.' In short, ensure the structures of the organisation support the direction and motivation. Alexander Forbes has become a much more profitable business, with a vigorous process of performance engagement, performance management, performance evaluation, and performance reward in place.

Kieswetter believes the first job of a CEO is to build leadership. Many top leaders say this but don't really show by their actions that they are serious about it. He finds ways to expose his Exco team to unique experiences. He invited me and Lewis Pugh, the British environmental campaigner, maritime lawyer and pioneer swimmer, to have breakfast with his team. Pugh was asked to spontaneously share why he does the 'crazy' things that he does. He inspired us with his story. And then I had to share something on leadership and why I am involved in this world. Jokingly, Kieswetter asked us to draw parallels between what we do. It was a great discussion. He seems to seek opportunities like this for himself and his team.

My contribution was to share the universal law of movement, because ultimately leaders are in the business of movement. The law states: 'All movement is governed by the integration of motivation (motive, reason, purpose, desire, and aspirations), direction (plans, vision, destiny, goals) and structure (resources, systems, procedures).' Nothing moves without the effective blending of these three components. Successful leaders such as Kieswetter find a way to activate this universal law. They push motivation on an individual and organisational level; they emphasise, simplify and personalise direction – what winning means; and they streamline and appropriate the necessary resources, structures that ultimately sustain movement – the goose and egg principle.

For Kieswetter this journey of change starts with 'first of all being clear about what you want to achieve; secondly, starting to evangelise the hearts and minds – persuading people – and that's why the conversation starts with who am I and why am I here?'

It is clear that good leadership is what intervened in the destiny of this organisation.

Q&A

|||||||||||||||||||||||||||||||||||||||||||||||||||||||||||||||||||||||||||||||||||||||||||||||||||||||||||||||||||||||||||||||||||||||||||||||||||||||||||||||||||||||||||||

Q: You believe in being yourself. Explain, please.

Kieswetter: I posted the following tweet recently – just be yourself, it's the path of least effort and maximum reward. Some say it must be difficult to lead the kind of life where everyone watches you. I say actually no, it's not difficult, if I was pretending to be someone and wasn't authentic it would be difficult because I'd always have to think about how I want to behave, but I don't think about it because if you are just yourself – just be yourself.

Q: If 'yourself' is a good yourself ...?

Kieswetter: Even if it's not the best yourself, people don't expect leaders to be perfect; they expect leaders to be authentic. You know if you can trust your leader you'll do a lot more with and for him than if you thought he was perfect but didn't trust him.

Q: But our society allows for unauthentic leaders to rise to the top.

Kieswetter: Look, democracy does, right? And it's the apathy of society that allows it. We are actually our own worst enemy in that regard. But nature doesn't. We foster mediocrity. And that's why I said the fifth point of engagement is to be very clear about rewards and sanctions. We don't engage, we don't sanction, we don't reward. And that's unfair.

Q: You believe in the abundance mentality, which stems from your character. Some leaders just can't access it, even though they have very responsible, massive positions. It has to come from your value system. The question is, can you train that in leaders when they didn't grow up that way, when it really is not part of their framework?

Kieswetter: Well I think you can 'conscientise' people to it – you can't train them to it. So if I think of how I grew up, my biggest two leadership lessons actually came from my parents. My father taught me the ethic of hard work; I saw that in him, he drilled that into me. My mother taught me the balancing lesson – that I needed to be a blessing. So two of the most powerful lessons I learned came from my parents. One, the ethic of hard work; and two, the purpose of life. You're here to be a blessing. And then you accumulate other lessons as you go along. When I went to Harold Cressy, my high school, and met people like Trevor Manuel and the teachers that we had, it 'conscientised' in me a sense of social justice, of acting in the greater good. So yes, you can condition, you can 'conscientise', and I think the role of leadership is to make that explicit and tangible for the next generation of leaders. So I hope they are not sitting in a class being lectured every day by Edward Kieswetter on what leaders should do, but in me living out my leadership hopefully some of it will rub off. That's why public leaders are so important.

Q: You seem to have grown as a leader, even though you have always had leadership capability in you.
Kieswetter: Hopefully growth is an on-going thing so it would be quite an indictment if one doesn't grow, and hopefully if we have a conversation in a year's time we would both have grown. Growth is integral to life. The difference between human beings and nature is we can resist growth – that's the difference. So the best gift you can give yourself is an open mind. I sat here earlier and I said to you I had a vision, I had a clear intent; it turned out to be harder than I thought. I always knew the technical stuff would be easy for me to get my head around as I demonstrate higher learning capability and complexity doesn't intimidate me. I always knew that changing the culture would be the hardest part – I didn't realise how hard it would be.

Q: A parting thought?
Kieswetter: Whether you take my younger life as a power station manager or at SARS or here, there is one thing that has consistently manifested itself – everyone wants to be part of a winning team. Everyone. Everyone wants to be part of something bigger than themselves. Everyone wants to know that they are making a difference.

Paul Harris – Co-founder and former CEO First Rand Group

Seamless Leadership Principles:

1. Look out for Harris's comments on how to empower and motivate people.
2. Try to identify more seamless leader principles and signs of a seamless leader attitude. There are many to pick from.

Although he says he cannot remember it, the story is told that Paul was voted by his fellow matriculants as the student most likely to succeed in life. Boy oh boy, were they right! Today he is a shareholder and former CEO of First Rand Limited, an organisation with a market cap of well over R100 billion. Successful? I would think so! However, although society at large may judge Paul by the size of his bank balance, the title after his name, and even by the tens of thousands of people he had working 'under' him, he judged himself and those who worked with him by 'how many people they liberated rather than how many people they controlled'.

The essential leadership principle of needing to empower (liberate) those around one was truly part and parcel of Paul Harris's – and the organisation's – leadership philosophy. In First Rand, he says, they 'believe in accountability struggles not power struggles. In power struggles you want to dictate things to people who know that what you are doing is wrong, but will do it anyhow because you are the boss. In a case where you liberate people and let them take accountability those people will put energy into the system and not take the energy out of the system.'

Ask yourself to what extent those around you are doing what must be done your way, as opposed to doing what needs to be done their way?

A financial manager I was coaching once told me how one of her staff wanted to do something in his own way and she simply told him to 'go for it!' She was liberating him rather than controlling him.

Although Paul attributes the remarkable success of First Rand Limited to him and his partners being at the right place, at the right time, their business philosophy of striving to create an environment for people to manage their divisions or business units as if they were their own is probably the greatest contributor to their success. An illustration that epitomises this philosophy is when a reluctant Michael Pfaff was offered the job of leading Rand Merchant Bank. Paul said the following to him: 'We appoint you to do what you want to do with the business, not what we want you to do.' Once again, can one only say this to someone who is about to be appointed as CEO of a major organisation? This statement can easily be adapted to: 'We appoint you to run this department in your way, as if it is yours, and you need to tell us how you plan on contributing to the region's targets.' In fact, go so far as to ask staff what they need from you in order to feel liberated.

Even when I discussed the expansion of First Rand from a strategic angle Paul's answer was steeped in the liberation theory. I asked him if his greatest strategic challenge was that of international expansion: 'We believe in de-centralised models. If some of our business units believe that their growth comes from doing business internationally, we would encourage it. We have 160 profit centres thinking of how to grow, and that's good enough for me.'

When Rene Otto, now CEO of MiWay Insurance, set up Outsurance several years ago, he sat down with Paul, who then proceeded to counsel him about guarding against mediocrity. Rene was slightly taken aback by the comment, but the way Paul described it resulted in this principle staying with Rene up until today, and he has quoted Paul many times since. He said one has to guard against mediocrity for two reasons: 1) mediocre people are boring, and 2) mediocrity casts a shadow. I asked Paul to expand on point 2 and he explained as follows: 'If you have a mediocre person at the top of the organisation think of it as closest to the sun, it will cast a big shadow. If you have a mediocre person at the bottom of the company, it casts a very small shadow. If you get the wrong person high up in the organisation, it casts a shadow and they will surround them-selves with other mediocre people.' Ask yourself what kind of shadow are you casting – mediocrity or excellence?

||||||||||||||||||||||||||||||||||||||||||||||||||||||||||||||||||||||||||||||||||||||||||||||||||

CHAPTER 9

Seamless leader attitude to connecting

WITH
- ❏ *Heyneke Meyer*
- ❏ *Chad Le Clos and Graham Hill*
- ❏ *Roelf Meyer*

Great leaders connect with their people. As former McCarthy Limited CEO, Brand Pretorius, commented: 'If you don't connect, you have no influence, and if you have no influence, you can't lead.' A strong/special connection is not something to be taken for granted – for example, a leader communicating with people may think that merely talking at them did the trick. But, if a connection was not really made, time and energy may have been wasted.

When we connect with someone a special bond develops. This is what happens with friends and couples. They meet, engage and somehow, something between them 'clicks'. When this happens it takes a lot to break that connection.

I regularly sit with executives for personal leadership conversations and listen to what they say about their leader. Often when they speak highly of their leader I probe deeper. What do we discover more often than not? They believe that they have a special connection with their leader. Somewhere in the past, the two of them had some interaction that meant more than the usual professional engagement.

Cast your mind back and think of an individual you have (or had) a connection with. I guarantee that – even if it happened years ago – so long as nothing specific happened to destroy this, even thinking about him or her now creates a special feeling. As leaders we need to ask ourselves if we have a special connection with every person who reports to us or works with us. We may be shocked to realise that most of our relationships are merely professional in nature. While this is acceptable, it is not ideal and not necessarily the way of a seamless leader, as such relationships will probably not get the absolute best out of our people, or we will simply not have as much influence as we could otherwise have.

Perhaps we feel that we do have the necessary influence – because, after all, we give an instruction and it gets done, though sometimes not according to our standard and at the preferred speed. But Pretorius adds to his quote: 'Issuing instructions simply doesn't work. You must get through to hearts and minds if you are to be effective.'

Seamless leaders work hard to develop a connection, as those with whom they have it will give much more and be more loyal to them and their cause. They believe it is this kind of connection that taps into the 'miracle-performing capacity' of human beings, that unleashes their seamless capacity to move towards their full potential.

Although there are leaders who have the skill to deliberately make things happen, seamless leaders don't believe in artificially planning a connection. What they do is to develop an approach or behaviour that naturally opens the door to a possible connection. Their seamless leader attitude automatically results in such behaviour.

There are many ways to open this door, such as creating a common, passionate purpose; sharing the same interest; etc. I want to touch on two specific principles that seamless leaders often use:

Lead beyond: In some cases the connection just happens. However, usually the seamless leader 'leads beyond expectation' in order to find the connection. Some ways in which they do this is to really care; express interest beyond the work environment; show genuine appreciation; listen to understand; give recognition, and so on. Basically, they go the extra mile. When someone in an influential position (the boss) goes the extra mile it surprises and so makes it easier to connect. And this leads us to the next point.

Surprise element: Another way used by seamless leaders to open the door to a possible connection is through 'authentic surprise'. In 1995

Nelson Mandela arrived at a rugby world cup game with a no 6 jersey on and surprised everyone. This surprise was so unique that he immediately made a connection with thousands if not millions of South Africans, including Afrikaners who still saw him as a terrorist.

Connect exercise – why don't you connect with someone?

It may be worthwhile to consider why leaders do not connect with their people. Evaluate yourself against the following possible reasons as you think of individuals you haven't connected with:

- ❏ Your personal motivations are just selfish – it is all about your career, position, recognition, etc.
- ❏ You are not sufficiently present 'in the moment'.
- ❏ Deep down, you do not really care about the individual/s.
- ❏ Your job is merely a professional occupation.
- ❏ You are too busy.
- ❏ You are out of your depth in the current position – it is too overwhelming.
- ❏ You are too task driven and not people focused.
- ❏ You do not feel comfortable within your own skin – confidence is lacking.
- ❏ There is a personality clash.
- ❏ Your ego is in the way.
- ❏ You are of the old school of command and control – you command and control your people.
- ❏ Deep down, you believe that because of your title you are more important than those who report to you.
- ❏ You have simply not been taught how to connect.

Try to *surprise, lead beyond* and *connect*. As you do this you and your people will navigate successfully through turbulent water towards success, which in and of itself opens up a door to connecting even further. Achieving success together deepens connection.

Heyneke Meyer – Springbok Coach

Seamless Leader Principles:
1. Look out for the way Meyer creates a connection with his players.
2. Try to identify more seamless leader principles and signs of a seamless leader attitude. Meyer deposits in several ways.

The response to the announcement that Heyneke Meyer was our new Springbok coach was largely positive. For him personally it was over-whelming, bringing him to the realisation, more than anticipated, that the responsibility that had befallen him was not only enormous, but that he 'carried the hopes, expectations and dreams of all South Africans on his shoulders'.

He was on the short list in 2003, but withdrew in order to build the Blue Bulls team and then came even closer in 2007.

Duty and honour is how he described the privilege of being entrusted with this responsibility. Though there will be pressure, he said, 'One of my philosophies is to always enjoy what you do.' And, he also believes that 'the best iron goes through the warmest fire', meaning that pressure is a good thing. He looked forward to growing as a person, while being very aware that this job required stepping on toes.

Being national coach means being busy, but this too fits in with one of his life philosophies: 'To be successful you only need to work half a day and you can choose whether this will be the first or second twelve hours of the day.' Though he worked hard at the Bulls his life settled into a certain work/home life balance. This changed when he became Springbok coach.

Being the national coach feels like a calling to Meyer. From a young age he listed his desired career as becoming the coach of the Springboks. In those days professional rugby seemed a far-fetched dream. But for Meyer, who is a 'big picture' thinker, it was always clear that professional rugby was his destiny. All his studies after school were directed at this goal.

In 2010, during the soccer world cup, Meyer was in the US for a week and was struck by the respect Americans had for South African rugby. He realised that our country may not be the best at many things, but we can actually be the best in the world at rugby. He returned with an even stronger commitment to strengthen South African rugby from his sphere of influence, which was of course at the Blue Bulls. Ultimately Meyer's dream has come true. His heart and passion are absolutely in this mission.

For some time now his main motivator as a coach has not been to collect trophies but to make a difference in the lives of the players and beyond. When former players contact him to thank him for the life and leadership skills they learnt it makes everything worthwhile. The other motivator for Meyer is a desire to unite the country, as was done in 1995 by the rugby world cup.

Meyer is of course both a coach and a leader. However, he sees himself leaning more towards leadership than coaching, the latter being the technical side of what he does. He comments: 'You can't push people to do things; you can't push someone up a ladder. Due to the position of coach one can push players to do things, but you will never be successful. As a leader I am very big on having a vision for the team, and then for every individual to have a personal vision. All these visions must then interlink; all the arrows must point in the same direction. It is therefore more about leadership. If you lead people they want to follow and make their dreams come true.'

He believes that there is some truth in what Andrew Carnegie said, that 'Every person out there can be compared to the gold mining industry. If you take layers and layers of dirt off them you will find the gold nugget. If you can help the person to nurture that, you will be successful.' Meyer's philosophy is to 'get people to buy into your philosophy, but it is more important to give them what they want. It is a question of what I can do to help that guy fulfil his dreams and then you fit it in with the bigger picture.' To illustrate this principle, he used the example of when one looks back at a school class photo, 'the first person you always look for is yourself.'

Focusing on the individual is crucial to long-term success. When he recruited young players for the Bulls he would speak to them personally and ask: 'What are your dreams? Most of them have not thought about it. Then I would ask them to think about what they want out of life. When they tell me then we discuss how we would assist them to achieve their dream.'

Though the individual is very important, Meyer believes equally in the need for unity of purpose and goals within the team. To illustrate the power of united goals, he likes telling his own story about two different individuals on a ship. The first person is newly married and on his honeymoon, enjoying the time with his wife. He falls off the ship, swims and finds an island. Then there is another man, a convict sentenced to death, who jumps off the ship and escapes, chains and all. He ends up on the same island with the first man. When these two individuals are threatened by dangers around them the first man will help the convict to take off the chains so that they can survive, live and hunt together. They will do this for ten years, if necessary. They have the same purpose and vision. Then another ship comes past. The first guy wants to get back on a ship to return to his wife. The escaped convict knows that if he gets onto that ship his freedom disappears and he dies. Now the purpose, vision and goals change and these two men will probably kill each other.

So, for Meyer, 'the person is always most important and needs to understand I am there for him, and then the art is to try and get the individual and team goals as close together as possible. You have to let people feel safe in the team, because as soon as they are under pressure and only look at their own goal you won't be successful. You have to create an environment of respect, camaraderie, work ethic, integrity and playing for the guy next to you.' For a courageous conversation along these lines, see the interview with Victor Matfield in chapter 10.

Though a visionary and 'big picture' leader, Meyer is also very strong on the detailed planning that follows the vision. When young coaches come to him for advice he asks how long their contract is and then requests their business or implementation plan. If they don't have one he predicts they will not last or be successful. He believes that without a plan, when the pressure is on one ends up all over the place. In line with this, he adds: 'I am very big on having set standards. I think the biggest thing for the coach is to set the standards, and to be consistent in the implementation, towards all players, including senior players. There is one set of rules for all players.'

Overall I sense this is a man who has been prepared for the challenge and consciously looks forward to it, radiating confidence rather than arrogance. He is the right man for the job. He thinks like a seamless leader – leading with a balanced big picture in mind, while, in an inclusive manner, confidently confronting barriers and boundaries to full potential of individuals, Springbok rugby and South African rugby in general.

Meyer's approach is a conscious leadership one. Therefore, as per his track record, my prediction is that the time will come when the team will gain momentum and a rhythm of excellence.

Chad Le Clos and Graham Hill – Olympic Gold Medallist and Coach

IIIIIIIIIIIIIIIIIIIIIIIIIIIIIIIIIIIIIIIIIIIIIIIIIIIIIIIIIIIIIIIIIIIIIIIIIIIIIIIIIIIIIIIIIIIIIIIIIIIIIIIIIIIIIIIIIIIIIIIIIIIIIIIIIIII

Seamless Leader Principles:

1. Look out for the connection between athlete and coach.
2. Look out for other seamless leadership principles, like being in the zone, focus, passion, disciplined consistency and much more.

IIIIIIIIIIIIIIIIIIIIIIIIIIIIIIIIIIIIIIIIIIIIIIIIIIIIIIIIIIIIIIIIIIIIIIIIIIIIIIIIIIIIIIIIIIIIIIIIIIIIIIIIIIIIIIIIIIIIIIIIIIIIIIIIIIIII

According to Graham Hill, Head Coach of Swimming SA and Personal Coach for Olympic gold medallist Chad Le Clos, his achievement was absolute destiny! He explains: 'Two years ago at the Dubai World Short Course, Chad races in the first race of the meet, a 400 medley, he finishes fifth. Three days later he lines up in lane five, with the world record holder from Brazil next to him. He wins the race in lane five by .05 of a second. Two years later we go to London, Chad lines up in the first race of the meet in the 400 medley and he finishes fifth. Three days later he lines up in lane five, with the world record holder Michael Phelps in lane six, and he wins by .05 of a second. This is destiny! How can it be explained in any other way?' Having interviewed both Chad Le Clos and Graham Hill separately, it seems destiny is where unmatched motivation towards a vision, detailed planning, disciplined execution, hard work, and a bond of trust and mutual respect converge. Surely this is a formula that serves any worthwhile endeavour; principles relevant in any leader's life.

Being on the national team since 1997, Hill has been closely associated with most of our successful swimming athletes, including Ryk Neethling and Roland Schoeman. He has been on countless trips with them, including four Olympic Games. He compares being a personal coach to one athlete like Le Clos with a circle: 'Chad and I are in the middle. Then we have different support people around us – a doctor, agent, the physiotherapist and family (athlete and coaches). To define my role – at the end of the day I am the boss. I'm the one who puts it all together. I say what can and what can't happen. And the team around us all understand that.'

Yet he understands the role of the coach is to remain in the background and believes 'the glory is there for the athlete that you coach. And if you are that good a coach you will be recognised along the way.' This has been the case with Le Clos's victory; both the athlete and the coach are receiving recognition.

The magnitude of Le Clos's achievement was in another league, especially after he beat his idol, the legendary Michael Phelps, at his favourite event. Hill describes the after-effects: 'It was a whirlwind; it went crazy. For about three days we would leave the Olympic village at 7:30 in the morning and only get back at about 23:30 in the evening, jumping from one function or interview to the next. We were driven by a driver and we would be in the back of the car talking and forcing ourselves to have quick power naps.' They spent a lot of time together, just the two of them, and were able to build an even greater relationship along the way, which included conversations about how to handle the future.

Hill explains the essence of why Le Clos won: 'Chad executed the game plan with exactness, one hundred per cent; you could not get better. The way he executed it, the only result was the gold medal. We knew we had to be at this point on Michael's shoulder; we knew where he had to be on the last turn and we knew we could beat him on the last 50 – we had trained for it; we prepared for it, exactly like he swam.'

So, detailed planning, hard work and execution with exactness constituted the formula. Hill adds: 'I don't think people understand, the amount of times we watched the videos; Le Clos would go home and watch, then we would discuss in detail.'

Before the race Le Clos mentioned to Hill that he felt nervous but relaxed, almost as if he did not realise he was in an Olympic final. Hill simply replied: 'Chad, we have done the work, you are confident, and that's why you are relaxed. You are ready for this.' Then, just before Le Clos walked through the door Hill looked at him and said: 'This is it. You remember one thing, you've dreamt this, and you want this so badly. This is your last chance to beat Michael Phelps. He is not going to swim another tournament butterfly ever again. You want your dream to come true, this is your only chance!' It was his attempt to get his athlete into the zone. It most certainly contributed. From Le Clos's angle, 'In the race I felt like I switched mentally, because it was something I wanted to do since I was a young boy. I remember thinking this is the last time to beat him and I want to beat him.'

The bond and connection between Hill and Le Clos is evident. Le Clos respectfully describes it as a fiery relationship: 'We have spent 12 years together. We know each other backwards. He is a nice guy outside the pool. I like to have him in my house and with my family. Seriously, he is a cool guy to be around. But, when we are training he is different; in the pool he is the boss and in charge. I can't think of a full week where he did not shout at me, to be honest.' But Le Clos does not take anything personally and realises fully he needs his coach; while Hill is very aware that he is now dealing with a man and not the young boy of the past, an Olympic champion, and 'this is now a whole different ball game, I have to change my ways and thoughts on motivating him, a whole new challenge, a whole new journey, so to speak, moving forward to 2016'.

Hill believes one of the factors that create top athletes is this bond between coach and athlete: 'The way you create the champions like Chad lies in the bond (connection) between coach and athlete. It is almost as if that sixth sense is there. If he does something he will look up at me and I will know what he is up to, just in everyday life. That's how close we are. We trust one another with our lives. The trust and the bond we have is what I believe makes great champions. Yes, obviously he has a natural gift and talent to be a winner, a champion, to be able to focus and finish events off. But I think it is the relationship of a coach and an athlete that makes the big difference.'

What made him different from other young kids who were even better than he was is that he wanted it more than anything, from the age of twelve: 'I wanted to be an Olympic champion. I wanted to be the best in the world. I wanted to compete against the best, and Michael Phelps was the best.'

Still, his resolve was often tested when other distractions surfaced

– different sports, girls, sleeping in, and much more. But the drive to become an Olympic winner against his idol trumped them all.

As with all top achievers, moments of self-doubt do rear their head, even for Olympic athletes. Le Clos confidently confirms this: 'The last two years I always had doubts in my head. I was always worried about what would happen if I did not get into the final; will I be able to come back from that?' After the win against Phelps, Le Clos mentioned to Hill that he hoped it wasn't just luck. The response: 'Great athletes make their luck.' According to Hill, in any game one needs luck, including in the business world – 'right place; right time'.

Today both the coach and athlete thank Phelps for being such a role model in the sport as to motivate Le Clos to achieve an Olympic gold medal. But what will motivate Le Clos in equal measure to move on and achieve even greater heights? Going beyond London has always been part of their thinking. Le Clos wants to beat Phelps's record of single medals. And, if they can be successful at developing other great swimmers to win medals in relay, then he even wants to challenge Phelps's overall medal tally, starting with eight medals at the next Olympics.

This entire story is a perfect example of an ultimate achievement because of a passionate vision that truly motivated detailed planning, hard work, disciplined execution and a deep connection between two individuals. Business, political and other leaders will do well to fine-tune their abilities to implement the same formula in their areas of responsibility.

Roelf Meyer – Chief Negotiator for the National Party Government in 1994

||||||||||||||||||||||||||||||||||||||||||||||||||||||||||||||||||||||||||||||||||||||||||||||||||||||||||||||||||||||||||||||||||||||||||||||||||

Seamless Leader Principles:

1. Trust brings the best out of people and situations.
2. Never act out of anger.
3. Try to identify more seamless leader principles and signs of a seamless leader attitude in this piece.

||||||||||||||||||||||||||||||||||||||||||||||||||||||||||||||||||||||||||||||||||||||||||||||||||||||||||||||||||||||||||||||||||||||||||||||||||

It is hard to describe my feelings and thoughts while meeting with Roelf Meyer. I could not stop thinking about his eventful journey through life thus far. He is the epitome of being in the right place at the right time.

In his own words: 'I must say that I was extremely fortunate in terms of the opportunities that came my way in politics. I was part of the transition of South Africa in a very special way and of course that was the highlight of my career ... There is nothing that could ever match that again.'

This awareness of his good fortune is not just a function of looking back from the perspective of hindsight and wisdom that comes with age. Meyer believes part of his makeup as a person is to do what he enjoys and since a young age he felt a desire to be part of something great.

As a South African it is so easy to fall into the trap of forgetting what a prominent role Meyer played in our country, together with individuals like Cyril Ramaphosa and many others. For several years these two individuals were the front men as negotiators for the preceding and incoming governments.

Meyer's full responsibility at the time stretched over a period of about four years. During this time his life was a never-ending process of negotiations; engaging; moving one step forward and two back; catching up with experience because the National Party government had to change its mindset from control to negotiation; high intensity for 24 hours a day, with just enough sleep to carry on ...

All this happened on an emotional stage that was under constant scrutiny, surrounded by media coverage and audiences that either admired or hated Meyer. A skill he had to learn quickly was to recognise what criticism to take on board and what to ignore.

While he paid a price in terms of family life, he learnt a great deal and today I sense that he knows who he is; he knows what he has done; he knows who he knows and I am sure he knows what he is capable of.

While interviewing Meyer I sensed an experienced, confident man. His posture and then looking into his eyes confirmed that during his lifetime he has been in some very pressured, high-powered meetings with 'heavyweights' in our and other countries.

Trust plays a very important part in leadership and the performance of individuals, ultimately bringing the best out of a situation. The truth is that one gets more commitment and unity out of a relationship where trust is the golden thread.

This principle is evident in Meyer's life. In his leadership role during the 1990s it seems the presence of trust impacted an entire nation positively, and could have had the opposite effect had trust been absent. He and Ramaphosa managed to build a trusting relationship during the negotiation period, despite their differences.

Part of this was a result of their establishing a personal connection. Thinking about the famous 'fishing' incident, Meyer says: 'One must never underestimate the value of social and more friendly engagement and interaction in the process of finding answers for difficult and serious matters. If we didn't strike the relationship that we did, and more particularly the level of trust that we had between us, the end result could have been quite different. Even though we differed and sometimes heavily differed, we still had the trust in each other and it is out of that that the friendship developed.'

Another principle revealed by Meyer is that one should never act out of anger when making crucial decisions. In the late 1990s Meyer left the National Party because he was angry with FW de Klerk and other colleagues for not wanting to change the party as he believed it should be done. Although he was tasked to transform the organisation, too many around him resisted the change. He predicted this attitude would lead to their downfall and so it did. He left and in anger started the United Democratic Movement with Bantu Holomisa. This action was an attempt to show some of his former colleagues what the new National Party should look like. The initial growth of the party was fairly good, but it never really rose to significance, partly because it was born out of anger.

Today Meyer seems to have found a home in business and civil society. He believes if we want to be a successful democracy we have to be strong in three areas – government, organised business and civil society. He continues on his remarkable seamless leadership journey and one can only hope this current initiative results in positive movement for all!

CHAPTER 10

||||||||||||||||||||||||||||||||||||||||||||||||||||||||||||||||||||||||||||||||||||||||||||||||

Seamless leader attitude to disciplined consistency

WITH
❏ *Victor Matfield*

In most if not all cases disciplined consistency plays a dominant role in seamless leaders' career and leadership success. Without it they could never achieve their full potential.

Ironically, while success requires disciplined consistency – and thus time – in whatever endeavour, it can disappear in an instant because of one single, irrational moment of weakness, even though at times hindsight proves that there was in fact a build-up to the obvious moment of weakness.

As mentioned in chapter 7, Malcolm Gladwell's '10 000 hours or 10 years' rule is convincing: it almost always takes this long to build something successful that has substance, which implies the ingredient of disciplined consistency.

A leader of or in any organisation, together with a team, carves out a vision with a direction and plan; then, crucially, follows up with disciplined consistency on how team members are performing against their responsibilities set out in the plan – consistent accountability sessions.

To turn around a struggling business or division – or one's personal life – does not depend as much on a brilliant strategy or plan as it does on implementing even an average plan with disciplined consistency. If, for example, one division of an organisation is not performing, while another seems to achieve consistently, closer scrutiny will probably reveal that the successful division implements certain actions, programmes or systems around the correct drivers of the business, with a disciplined consistency.

More often than not, it is the 'boring' disciplined consistency that results in organisational and personal success, rather than the more romantic once-off exhilarating activities.

Seamless leaders believe that senior teams of organisations are mostly clear about what their challenges are and what they need to do to be successful. But despite their expensive yearly strategy planning session it would seem many of the same issues surface a year later at the next team session. They realise that the true test is often not about finding a solution to their challenges but about how to entrench a culture of disciplined consistency without being so rigid that leaders feel disempowered.

Naturally, the principle of disciplined consistency also applies if we want to be fit and healthy. The answer lies in consistently disciplined exercise and eating habits, not overnight diet or fitness programmes. Seamless leaders realise that if they want to be good parents, they need to spend quality and even quantity time with their children, with disciplined consistency. Want good academic qualifications? Study year in and year out, with disciplined consistency.

I have met some 'boring' individuals with limited charisma or people skills who simply managed to take one step at a time in their business or corporate career to eventually reach a high level of success, but they did it with disciplined consistency. Then I have also met some very charismatic individuals with all the people skills one can possibly dream of, but they jumped around from one opportunity to the next and never settled down into a rhythm of disciplined consistency and therefore never really reached their full potential.

Wonder why you are successful in one area of your life yet 'hopeless' in another? A seamless leader would suggest you find a quiet moment and examine these two areas of your life. You are bound to find that you have applied disciplined consistency in the area that you are successful at, and that the reverse is true of the area in which you are not successful.

Seamless leaders know that what fuels the disciplined consistency in the successful area is the other ingredient of the seamless recipe, namely motivation or passion, as mentioned in chapter 5. You see, when you do what you love (passion) it is easier to apply disciplined consistency, even to those 'mundane' things that you don't enjoy but that are crucial to being successful in that area, because these will always exist. One may of course be motivated by duty or fear, which when combined with accurate disciplined consistency may yet be followed by a measure of success. However, passion is the longer lasting and often more successful ingredient and plays a big role in not only achieving success but also being happy along the way.

In essence, to become more successful in the unsuccessful area we need to replicate the principle of disciplined consistency that we are demonstrating in the successful area. Therefore, sit down and make a list of what needs disciplined consistently. More often than not we know the answers – personal and organisational. If, for example, an important relationship does not seem to work out, find ways to say and show that you value the person, with a disciplined consistency. Don't try to bring it all back on track through one act of consideration. This hardly ever works, because deep inside all human beings subconsciously link disciplined consistency with integrity. So, when we try to rectify consistent failure through one act, others around us will be suspicious of our level of integrity and sincerity.

Some people may feel that disciplined consistency has not paid off. Well, the truth is that one could be applying disciplined consistency in the wrong direction. As in business we need to focus on the right things. So, do not abandon your disciplined consistency ability, but following some objective evaluation start tweaking the focus and at the right pace start doing the right things with a disciplined consistency. Of course it will help to shift the focus in the direction of passion rather than dutiful or fearful motivation.

Finally, as seamless leaders focus on the principle of disciplined consistency in their lives – personal, family and work – more often than not they attract another important ingredient of success ... consistent 'luck'. Somehow 'life' or 'influential stakeholders' hand 'unexpected' opportunities to them on a plate because they prove that they can apply disciplined consistency. Doing so demonstrates character, discipline, respect and gratitude, which are seamless leader attributes deserving of even more opportunities.

Victor Matfield – former Blue Bulls Captain and Springbok Vice Captain

Seamless Leader Principles:

1. Look out for how Matfield emphasises the principle of disciplined consistency.

2. Also notice his attitude towards personal development, movement and growth.

3. Try to identify more seamless leader principles and signs of a seamless leader attitude in this chapter. There are many to pick from, including:
   - ❏ Be humble enough to want to improve
   - ❏ Make time to think about your key strengths and weaknesses, what you want to change and what your principles and values are
   - ❏ Consistently work on your list
   - ❏ Confront the obstacles in your life
   - ❏ Work hard consistently towards the next level, lead by example and be professional
   - ❏ The more pressure the calmer you should become
   - ❏ Accept feedback and be humble enough to change
   - ❏ Consistent and correctly channelled passion more often than not leads to consistent peak performance.

During my conversation with Victor Matfield he took a piece of paper from his pocket. The information on the page was entitled 'self knowledge' with headings: strengths, weaknesses, changes, and principles and values. Under each of these headings were written four or five points. After the interview I annexed the document.

He wrote this page in 2004, after his first and not so successful year as captain of the Blue Bulls, and then started working on the things he wanted to change to become a better leader. Obviously this exercise made an impact, as he still had the list almost five years later. Today he feels confident that this simple process made a huge difference in that he is a better leader as a result of it.

What did he do? First, he was humble enough to want to improve; second, he made time to think about his key strengths and weaknesses, what he wanted to change and what his principles and values were; third, he wrote it down; and fourth, he worked on the list with *disciplined consistency*. What does this tell us about the man?

He has an attitude of improvement, growth, being better today than he/ the team was yesterday and confronting the necessary obstacles to full potential, which I would call a seamless leader attitude. Heyneke Meyer (former Blue Bulls coach and now Springbok coach) confirmed to me that Matfield transformed as a leader and grew a lot; that he was always a hard worker; that he led by example; that he was professional.

One of Matfield's weaknesses in the early days, which is listed on his 'self knowledge' page, was staying calm under pressure. He lost it with referees; he was impatient with people around him. So he had to learn to calm down; think about what happened; think what could be done; then only act. Eventually this weakness became a strength that he brought into the Springbok team. Today he believes that the more pressure there is, the calmer one should become.

He was undisputedly the best lock in the world! He was an integral part of teams that played in and won several titles, including World Cup, Super 14 and Tri-nations. In some of these games he was the captain or vice-captain on the field.

Still, he comes across as a humble, down-to-earth guy. But this humility has of course been tested over the years, as is the case with every young sportsperson suddenly catapulted into a life of stardom. He too went through a phase where the threat of becoming more passionate about all the 'fringe benefits' of being a top sportsman was looming. In other words, the passion for rugby that brought him stardom was almost replaced by more passion for 'sideshows' – attention, money, and so on. But, a caring coach with vision and passion for his players had the courage to sit him down and confront him about this diversion. The coach was of course none other than Heyneke Meyer.

This courageous conversation managed to capture Matfield's attention and change his behaviour and attitude, because there was mutual respect. More specifically, he respected Meyer – and as a result all rugby lovers can be grateful for a coach who did what was necessary and a player who was humble enough to listen and change. This is seamless leadership in action!

We have enjoyed watching a world-class player who somehow managed always to stay in peak form mentally and physically. Matfield seemed never to hit a slump! He was consistently excellent, smart, committed, and hard-working! How did he do this? Well, the man remained passionate about rugby. He never got tired of playing, training and thinking about the game. When other players walked away from practice he remained behind to talk, discuss and think about how to improve even more. He drew his energy from doing what he loved, and of course his values also indicated where he believed his strength came from. The first value on his list was 'believe in God'.

Matfield loves rugby and he can clearly imagine being involved in the sport for many years to come. I believe the sport will be better off for it. It is fairly common knowledge that the Springbok coaching team involved him a lot in planning and strategising games. His opponents had respect for the intelligent way in which he played.

While his passion and mission was rugby, it expanded over time to include making a difference to people through the sport. He remembers seeing a disabled lady in a wheelchair with her Springbok jersey on and realising that even to her he and the team meant something; that they were somehow impacting on her life.

I asked him how one motivates a winning team to consistently win, rather than become arrogant and then go down the slippery slope of consistently losing. His answer was very interesting. He believes it is easier to criticise or point out areas for improvement of a winning team than it is for a losing team. A winning team is confident and their self-image is healthy, so one can point out areas for improvement with boldness, while this is not always possible with a losing team.

To him it is logic that when one is on top others are going to keep striving to climb on to your level, so you need to make sure that you are working hard to climb even higher, with a disciplined consistency.

He believes the core of a successful team is when they are like a family; when every member feels like he wants to walk the extra mile for the other team members; when one plays for one's team; when every individual knows what the team stands for; when there is character.

He really believes that to be successful one must apply disciplined consistency. To be consistent there must be passion and hard work. One needs to do the same things over and over every week. In my view this principle applies in every area of our lives, especially those areas in which we want to be successful – family, at work, exercise, health and so on.

Matfield loves South Africa and dreams that we will continue maturing in our ability to see the positives and work on solutions together. Sometimes we are quick to complain and forget to look at how to improve.

||||||||||||||||||||||||||||||||||||||||||||||||||||||||||||||||||||||||||||||||||||||||||||||||||||||||||||||||||

CHAPTER 11

Seamless leader attitude to title and position

WITH
❏ *Michael Jordaan*

In general people are respectful or even wary of title and position. People mostly care what their leader thinks of them, whether it is because he determines their bonus or next promotion or that they simply respect him. So, they often fall into the trap of showing and reporting selectively what they believe the leader should know, showcasing their best side in many instances; or they withhold the bad news for different reasons, including a belief that they will sort it out before the leader finds out. This is a natural consequence of a title or position of authority.

Seamless leaders are aware of the limitations that title or position bring and never underestimate them, so they constantly fight this barrier to them being in touch with reality and establish its nature as exactly as possible. Symbolically such barriers may seem like a high wall between leader and follower, which means the leader cannot 'see' or 'hear' what is going on in the organisation.

When followers move over to the leader's side of the barrier they behave differently to when they are on the side where the leader can't 'see' or 'hear' them. The barrier may seem like thick glass, in which case the leader can sort of 'see' the behaviour on both sides, but not 'hear' it. So, followers can smile while actually uttering negative comments and so fool the leader. Or, the barrier may seem like thin glass, in which case the leader can 'see' and 'hear' most of what goes on, but not the exact truth.

Seamless leaders realise that one of their functions is to try and see the situation that has been thrust upon them as it really is. Lacking this ability to see the truth means moving in the dark – and no doubt acquiring some unnecessary bruises as you bump into all sorts of obstacles. It is essential to be aware of this dilemma, which is a need to acquire accurate information on the one hand, while on the other hand the very people that provide the information report selectively, for various reasons.

The seamless leader's aim is to continually break down the barrier. Anything that threatens an authentic open environment helps build the barrier. Anything that enhances an authentic and open environment breaks down the barrier. There are a number of different strategies to be used:

1. Give instructions to your reports and not below them, but insist that you will access information at any level. This means you can walk the floor and ask questions of anyone.
2. Promote absolute openness and insist that reporting must include positives and negatives. Then, don't only focus on the negatives but recognise the positives as well when someone reports both.
3. Connect with people, at a deep level. A person who is truly connected to the leader will probably act more consistently – the same on both sides of the barrier (see chapter 9 on connecting).
4. Ensure your passions – and therefore your intentions – are in place.
5. Ensure an accurate management information system.
6. Trust your 'gut' feel. When you feel something somewhere is not right, dig deeper.
7. Understand yourself, to the point that you know what weaknesses may prevent you from following through on your 'gut' feel.
8. Share your views on given situations after your direct reports share theirs. Realise that should you share your views first, most will simply agree.
9. Ask probing questions when you feel that the person reporting to you may be volunteering selective information.
10. Don't emphasise title.
11. Create opportunities to make direct contact rather than depend too much on mediums like phone and email.

12. Have a clear vision that inspires and unites.
13. Know your industry well, so that you know what to ask.

As a leadership barrier exercise, rate yourself objectively on a scale of 1 to 10 on the 13 points above (1 = useless; 10 = perfect). Those who score high, continue implementing these. Those who score low, strive to improve these.

Michael Jordaan – former CEO FNB

Seamless Leader Principles:

1. Notice how Jordaan's style naturally broke down title barriers. He and his team created extraordinary movement towards becoming the most innovative bank in the world.
2. See the importance of multiplying leaders to take over from you.
3. Also look out for his empowering approach.
4. Notice his passion and sense of purpose.
5. Try to identify more seamless leader principles and signs of a seamless leader attitude in this piece.

When I sat down with Michael Jordaan he had been the CEO of First National Bank for approximately nine years.

In some ways Jordaan differed from other banking leaders – his almost 30 000 followers on Twitter serving as a case in point. I would not be surprised if this is the largest Twitter following of any CEO in South Africa. Being different would however make sense as he heads up the most innovative bank in the world.

During a previous interview I had described him as follows: he possesses fortitude, courage, is not afraid of the unknown, believes a leader should be himself, is authentic, asks for feedback about himself specifically, believes in situational leadership – letting the best person take the lead; and surrounds himself with the best.

He explains more: 'You surround yourself with people who are better than you – if you can do that, that's half of it. Together you agree on what the goal is, where you're going, and then you must largely get out of their way. You can't get good people and then frustrate them and micro-manage them, just get out of the way. And then if you have made the right decisions people tend to surprise you, it's the most amazing thing.'

Of course getting out of the way does not mean he disappears completely off the scene: 'You set challenges, you question, you debate intensely – but intentionally, you never tell, you just challenge people.' Good people are inherently proud, they want to do well and want to achieve, and so 'wonderful things happen', explains Jordaan.

Upon reflection, his basic leadership philosophy hasn't changed over the past few years. However, he comments: 'Maybe I have changed – over time you can relax a little more, things become clearer and you become a little more self-assured about letting go.' And Jordaan does not feel this need to prove himself to everyone, as a younger CEO may tend to do. Because of this he says 'you're happy for anyone else to also get the credit because they actually deserve it and then people perform even better.'

He has continued down this road and together with his team they have taken First National Bank from strength to strength. For him the ultimate achievement has been the award as the most innovative bank in the world. Quite an accomplishment when one considers that it was soon after he became the CEO that they consciously set out to differentiate through innovation more aggressively.

Of course they had resistance to this vision when the global banking crisis struck. He explains: 'We took a dip during that crisis, but then we challenged everything. We said to ourselves, bankers are either in denial or behind the curve and we want to be neither. At the time we relooked everything completely – business model, positioning, cost structure, where the market was going.' In short they realised they could no longer just be beneficiaries of the economy; they had to go out there and grow market share. First they wanted to make sure their existing customers were really happy, before attracting new ones. They cut fees, lowered prices: 'So in the midst of the crisis we did what most companies don't do which is we actually lowered prices,' comments Jordaan. Then they went to the market aggressively, telling new prospects how much money they could save by joining the FNB stable. As Jordaan states: 'That's a very tough thing to do. Had there not been a crisis, we may not have taken the type of decisions that we did.'

Key message: It takes time to achieve any prestigious accolade, especially when it needs to happen on the back of a culture change. And, there will always be resistance on the road to significant achievement, but this very resistance could turn out to be your friend.

The decision to take innovation to another level came alive at one of their first strategy off sites soon after Jordaan became CEO. After two intense days they arrived at what seemed to be the final plan – vision, mission, measurements and the whole package. Jordaan says: 'All I wanted to do was to go have some red wine with everybody.' But one of their team members challenged the final product, stating that it wasn't strong enough, that it was boring. One can imagine that he wasn't too popular at that moment. But the team listened, probably because the leader was willing to do so. The observation was that what would set them apart would be their culture, which had to be one of innovation. And this is what they did.

Another message: Team members must feel that they can challenge at any stage of the strategy crafting process. The process itself and the leadership culture should allow for this. Why? Because the birth of a great idea or essence of a winning strategy can be born or dismissed in a moment, and for this to happen there must be a very high level of trust within the team.

How exactly did they achieve this innovative culture and consequent global recognition? As is almost always the case, the answer is simple, but the doing takes discipline, focus and endurance. In my view the leader always remains the kingpin, the heart, the driving force, hence the reason for a leader to remain in the seat for as long as it takes, within reason of course. And Jordaan adds: 'In our case, we kept at it, we learnt along the way, we made many mistakes and then you just tweak it and tweak it until it becomes better. So our strategy hasn't changed since I've been around. Our structure has barely changed. This is our strategy and we're sticking to it.'

In essence they told people that innovation is important. Jordaan says: 'It sounds very obvious – you're not going to get innovation unless you're saying that innovation is important. For example, how many companies in South Africa have, somewhere in their strategy or mission or values, the word innovation – very few.'

Also important is to measure innovation. How many companies actually do this? Jordaan believes 'if you don't tell people it's important and then measure it, then it doesn't happen'. And then, for innovation to thrive, an empowering culture is essential. Jordaan adds: 'That can take time – this is where it's important how leaders behave. Your behaviour has to be incredibly empowering'.

FNB is fortunate in that Jordaan's style and matching behaviour are naturally empowering, and this cascades over time – the key word being time. Where do corporates get it wrong? 'People must be able to take risks and make mistakes,' says Jordaan. He believes that organisations grow large and start bureaucratising, systematising, often putting in place necessary rules and processes, mostly to minimise mistakes. While this may be good it also stands in danger of becoming a barrier to an empowered employee and culture. As he explains: 'It's very important if somebody suggests a great idea and we all debate it and agree to give it a go and then it doesn't work out, that that person isn't taken to task for it. It sounds obvious but I think it's very difficult for a lot of companies to allow this risk pattern to actually happen'.

At FNB they realised that the world is changing so fast, that technology is changing the world so quickly that the risks of not innovating is bigger than the risk of making mistakes along the way. Of course this does not mean they condone silly mistakes or careless behaviour. Together with encouraging innovative ideas they also encourage the principle of 'don't fly solo'. When someone comes up with a great idea they are encouraged to discuss with other people, 'just like a pilot who is about to fly will first log a flight plan – that's what you do so people know where you're going, where you're going to land so that if you don't land they know where to go look for you. So we say, whatever idea you have, don't fly solo – internalise it, kick it around – often it becomes better in that process – and then you can go out and do it. It's about taking calculated risks, and many of them,' says Jordaan. Finally, 'recognise and reward people who have innovated – make them heroes'. At FNB they are known for handing out prize money that borders on ridiculous. In essence they put their money where their mouths are.

Every single year they just add more and more innovations. As Jordaan says: 'Right now we are in this wonderful phase where there is a great pipeline of innovations happening and it's a system that is building up momentum. I can't tell you how much fun it is to be at the helm of a system now that looks after itself.'

Of course their competitors copy their innovations. Question is do they always understand exactly what's behind each innovation, and as Jordaan says: 'More importantly there are hundreds of innovations that are internal only, that's not visible to the public, ways in which we do things and you can't copy a culture, I'm convinced of that. It takes a very long time.' Jordaan is correct in his assertion. They have secured the innovation space, not only in the banking sector but in general. It almost leaves their competitors with no alternative but to strive to occupy other spaces by way of branding, perhaps at their peril when one considers the strategic need for banks to innovate in these difficult times. And remember that an innovative culture is a reflection of an empowered culture, which is an essential ingredient to a successful bank or any large organisation these days.

Being a 'different' leader, Jordaan has served FNB and quite possibly the corporate landscape well. He has left his mark.

Q&A

Q: You obviously believe in internal succession?
Jordaan: Yes, if at all possible. There are studies that show internal guys do better than external guys, unless the company is in trouble and you need a real turnaround. I do believe in this concept of an insider outsider – you want somebody who really gets the company but also has the ability to think just a little bit differently, because the world is changing so fast right now. Sometimes companies become a little defensive about the way they do things and they've always done it in a certain way. So I believe in an insider but also an insider who can think outside. [Jacques Celliers, who took over in 2014, having been a member of the FNB Executive Committee, is such a leader.]

Q: For me, one of the signs of good leadership is if you're able to hand over to someone internally – it means you've multiplied leaders.

Jordaan: It has to be – it is the most important task of a leader. It has to be succession. If you leave, even if you've done a marvellous job and you leave a big void, then you've failed.

Q: Had you left five years ago what would you have missed or missed out on?

Jordaan: What gives me a kick is my team and when they do well. It's a bit like a family because most of your time you spend at work. Typically, the modern professional, and especially when you are the CEO – will spend far more time at work than you will with your family – so in a way, they also become your family. So seeing how people have grown and how teams synergise and form and become better and better at what they do is one of those amazing privileges that you have in a leadership position. The bank has had certain successes since we last spoke and clearly I would have missed out on living through some of those things.

Q: What more have you learnt about leadership?

Jordaan: So often in life you have to invert things and leaders for example should always think 'who is the type of person you would voluntarily submit to?' – because that's what you do, you submit to someone who is in authority. If you were not forced to work anywhere – where would you voluntarily do it; who would you happily work for? Probably where someone has your best interests at heart and wants you to do well? So if you can demonstrate that to people – that you actually want them to do well, you want them to grow, that you actually care for them ... this is my fundamental belief: You surround yourself with better people and you set them up for success. Clearly that doesn't mean that results aren't important, but they are just a yardstick by which you measure how well they are doing in the business. And if people feel that, and I do believe people can intuitively feel that – we all have that ability when you sit next to somebody and you know if they are using you or have your best interests at heart. Now that takes some time, but people get that.

II

Seamless leader attitude to courage and courageous conversations

WITH
- *Bheki Sibiya*
- *Herman Mashaba*

The American essayist and poet Ralph Waldo Emerson said this: 'Whatever you do, you need courage. Whatever course you decide on, there is always someone to tell you that you are wrong. There are always difficulties arising that tempt you to believe that your critics are right. To map out a course of action and follow it to an end requires some of the same courage that a soldier needs. Peace has its victories, but it takes brave men and women to win them.'

Seamless leaders demonstrate courage in many ways. Within their sphere of influence they stand up and say what needs to be said, with the right motive driving them and in a way that is generally considerate and not unkind to others. With those closest to them they hold courageous conversations when needed: remember Heyneke Meyer's confrontation with Victor Matfield in chapter 10. A seamless leader views a courageous conversation as a difficult, assertive, honest and even confrontational discussion that most individuals prefer avoiding, even leaders at the highest levels of organisations, up to presidents of countries.

When you need to have a discussion with someone or to raise a controversial, unpopular yet necessary topic and your first inclination is to avoid it, chances are you are staring a courageous conversation in the face. For a seamless leader the intent of such a conversation is to help someone or something grow or develop, or to spark a breakthrough in a dysfunctional relationship. And the reason why the conversation needs courage is that it seems to clash with our instinct to avoid contention (argument or quarrel), to belong and be accepted; it can either build or destroy an important relationship or situation; it is often held with someone close – a spouse, a child, an employee, a boss or a friend; or about something that matters in our life.

Seamless leaders are confident that this kind of positive breakthrough seldom happens without some form of one-way courageous message or two-way courageous conversation – parent and child; manager and employee; public figure and society; wife and husband; friend and friend; and so on. In most cases the conversation should be 'with' rather than 'to' someone. But, this is not always possible.

Why do so many of us shy away from holding courageous conversations? There are of course many reasons, like fear of rejection, lack of caring, concern for what people think of us, hidden motives leading to guilt feelings and avoidance, and so on. Often people don't confront because they confuse the word or concept of confronting with two other words – conflict and contention. Most people don't like contention, which is a good thing. Even seamless leaders don't like contention. But, most leaders don't know how to confront skilfully without contention, so they decide to ignore, rationalise or procrastinate.

How do they rationalise? They say things like: 'I don't enjoy fighting with people', 'We need to be patient with him' or 'Raising this issue in public won't serve any purpose'. They procrastinate for the same reasons, or provide reasons like: 'I'm too busy' or 'I have more important things to do than to go over there' or 'This public issue has nothing to do with me'. The real truth is that they have not yet developed trust in a confrontation process that leads to success, or in how to raise confrontational issues maturely on a public platform for debate. In other words, they are not 'confident confronters' and quite possibly lack courage.

Unfortunately most people possess this weakness, and this is why we have unresolved grudges that eventually lead to contention that is irreversible, or even war. The word 'conflict' does not have to mean quarrel or argument. It should rather mean disagreement or difference, which mostly is a good thing. All human beings are different and complex. It is therefore reasonable to expect conflicting ideas, perspectives and views. Imagine what the world would be like if we all agreed, all the time.

Many people believe confronting means not being a 'nice' person any more. They forget that great or seamless leaders and individuals in the history of the world learned to confront those resistance factors that prevented them from moving towards their full potential.

Broadly there are three types of reaction to confrontational situations:

- ❏ **The non-confronter** simply avoids confronting and is terrified for many reasons, some mentioned above. This person will never become a seamless leader!
- ❏ **The aggressive confronter** has realised the importance of confronting in order to create successful movement, but having never learned how to do it skilfully or seamlessly, he or she confronts aggressively and gets away with it. Most people in general are poor confronters so this person scares them off and gets what he wants. The aggressive confronter may become successful in life (a P&L success), but will struggle to connect with people to move them willingly, so their attitude towards him will mostly be negative. He will not become a seamless leader.
- ❏ **The seamless and skilful confronter:** There are unfortunately too few of these individuals walking the earth. If only we had more, then there would be fewer divorces, unsuccessful partnerships, wars, and so forth.

How to hold courageous conversations or confront a difficult situation

Seamless leaders instinctively use the Destiny Chain as a guideline process when they confront a difficult or potentially contentious situation between parties:

1. Where possible, define the facts of the situation, without emotion.
2. Allow for listing of the perceived or real issues, problems or challenges that seem to cause the contention as you and the other party/s

see it, but keep in mind the following rules – try not to judge while the listing takes place, not to defend comments, but allow for clarification, openness.

3. Allow for the listing of the perceived or real positives (even the alternative views) of the situation so as to create perspective; be aware that almost no situation in this life is negative only. Listing the positives or alternative views also creates an atmosphere of tolerance for different perspectives. Again, try not to judge while the listing takes place, or to defend comments, but allow for clarification, openness.

4. Allow parties to express positive desires, aspirations for the specific situation. In other words, what positive outcomes do relevant parties really want?

5. Together, agree on some actions for the way forward. These actions move parties closer towards the positive desires listed in step 4 and address the perceived or real negatives or problems listed in step 2.

6. Allow for agreement on some form of follow-up to evaluate progress.

An overall principle that assists seamless leaders in a successful courageous conversation is to qualify the intent of the conversation in your mind. This creates an environment of authenticity. Do this before you launch into point 1 above. Then, stay calm and try to be like Roger Federer during a grand slam final. This is more difficult for some, but it is essential. The ability to control their emotions is one of the things that makes sportsmen great.

Raising issues publicly

Seamless leaders will not shy away from raising issues publicly when this is the best way to initiate action towards confronting barriers to full potential. Keep in mind the following principles:

1. The motive for raising the issue should be a pure one, not simply to enjoy attention or boost reputation. In short, your motive serves the bigger picture and not your own selfish agenda.

2. Stick to the facts and don't make sweeping negative statements, like 'All politicians are corrupt' or 'The entire education system is failing'.

3. When you raise a negative concern or issue and it is a mere perception, emphasise that it is a perception – for example: 'It is my and many others' perception that crime has spiralled out of control', or 'Most people seem to feel that the education system is failing horribly'.

4. Where possible, recognise the opposite side or possibility of your statement, for example: 'Most people seem to feel that the education system is failing horribly. However, there certainly seem to be clear pockets of excellence, for which we are grateful.'

5. Give context to your reason for raising the issue. In other words, link it to the bigger picture: 'Most people seem to feel that the education system is failing horribly. However, there certainly seem to be clear pockets of success, for which we are grateful. As per the aspirations mentioned in the National Development Plan, as a society we have to address the barriers to a successful education system for the good of future generations – your children, my children.'

6. Raising a controversial issue may end with point 5. However, where at all possible and relevant, don't just raise the issue, but propose a possible solution, direction and structure, admitting that the proposed solution may not be the only and comprehensive one out there, but it is the best one you know of at this stage.

The seamless leader approach is to do all of the above without getting too personal or singling out individuals unnecessarily. It's all about the issue, so keep your eye on the ball. Finally, if it is at all possible, go straight to the source and address a contentious issue with the concerned person direct rather than via a public platform. Have the maturity to avoid a public spat and attention for the greater good.

Bheki Sibiya – CEO Chamber of Mines

Seamless Leadership Principles:

1. Notice Sibiya's fearless attitude to courageous conversations.
2. Notice how his leadership approach breaks down barriers.
3. Try to identify more seamless leadership principles and signs of a seamless leader attitude.

The first time I met Bheki Sibiya, he was a guest speaker and talked about leadership. He was impressive, to say the least. His comments on courageous leadership, which seems to define his approach to life, stood out.

Sibiya is fearless. He is a straight talker and speaks his mind without hesitation. About this he says: 'If I were to be fired here, I would be able to retire; I would have a car, a home, food on the table and will be able to go on holiday until I die. At what stage am I going to be fully me? At what stage should I express my views to whomsoever I meet, as articulately as word allows me, as respectfully as my mother taught me? If it does not happen when I am 54 I may just as well drop dead.'

He was born in the slums of Durban and raised in rural KwaZulu-Natal. His father was a polygamist and married two wives, so there were many siblings around. As young kids they worked so hard in his father's expanded general dealership business during school holidays that they could not wait to get back to school. As he explains, 'We would realise that relaxation for us was during school term, because during school holidays we would be working extremely hard, often 18 to 24 hours per day.' This 'classic child labour', as he calls it, instilled three things in him: the ability to work hard; the desire to qualify himself well, because he realised 'if you are uneducated you are going to live a hard life for a long time'; and that one could make a living as an entrepreneur and not only through standard career choices like doctor, teacher, ministry, etc.

His view today is therefore that the first ingredient of success is hard work. It is the foundation principle upon which 'working smart' can be built. Further to this, he has come to believe that one should not force oneself into a leadership position but that it is something that one should be entrusted with. In his career he has been entrusted with several leadership responsibilities, which included being National President and MD of the Black Management Forum, founding CEO of Business Unity South Africa, several chairman, director and non-executive director positions, and currently the challenging position of CEO of the Chamber of Mines.

A breakthrough for Sibiya came early in his career during his first job, at Ford Motor Company. He was a junior personnel officer with an industrial psychology, public administration and political science degree from the University of Zululand, working extremely hard after hours to understand the business and his environment. His first expertise that put him on the map was leave administration. He became the top expert around. Eventually he was granted a fellowship to study for an MBA full-time in the US.

To Sibiya, leadership is 'the ability to listen, observe, and understand what is required at a point in time and in a sense responding to the needs of a particular community by looking at the resources that need to be utilised to achieve the goals'. His personal leadership philosophy is to lead 'through my ears, my eyes and my heart – my ears to understand what the situation demands, to listen to the people who are the recipients; the eyes observe, because whereas we wish that people are articulating issues as they should, sometimes their actions say more than their words. Therefore my eyes can observe what they do and I am then able to bring together what I hear and what I observe to get closer to the full picture.' The heart is about being passionate about what one does, 'to ensure that the flame and passion for excellence within yourself and those you interact with is high'.

Also, leadership to him is about being courageous, which means 'doing what is necessary irrespective of what some of the personal consequences are going to be; believing that the cause is bigger than self'. In his view, so long as a leader sees it this way he can act courageously. When he sees himself as bigger than the cause, courageous leadership is replaced by self-serving leadership, which, according to Sibiya, 'in our country we are seeing a huge amount of'.

Courageous leadership requires being happy and confident within your own skin so that you will be yourself no matter what the situation; and your attitude should be 'no matter what title I carry, I am a very small cog in a major wheel, but the cog I am may enable the larger wheel to move more effectively' – in other words, humility.

He has done some courageous and different things as leader of the Chamber. For example, getting mining bosses to march with the unions (only the second time in history) about safety issues; or greeting ANC Youth League marchers with a huge banner outside the Chamber, indicating that there are issues on which they agree, though they differ on the solution. This was brilliant leadership that was about highlighting commonalities, creating a foundation on which future discussions and relationships can be built.

In his current position he certainly has several challenges that will require him to utilise all his acquired leadership skills. In his view, 'first and foremost is the issue of safety'. Sibiya says: 'Some would say the nationalisation challenge is out there, but I would say if nationalisation were to take our eyes off the safety ball it will hurt this country terribly. We must just focus on safety and environmental issues.'

Sibiya's courage featured strongly when I engaged him about challenges that hold South Africa back from achieving its full potential. He believes the political scene has changed 'because of the cushiness of the private sector, resulting in some pulling out of politics. Some remained to reap the rewards of business. Those seem to be the ones that are succeeding.' He also feels strongly that 'many politicians have lost the spirit of Madiba, in being of service to the majority of South Africans. Generally people are now self-serving.'

His question was 'How much is enough'? In his view, within the 'next five years we are going to see significant shifts in leadership', unless the ANC makes an absolute U-turn.

Sibiya ends our conversation with strong words: 'Unity is strength. With unity, let's fix these problems. We are all on the same boat and if it is not fixed it is going under.'

Q&A

Q: In terms of modern leaders, who would you say have been your role models in respect of leadership?

Sibiya: That is extremely difficult to say. There are quite a number of popular leaders that influenced me. For example, aspects of Madiba are absolutely exciting and if one does not emulate a lot of his leadership aspects one would not have learnt to be fully South African. He is a beacon of hope, of light and confidence for us. Looking at business in for example the mining industry, Sipho Nkosi, CEO of Exxaro, was my university mate when we were at university. We worked at Ford Company together and for about 15 months we shared the same room. He was retrenched at Ford and decided to do an MBA full-time at Boston, came back and eventually concentrated on coal. Today he leads Exxaro, which is worth between R65 and 70 billion. Exxaro stands out in terms of developing necessary skills. Sipho's net worth is about R1.6 billion. He is still humble and drives a simple car.

Q: How has your experience over time helped you in your current position?

Sibiya: Experiences like watching Madiba come to KZN at the height of tensions between ANC and IFP and how he would listen, listen and listen to people's views and comments. There were times I would wonder whether he took everything in. But with his incredible memory he would pause and then summarise in detail and suggest a wise way forward. People wanted to feel they had been heard and he allowed this to happen. When Saki Macozoma was MD of Transnet I asked him how he dealt with challenges and being exceptionally busy. He just encouraged me to focus on priorities of today, linked with a long-term goal. I apply this advice today. There are many challenges in mining, but we can simply look at what we can do today; ensure that the members are united around the priorities of today. We can't fix all the challenges now, but we can put structures in place today that will help solve other problems in the future.

It is the balance between what we can do today and what should be done in the future.

Q: Why are you against nationalisation?
Sibiya: I believe nationalisation is amputating the toe to address a headache. It is an inappropriate intervention. We don't know of any country where it has worked. It may create short-term employment but then it will be gone. If you look at a bird and a fish, there are some birds that can swim, but there are no fish that can really fly high. Government has a certain skill to govern and that is where it needs to remain, perhaps as the 'bird', in my analogy. Commerce and industry has a certain aptitude to manage businesses, probably represented by the 'fish'. Some birds can swim but for a limited period. So there are no financial and human resources that would be appropriate for the government to effectively manage nationalised mines. Mines will go south. So we need to reason together about how to fix job creation, poverty and much more in a sustainable manner. Mining could contribute to service delivery by partnering with local government, but it would need the blessing of national government. Private sector delivers while government tenders and tenders and tenders. What we also need to do is engage several relevant Ministers on what we as a mining industry can really do to address the real issues.

Q: What are you doing to reposition the image of the industry as a dirty, dangerous place to work, yet does do a lot of good?
Sibiya: People talk about do and tell. Sometimes when one tells, but the reality is not that great, the message is lost and credibility gone. From where I sit, I focus less on the credibility or image issues but rather on improving the reality. The mining industry will always be dirty and potentially dangerous. For us, we want to say that the potential danger does not eventuate. Places like Australia and Canada are achieving this and we role model ourselves on them. We are for example looking at re-engineering production bonuses. Unions are very against the current system because people start depending on their total remuneration, which includes bonuses, and structure their lifestyle accordingly. Bonuses come down and they are in trouble. Employees then cut corners in order to achieve

production targets for bonuses, because their debt must be serviced. We are debating this issue.

Q: The relationship between the Department of Mineral Resources and mining leadership seems to be tense and challenging. Your comments on this?

Sibiya: When there is a fatality and the DMR stops the mine for the right reasons we of course cannot blame them. It's where the DMR may come and for a tiny administrative issue stop the mine and declare it is for safety reasons, which is not right. Where I am working hard on is for stakeholders to understand the positive impact of the mining industry and so support it, as is generally the case in Canada, Australia and other countries. In South Africa, because of our racially divided past it is more difficult. The mining industry has to cleanse itself of the bad acts of the past. But it also needs to let South Africans understand that they can't be theoretical about life. The mining industry is a major contributor. Sometimes one gets some uninformed government officials who very flippantly deal with the mining industry and its losses. They forget the mining industry spends close on R400 billion per annum on investments.

Herman Mashaba – Owner Lephatsi Investments; Founder Black Like Me; Chairman Free Market Foundation

IIIIIIIIIIIIIIIIIIIIIIIIIIIIIIIIIIIIIIIIIIIIIIIIIIIIIIIIIIIIIIIIIIIIIIIIIIIIIIIIIIIIIIIIIIIIIIIIIIIIIIIIIIIIIIIIIIIIIIIIIIIIIIIIIIIIIIIIIIIIIIIIIIIIIIIIIIIIIIIIIIIIIIIIIIIIIII

Seamless Leadership Principles:

1. Look out for Mashaba's attitude towards getting involved in the bigger picture; leading beyond his area of responsibility; speaking up.
2. Try to identify more signs of a seamless leader attitude.

IIIIIIIIIIIIIIIIIIIIIIIIIIIIIIIIIIIIIIIIIIIIIIIIIIIIIIIIIIIIIIIIIIIIIIIIIIIIIIIIIIIIIIIIIIIIIIIIIIIIIIIIIIIIIIIIIIIIIIIIIIIIIIIIIIIIIIIIIIIIIIIIIIIIIIIIIIIIIIIIIIIIIIIIIIIIIII

Herman Mashaba is a businessman, entrepreneur, capitalist, and now crusader – a man on a mission. As the founder of Black Like Me and owner of Lephatsi Investments (assets under management of R600 million, stakes in 12 different listed and non-listed companies), he has been a leader in the business community for years. Recently however he decided to extend his leadership beyond the boundaries of his business empire. He takes his leadership position as the newly elected Chairman of the Free Market Foundation (FMF) very seriously, to the point that he spends about half his time campaigning for a more free market system in South Africa. He says: 'Obviously all of us as South Africans are concerned about what's happening at the moment with the threat to our free market principles.'

He feels strongly that the voices for nationalisation and socialist principles have dominated the public platform for too long. In his view, 'this is unfair, but at the same time we have to take responsibility for raising our voices in our democratic society and present another view, which is precisely what I am doing'. He has chosen the FMF as his vehicle and is willing to go all the way to achieve this, even the Constitutional Court if needs be.

Mashaba pulls no punches in making his opinion known that South

Africa's current labour laws are destroying job opportunities. Though there were no doubt good reasons for the final product, time has passed and he and the FMF believe they do not serve the desperate need for job creation at this time. He speaks as a businessman and employer over the last 30 years.

He comments: 'There is no way you can force employers to pay salaries that they cannot afford. So what happens? They don't employ. And when you do employ someone and they don't deliver you struggle to get rid of them. Why then take that risk. Business on its own is already a risk.'

According to him we simply need to create a high employment market 'so that employers know that when they don't pay someone enough they are going to move next door'. For Mashaba, this is not rocket science, in that employers know they can't hire and fire randomly after investing in people, because this costs money and time. He adds: 'No employer any-where in the world would want to employ people just to exploit them. From a logical point of view it doesn't make sense. Because once you em-ploy someone, for that person to be valuable to you they must be trained, and you don't want to lose people and continually train new people. For you to really stabilise your business you need loyalty.'

While this is the angle from which Mashaba comes, when one pushes him he is astute enough to realise that there is a huge need for labour or-ganisations like unions, because 'we should not take it for granted that all employers mean good'. Advocating a free market system includes systems that ensure it is all done in a fair and responsible manner, which is where we need 'all the role players, including labour, to ensure that unscrupu-lous business people are kept in check. So I think labour has a big role to play. Personally I support them to be there to protect the ignorant with an oversight role.'

We have thrown the baby out with the bath water, according to Mashaba: 'Absolutely. That is where I believe we made a terrible mistake, to ignore the basic fundamentals of how an economy works. An economy works on the basis of creating entrepreneurs who must be able to employ people where it makes commercial sense. If it doesn't then people don't employ.'

When Mashaba visits less-privileged communities he notices the levels of unemployment and the desperation of people, which many of us do. He says: 'It is actually quite scary; it hurts me that I am unable to assist them. The only way I can assist them is to engage the law makers to understand the devastating effects of this legislative framework.'

He explains his real gripe as follows: 'The responsibility lies with Parliament. They are the ones that developed and approved this legislative framework. They need to understand and appreciate the fact that South Africa is not made out of 2 million union members, it is made out of 50 million people and all of them are stakeholders. I think that when we come out with legislation, we should make sure we come up with something that is equitable to the 50 million South Africans and not the minority.'

Mashaba referred to the millions of South Africans who are unemployed, many of them within the youth category, and he is convinced government is not helping with this. Sooner rather than later this time bomb will explode, and signs are already evident.

At least 90 per cent of the waitrons in restaurants across Gauteng and other places are from countries up north, mostly Zimbabwe. And many gardeners and domestics are also from Zimbabwe. The reason for this speaks to Mashaba's argument that labour legislation prevents free negotiations between prospective employee and employer; that government interferes with a citizen's freedom and right to decide whether he/she wants to work for a certain income. Because of this barrier, employers employ foreigners who are not bound by these restrictive laws. As a result, and understandably so, millions of wonderful Zimbabweans enter the South African economy, which logically adds to the burden placed on basic services like health and education.

According to Mashaba, short-term interventions to create income, like grants, may be necessary. However, his view is that it 'destroys the dignity of our people, if we see it as a long-term solution. It can never be a sustainable way of addressing our social issues.' Dignity and determining one's own future are principles he believes in passionately.

This leader is on a mission: what motivates him personally is to succeed at whatever he does. His biggest fear is failure. And he believes 'the only way to avoid failure is to work harder every day and to be conscious not to take anything for granted, because life can change overnight.'

||||||||||||||||||||||||||||||||||||||||||||||||||||||||||||||||||||||||||||||||||||||||||||||||||||||||||||

Seamless leader attitude to honesty and openness

WITH

❏ *Bill Child*
❏ *Nick Badminton*
❏ *Zwelinzima Vavi*

Thomas Fuller, an English churchman and historian who lived in the 17th century, penned this truth: 'He does not believe that does not live according to his belief.' Seamless leaders do not fall into this trap. They strive to be honest with themselves, others and society as a whole.

How many times have we wanted to say something in a meeting but haven't because of fear or concern for what others may say or think, or what the boss may do to us? When this happened we were not being honest and therefore authentic and chose to be manipulated by fear.

Some leaders who are striving to be honest in a diplomatic or 'caring' way go so far down the road of diplomacy that they forget to be honest and therefore authentic. For seamless leaders it is honesty first and diplomacy second! They realise that when they are honest and not diplomatic many will respect them and few will like them. If they learn to be excellent with both, many will respect them and many will like them – but never everyone, because leaders have to do the difficult and unpopular thing.

Being honest is a decision based on principles and values. To become diplomatically honest is an acquired skill and can therefore be developed over time.

Are honest conversations being held in South Africa about sensitive issues? For example, is there honesty as far as the agenda to eradicate poverty is concerned, or is the real agenda materialism, the selfish acquisition of wealth? Is the employment equity agenda an honest one – in other words, are real issues being addressed with real and honest facts and in the best possible way, or is the agenda of some a black and white issue only?

Is the constitution an honest one when it provides for a certain level of discrimination against a specific sector of the working population? Can organisations honestly perform against sector charters when the facts about available skills indicate otherwise? Is there honesty about transformation when, almost 18 years into a democracy, most of the CEOs in the top 100 listed companies are still white males?

Being honest in every respect makes you authentic – honest with yourself; honest with others; honest about what is happening around you; honest in how you address the reality; honest in your agenda. An authentic environment must be honest! Then there will be fertile ground for the growth of seamless leaders who will rise to the occasion to achieve our full potential.

We challenge leaders to have a bold conversation with their teams about honesty; about how they can create an honest environment where people report honestly; express their views honestly; do performance appraisals honestly; prepare their budgets honestly; set honest targets for growth, finance, etc.

Simple honesty exercise

Do the following simple exercise with your team, on a regular basis. Hand each one two blank pieces of paper. Ask them to rate the level of honesty in the team from 1 to 10, one being no honesty and openness exist and ten meaning the team members are 100 per cent comfortable and open when they express their views and thoughts. Team members need only write a number on the piece of paper, fold it and hand back to you. They do not have to write their names on it.

On the other piece of paper they can write down what they believe should happen for the suggested rating to go up, in other words for more openness and honesty to exist. Again, they need not write their name on the paper. As a leader you can then collate the scores and share the final average with the team. Try to implement some of the suggestions and do the rating again one month later. As you continue this exercise the average rating should improve – look out for more and more names on the pieces of papers. This is an indication of the level of openness and honesty.

Bill Child – RC Willey, USA

IIIIIIIIIIIIIIIIIIIIIIIIIIIIIIIIIIIIIIIIIIIIIIIIIIIIIIIIIIIIIIIIIIIIIIIIIIIIIIIIIIIIIIIIIIIIIIIIIIIIIIIIIIIIIIIIIIIIIIIIIIIIIIIIIIIIIIIIIIIIIIIIIIIIIIIIIII

Seamless Leadership Principles:
1. Notice Child's and Buffett's emphasis on honesty and integrity.
2. Notice the principles on which Child built a very successful business.
3. Try to identify more seamless leadership principles and signs of a seamless leader attitude in this piece.

IIIIIIIIIIIIIIIIIIIIIIIIIIIIIIIIIIIIIIIIIIIIIIIIIIIIIIIIIIIIIIIIIIIIIIIIIIIIIIIIIIIIIIIIIIIIIIIIIIIIIIIIIIIIIIIIIIIIIIIIIIIIIIIIIIIIIIIIIIIIIIIIIIIIIIIIIII

Bill Child took a struggling 600 square feet appliance store in the State of Utah to a point where the iconic Warren Buffett bought the business from him in the mid-1990s. I sat down with Child, now retired, while visiting the USA recently.

Today he is the Chairman of RC Willey, a successful American home furnishings and appliance retailer. The business is led by his nephews. He tries to fulfil the duties of chairman while involved in a condominium project on the island of Kauai and enjoying his other passions of family and golf.

When Child was a youngster his father worked three jobs, with a small farm on the side. They never had a lot of money. He learned the value of hard work, frugality – and also realised he wanted to do something different, not depend on the price of a product, unpredictable weather and other outside factors.

In the 1950s Child worked part-time for his father-in-law, RC, in their small local furniture store. He had to take over the struggling business in 1954 when RC unexpectedly passed away. The estate recorded assets of $25 000, including the business accounts receivable, eight acres of land and a house. Liabilities were $37 000. In those days it was a lot of money, especially when one considers Child's house cost him $6 000. The bank suggested they close doors. Child could not accept this option as – apart from the fact that his mother-in-law was dependent on the income – he just did not want to fail, and he saw something positive in their good reputation. He decided to put his head down and do his best. At first the goal was to survive and get out of debt. There was no vision to become the greatest in the state.

But they did become the greatest in the State of Utah. Buffett once commented to Child: 'Bill, you moved from being just an insignificant player in the field of home furnishing, electronics and appliances to being the number one in Utah. How did you do it? What happened to these other companies?' Child then wrote a paper attempting to give an answer, and Buffett forwarded a copy to top business leaders like Bill Gates, Tom Murphy and about 20 others.

Child believes in eight simple principles to live by within the business environment, which no doubt contributed towards its success: 1) Treat every customer the way you want to be treated; 2) Little things make all the difference; 3) Be honest; 4) Do the right thing; 5) Don't follow the herd; 6) Hire the right personnel; 7) Treat employees like family; 8) Build a business to keep, not to sell.

In the mid-1990s several factors led to a desire to sell the business, and not just to anyone, but to Warren Buffett, primary shareholder, chairman and CEO of Berkshire Hathaway. It is rare that a so-called dream acquisition turns out to be what the acquirer or acquired expected, but life after the fact was certainly not a let-down in the case of RC Willey and Berkshire Hathaway.

About Buffett, Child says: 'Our relationship with Warren has absolutely been first class, perfect. He leaves you alone. He is a wonderful guy; his integrity is unquestionable; he is very bright of course; he is very focused. As a businessman I learnt a few things from him. I think my business IQ has increased by 10 points over the 15 years I have associated with him.'

According to Child the only thing Buffett gave him any trouble on was moving the business out of state. After becoming the largest furniture store in Utah, Child wanted to know if their model and approach could work outside the state. The challenge was that they also believed in not trading on Sundays. The opinion all round, including that of Buffett, was that RC Willey would fail outside Utah should they continue the practice of not opening on Sunday. Child remarks about this practice: 'Our contention was that you could get better employees if you don't force them to work on Sunday. There is a little bit of a cost saving because you cut your overheads down from seven to six days, which helps a little bit.'

After taking a helicopter flight with Buffett over Vegas and a town called Henderson, which at the time had been the fastest growing town in the USA for 10 years running, Child asked Buffett what he thought about opening a store there. He had also done his homework by asking for the opinions of other experts in the field. They believed RC Willey was good, but not good enough to succeed without abandoning their Sunday policy. Buffett could not be convinced and turned down proposals for building in both Las Vegas and Boise, Idaho.

Child came up with a plan that would get the ball rolling. So he proposed a deal that Buffett could not refuse. It was to personally buy land in Boise, Idaho and set up a store sticking to the 'closed on Sundays' rule. If it wasn't successful in six months, Child would close it down and take his losses. Buffett agreed, telling Child: 'If we can't do $30 million, we'll close it. If we can do it, I'll rent it from you and pay your 4 per cent of gross sales.' But if it was really successful, Child said he would sell it back to Buffett for the price of what it cost him, without charging interest. Buffett agreed. A few weeks later Buffett called Child to mention that there was no upside for Child. His response was: 'There is an upside. If we are successful you will let us go to Vegas, won't you?' Buffett seemed to agree. Thereafter he showed personal interest by often calling Child to find out how the project was progressing. He even started calling it the Buffett store.

Well, the store was successful beyond expectation and Buffett wanted to buy it back, with interest. Child did not want to relent as the agreement was without interest. And so there was a standoff between two leaders who are ruled by their sense of integrity. Buffett said to Child: 'Bill, we have never had an argument, but we are going to have it over this one'. They came to an agreement that some felt did not make sense for Child from a business point of view. But, to Child it felt like the right thing to do, which is how he chose to live his magnificent life.

Child is a simple businessman and a leader who believes that 'if a leader has principles his followers will admire and respect him and know when you tell them something, you are telling the truth'.

RC Willey did eventually move into Las Vegas successfully. The world needs more courageous leaders like Child whose lives are governed by simple, universal principles that will always withstand the test of time.

Nick Badminton – former CEO Pick n Pay

Seamless Leadership Principles:
1. Notice what Badminton did to break down the leadership barrier.
2. Notice how he confronted barriers to full potential by courageous conversations.
3. Notice how he creates an open and honest environment.
4. Try to identify more seamless leadership principles and signs of a seamless leader attitude.

Cape Town and Bishops boy Nick Badminton was with Pick n Pay for over 30 years, since just after school. It was interesting sitting in his Gauteng office, as it was the same office I sat in when I interviewed Sean Summers many years ago.

Summers was one of my first top leader interviews when I was still very intimidated by title and the perceived power behind it. I remember being totally surprised when he collected me in reception himself. Back then I wasn't interviewing Summers for any media platform but as part of research for post-graduate studies. So he certainly did not collect me to impress anyone.

Meeting with Badminton I sensed the same relaxing and comfortable approach. Like Summers, he radiated a sense of 'I am comfortable with myself, and not because I believe I am better than others.' I did not have to wonder whether I should call him by his first name or address him as Mister. I knew instantly that we were going to have an easy, open discussion about leadership and life.

He compares life with a filing system that looks something like a concertina file. Every single experience you have is filed in the system. Later in life one tends to dig back into that concertina file for previous experiences to assist in dealing with challenges and situations.

The first part of the file is filled up by childhood experiences. Therefore a child who for example plays sport and captains a team here and there fills his filing system with leadership experiences. A child who learns to play chess will fill his file with the ability to think more strategically; a child who walks her younger brother to school early every morning fills up her file with the ability to be responsible; and so forth.

As a young man after school there came a time when his Dad decided to 'kick' him out of the house. He had to get into his old, rusted and beat-up car and find a place to sleep. He believes this was an important experience to deposit into his filing system. The more valuable and often challenging experiences one dumps into that concertina file the better one will cope with life and leadership later on.

The principle is therefore that ultimately all experiences are for our good, no matter how challenging or difficult they may be at the time. Embrace every day with open arms because it is filled with valuable experiences. If you want to develop as a human being and leader or if you want your people or children to grow, shower them with interesting and difficult experiences that they can place in their concertina file.

Somewhere in the interview I put Badminton on the spot by asking – suppose he was on his death bed and important people asked him what he had learned about what it takes to be a great leader, what would he say?

1. Humility is important! A leader must not be bombastic, larger than life, striving to take all the credit. A great leader is more than happy to push people forward for recognition.

2. Leaders can never communicate enough! Even when a leader feels that he/she is on top of it all and that everyone understands the particular message it is still not enough.

3. Thank people incessantly! Every day almost every person in an organisation does at least one thing well enough to be thanked or recognised. But, instead we often prefer to find what is wrong and highlight that.

Isn't leadership simple? There is just nothing complex about these three principles, yet many leaders more often than not get them wrong! What many fail to realise, or eventually forget as they get used to their position, is that they are on the back foot simply because of the position and title that they hold. In other words, just because you have position, which followers then automatically associate with power, you will often be perceived as arrogant, sometimes simply because you were human and just once forgot to greet someone. Or sometimes because the person making the judgement actually has a low self image.

Just because you have position those around you will often fail to be fully open with you, communicating what they believe you want to hear or what is perceived to be favourable to their future career prospects.

Just because you have position, it is often the 'in' thing to speak negatively about you around a braai with colleagues. By the same token, people may be reluctant to assertively say something 'nice' about you.

A leader who believes his team is 100 per cent open and frank during discussions in meetings probably has a team that is 60–80 per cent open. If he believes his team is 60 per cent open they are probably 40 per cent open, and so on. Very few leaders are able to get their teams to be 100 per cent open and honest with their comments and views. I believe it is possible, though.

Badminton agreed with this principle. He believed however that placing the right people in the right seats goes a long way towards gathering a team that functions openly and candidly.

When he became the General Manager for Western Cape he did something interesting that would go a long way towards getting a team to be open, and it coincides with the universal Destiny Chain process. If most leaders did this during the early stages of their appointment to a position we would see more miraculous movement in organisations. In fact, I wish our newly appointed Ministers would do this.

He rolled out 'grievance' or 'gripe' sessions across the province. He called in managers and then assistant managers and challenged them to fill up a board with their frustrations and what annoyed them. They did this after he left. Later he would come back and go through the list. On most occasions they would solve about half of the issues; 30 per cent they could do nothing about, and the rest were deferred to the next meeting. As

Badminton said: 'The real issue was that they were able to talk and many of the issues faded away after that. It really got everyone very positive.'

This is powerful leadership! If you as a leader would learn to do this type of exercise effectively and with confidence I promise you greater success! However, balance this process with Badminton's advice that 'a leader should never be too democratic'. Discussing and even debating; listening to people's concerns; valuing suggestions; arriving at solutions together; getting buy-in and so on should not result in slow decision making. Your people need you to be decisive as well.

Like all other leaders, Badminton is not perfect, but he served his time and made a contribution.

Zwelinzima Vavi – General Secretary of COSATU

Seamless Leadership Principles:

1. Notice the lessons Vavi learnt from trying to hide behaviour that was not honest and open.
2. Also notice principles around how to lead COSATU out of the hole it finds itself in.
3. The importance of values comes out strongly in Vavi's story.
4. Try to identify more seamless leadership principles and signs of a seamless leader attitude.

I have met many leaders from different spheres of society. Surprisingly few of them have presence, or gravitas. Vavi has this, with his tall physique and authentic confidence to back it up. From the moment he walked into the CliffCentral studios for the Leadership Platform show he greeted every single person with a pleasantness that obviously comes naturally. Our actual interview touched on the man; the interaction in studio was a worthwhile experience, but the personal interaction before and after communicated even more about him as a person and leader.

This is a man who without doubt was destined for greater things, even beyond being General Secretary of COSATU. He somehow embodied integrity, honesty and the courage of speaking truth to power, which in large measure seem to be disappearing from our leadership culture as a nation and in fact across the globe.

Some time back a successful capitalist suggested to me, without hesitation, that South Africans should support Vavi, even for President. I was gobsmacked, because clearly Vavi would not necessarily promote policies that a capitalist appreciates. But this was the status and respect that Vavi commanded from all quarters of society. It seems that to many the value of integrity and honesty weighed, and perhaps still weighs heavier than economic and political views, possibly suggesting how desperate society is for leaders of real integrity and stature.

This is why Vavi damaged himself and possibly his future so severely when his scandal hit the press mid-2013; this is why so many were and are still disappointed in what happened. But, can he recover; has this been a mere bump in the road, or a detour on his road to destiny? Can he again become that man so many admired and respected; can he gain momentum once again?

I suggested to Vavi that we bed this traumatic scandal down by discussing what he learned from it, to enable other leaders to learn from him and avoid the unnecessary pain that follows not only for the leader but also for those closest to him and in some cases millions that depend on him for leadership.

The central learning for him was that 'you can do something behind closed doors, but nothing that was done behind these doors remains there forever. When you do things hoping no one would ever know about it you must know you are risking and at some point those things will come out and hurt you and your family badly.' Vavi commented that his family and everyone who believed in him and his leadership, what he represented, were badly hurt. He has learnt that 'nothing is irreversible'. The man is sincere about what he refers to as a 'terrible mistake', which of course he apologised for 'a million times over', he says. He adds: 'Sometimes it is not the words that convince people but the actions thereafter.' The truth is that one 'stupid incident', as he puts it, can destroy the credibility of a person, and he accepts that some may never support him again. The counter view is also true: many realise that he made a mistake and that the challenges South Africa faces are more important than focusing on Vavi.

Let's view Vavi from this angle. When a leader moves into a space where he becomes a real threat to the powers that be, certain influences enter that same space. These influences are not understood by us ordinary human beings, who pose no threat at all. Leaders like Vavi and even Julius Malema can attest to this truth with authenticity. It is therefore all the more crucial that someone like Vavi remains true to his own moral compass, a lesson he has now learnt with pain.

Remaining true to his moral compass will still not ensure an easy journey, because part of that influence of detractors that we underestimate, is the use of structures and resources that can either fabricate falsities or uncover human mistakes, then blow them up to serve a particular agenda. And this may be why in the political domain, more often than not, the most authentic and qualified leaders don't survive that treacherous climb to the top. Yet, what society needs most is for someone like Vavi to learn from his mistakes, change authentically and then continue ascending the steep mountain towards his destiny, whatever that may be.

Of course one is hesitant to state that he possesses the makings of becoming our number one citizen or that this is his destiny, one reason being his political and economic views – surely the correct model for our country has to be somewhere between what he currently advocates and what a party like the DA stands for. However, a leader worth his salt (Mandela comes to mind) realises, when that mantle of President falls, that his responsibility now transcends all boundaries and touches all citizens. He is then mature and wise enough to allow his mind-set to elevate to that of a statesman, sensing the need for more balanced policies and strategies. Vavi could be such a man.

His immediate leadership challenge however is COSATU. Vavi admitted that the organisation is currently 'completely paralysed because of leadership divisions that exist'. He explained quickly that this has nothing to do with his scandal. It existed before, and some even argue there are class divisions within the organisation. The contention 'is about how the federation should position itself in a democracy when it is in alliance with the ruling party. It is about how to relate to Cabinet; how to relate to demonstrators in the streets. We are calling for improved accountability and service delivery. This is the nature of the divisions', explained Vavi.

He hopes of course that they will succeed, because the alternative is a continued paralysis. They need unity in COSATU. Their disunity results in people finding solutions outside the organisation, and this takes them on a road to becoming irrelevant. We see this happening all around, especially on the platinum belt.

Vavi is convinced their solution is to unite behind important principles and not an important name. He says: 'People relate to the realities of today, and not to something that happened long ago. I think that's the lesson we must all learn as we try to find the unity within the federation.' He needs to consider the possibility that before the needed unity will emerge, courageous, tough decisions and actions, which are never risk-free, are necessary. When an organisation has descended as low as COSATU has, even continued engagement tends to result in a dead end, and that means tough action alone can bring it back on the path of unity.

COSATU is anything but a team. Currently it is all about the different 'I's' and perhaps even 'we's' in the organisation. It will take remarkable leadership to bring back a 'one united team'. Is this a final leadership test for Vavi before his summit to the peak?

II

Seamless leader attitude to making meaning

WITH

❏ *Mardia van der Walt-Korsten*
❏ *Ian Donald*

When I held a leadership conversation with Mardia van der Walt-Korsten, chief executive of T-Systems, she quoted Guy Kawasaki, who believes you should start or run a company not to make money but to make meaning. This could happen in one of three ways:

❏ Your product or service can increase the quality of life of people.
❏ Your product or service can right a wrong.
❏ Your product or service can prevent the end of something good.

And, as Kawasaki says, if you make meaning you will probably make money anyway.

As I gave this some thought and discussed it with a couple of leaders, it became clear that 'making meaning' – or purpose – can be more difficult in certain businesses and perhaps industries. For example, clearly seamless leaders do adhere to all three of Kawasaki's criteria, and hence feel an incredible sense of meaning. Inspiring a leader to move towards seamless leadership affects the quality of followers' lives too, and of society as a whole. Encouraging leaders to shun bad habits and to lead others in the direction of seamless leadership rights a wrong; and finally, fighting to keep the leadership legacy of our country alive prevents the end of something good.

If, however, you work for a gold mine, a high-end clothing store, or an IT outsource company, how are you making meaning? Seamless leaders find meaning in most businesses because they really look for it, and they really look for it because they understand the need for creating meaning, giving purpose, eventually linking up with the core purpose of life.

In the case of T-Systems, management started realising that when they assisted Eskom to run its business more effectively, they also contributed towards bringing power and light to South Africa. Their road towards significance and more meaning also includes becoming involved in various platforms that drive values and ethics into society. They stand for ethical business and, among other activities, also co-sponsor the National Values Campaign.

A friend recently told me about his company's development of a large golf estate. Successful completion would, of course, ensure financial freedom and open the door to many other opportunities. When we discussed the Kawasaki theory he surprised me with how quickly he saw meaning in his project, because all I could see was that his company was making money. He said that when he drove through the golf estate and saw families spending time together, enjoying a safer way of living that many of our citizens don't have, it excited him. The project has improved the quality of the lives of its recipients. We could also argue that the project adheres to the other two criteria. His outlook took our conversation to another level.

Often the issue is not necessarily whether or not the product or service is making meaning but whether the leaders of the organisation are succeeding in promoting the organisation's meaning or sense of purpose. Seamless leaders believe this often does not happen because the leader has not caught the vision of the meaning, or cannot communicate its essence effectively, or does not come across as passionate and authentic.

A business may start out making meaning, but as it grows and the owner or originator starts moving into the background, so does the meaning. It takes great effort, passion, focus and skill for leaders to ensure that the meaning in the business becomes part of its DNA.

Businesses such as First Rand and Pick n Pay have entered this phase where the founders are no longer fully active. So the question is: 'Can

Sizwe Nxasana and Richard Brasher continue making meaning, or are they struggling so hard to grow their businesses in a very challenging economic environment that they risk losing the focus on making meaning?'

For us a great case study is retail giant Walmart, which has now entered the South African corporate landscape, and not without resistance. Its slogan says: 'Save money. Live better.' It speaks to Kawasaki's first point and perhaps even the second and third.

In my associations with Massmart executives, it is becoming increasingly clear that Walmart actually means what it says and really tries to live by this simple slogan. It seems that everything it does is geared to saving money so that customers can live better. This simple philosophy of making meaning has most certainly contributed towards it becoming one of the largest companies in the world and enables it to enter diverse markets successfully.

It does not take long for employees of companies that have been taken over to buy into their way of making meaning. This is the power of simplicity and an authentic agenda of making meaning

Another effective way to make meaning is the creation of, and absolute buy-in to organisational values. Again, Walmart has three simple values only: respect for the individual; service to their customers; and striving for excellence. When it explains these simple values it cannot do so without also emphasising its slogan of saving money so that customers can live better.

I have worked with leaders in businesses where the organisation does not make meaning or it does not passionately promote the meaning. These leaders eventually find it difficult to motivate staff or to create a healthy culture of excellence throughout all structures. Money and bonuses can go only so far. To build a lasting organisation, one that can grow internationally, with a legacy that will outlast a generation, I am convinced that clarity by all regarding how the organisation makes meaning is absolutely essential. This is in line with the core purpose of life. In other words, making meaning is a key ingredient of seamless leadership.

Mardia van der Walt-Korsten – CEO T-Systems SA

Seamless Leader Principles:

1. Identify where Van der Walt-Korsten demonstrates a seamless leader attitude.
2. Try to identify more seamless leader principles, for example –
   - ❏ A focus on creating meaning while making money
   - ❏ Purpose-driven leadership
   - ❏ Moving one's organisation from success to significance.

When I wrote my first article about Mardia van der Walt-Korsten, CEO of T-Systems and former Businesswoman of the Year, I noted that towards the end of 2008 T-Systems SA was way over its targets set for the year. They moved from being a R600-million revenue company to becoming a close to R3-billion revenue company; from 600 employees to almost 2 700. When she became CEO their challenge was that they were shrinking and becoming irrelevant in their market space. They set a target to achieve 1 billion revenue by 2010, which they achieved by 2008. By 2010 they doubled their 1 billion revenue to 2 billion. All this happened in the middle of a recession.

They needed to expand their footprint, become a known entity and build scale in order to serve large customers like Transnet, Sasol, Eskom, government and so on. The big leap was the acquisition of Arivia.com, following which they became the number one ICT Outsourcer in the market.

This acquisition was a huge challenge, but it is something they are very proud of. As with all acquisitions there were challenges because at least 15 per cent reductions in staff had to happen due to overlap in responsibilities, especially at managerial levels. And since they preach values, they had to stay focused on aligning actions with these values, to set the tone for the culture of their much larger organisation, rather than destroy it.

They decided to be incredibly fair by not favouring T-Systems employees over Arivia employees, to simply look at who would be the best person for the job. At one stage they had about 60 internal and external consultants working on the integration process. The aim was to do it 'with heart'. People were taken through CV writing skills sessions, counselling sessions, training sessions and much more.

Finding the balance between saving costs yet putting in place a winning structure and culture was challenging. For example, Van der Walt-Korsten noticed the chairs of many Arivia staff were dilapidated because they were in serious cost-saving mode in order to prevent a takeover. She decided to buy a new chair for every person. Some felt this was an unnecessary cost to incur while jobs were being lost, but she argued that someone sitting on a chair balancing on a brick could not be expected to deliver a world-class service for a world-class customer.

As CEO she did a lot of the communication, discussions and interaction with people. Of course the process wasn't perfect and people did get hurt, but feedback indicated employees felt like human beings. The way they went about the entire acquisition was recorded and presented overseas in Germany (Head Office) and today serves as best practice throughout the group worldwide.

The road forward is a different one. The management team's decision on 'where to' was to move from success to significance, rather than simply staying number one. And how would they know when they have become significant? When: 1) they are the best partner for their customers, where customers truly believe this – few ICT companies achieve this status as there are so many things that can go wrong in this game; 2) they are the best company for their employees.

The management team also decided that all of this should be achieved in the context of 'becoming the best FOR South Africa'. This is different from becoming the best IN South Africa. The latter does not necessarily mean the company achieves significance while the former steers more clearly towards also becoming significant, while succeeding at indicators like EBIT, revenue, size, etc, after all, they are running a business.

This clinical psychologist by original trade is a strong believer in driving a sense of purpose within the organisation. T-Systems' road towards significance includes becoming involved on various platforms that drive values and ethics into society. Van der Walt-Korsten and her team started 'making meaning' at T-Systems, and her successor had a great foundation to build on.

Ian Donald – CEO Nestlé SA

Seamless Leader Principles:
1. Notice how Donald creates meaning or instils a sense of purpose.

2. Identify other instances of a seamless leader attitude, such as –
   - ❏ Remaining humble, teachable yet confident
   - ❏ Behaving according to the values you believe in
   - ❏ Seeing the big picture.

Every now and then I meet a leader who comes across as truly authentic, with a healthy confidence. Ian Donald, the newly appointed CEO of Nestlé SA, is such a leader. He has led in the Philippines, in Pakistan, together with war-torn Afghanistan, and in East Africa. And now he is back in South Africa to create movement in his motherland.

Confidence is 'trusting processes that work', and this is the same for leadership. To be a confident leader one must learn to trust leadership processes that work, which presupposes doing it over and over. Authentic and confident leaders have a track record of having created successful movement over and over. Donald has done this in several diverse geographical locations, which is part of why he projects confidence. In fact, because of this track record, his reputation precedes him. The mere announcement that he is coming to a country, division or branch triggers movement, action and people anticipating what he wants or expects of them. This is a powerful position to be in, which is part and parcel of an authentic and confident leader. Unfortunately, in a world of 'immediacy', where leaders want career progression now and where movement from one position to the next happens fast, together with overall societal change that happens at breakneck pace, these kinds of leaders may become rarer.

Authentic and confident leaders possess the courage to make themselves vulnerable, probably because they have learnt to manage or suppress their ego. They really believe that they are still learning; they admit when they don't know something or when they have made a mistake; while it may not be easy, they accept when others point to their incongruent behaviour; and they are comfortable with engaging staff on all levels. Donald says: 'I'm now 63 but still believe in this principle of learning all the time. I am conscious of what I learn. So going to Pakistan for example, I hope I made a contribution, but boy did I learn, and did I grow as an individual.' And he adds: 'I find the biggest journey I have been on all my life is knowing myself. And that's still the journey I am on most.' This attitude manifests in his everyday behaviour, like wanting to connect with people.

Authentic and confident leaders buy into the truth that human beings are driven by deep-rooted values, and so they fanatically drive values inside their business, while striving to remain true to their own. They work with the big picture of matching individual needs and values with their organisations and even broader society. As Donald comments: 'It comes back to values all the time – the importance of respect, and the importance of understanding other people, other cultures.' He has had to apologise because a staff member challenged his behaviour as being incongruent with values.

Authentic and confident leaders achieve greatness because they usually care relatively little about what others think of them. They are driven by what is right, rather than by how others perceive them. They don't act for approval but for successful movement, what the particular situation requires. Because of a tamed ego they don't just change things around them for the sake of changing. They move in, listen and do what needs to be done. If the situation requires radical change, they do it. If the situation requires them to merely build on what has been achieved, they make this happen as well.

When Donald moved into Pakistan he didn't just change everything. At the time he commented: 'The correct approach in a business that did not require turnaround but merely wasn't living up to its full potential was not to change everything. In fact, coming in and changing everything, especially as an expat, sends out a clear message that what was done up until then was not respected.' He was conscious of showing appreciation for the past and building on it.

It would have been easy for him to settle into the new job and simply manage professionally. But he was not comfortable with this: 'I realised the team needed a strong sense of purpose, a dream, vision and values about which they could feel passionate. Previous visions were very financially driven, for example increasing the turnover, and I had to build on this.'

He also realised that a leader with a dictatorial approach could be fooled into thinking that he had connected with the workforce, because it was within their culture to deliver, respect authority, receive instructions and do it to the best of their ability. Donald adds: 'But I felt a need to connect with the workforce on an emotional level.' He and his team engaged employees and they collectively bought into a vision which ultimately happened to be the broader Nestlé vision of enhancing people's quality of life – inside and outside the business. For example, they assisted in trying to find a solution to the current water crises, partnering with McKinsey, Harvard University, government and other organisations; they trained farmers to improve their skills in delivering more milk, resulting in positively impacting at least 1 million people directly.

Donald says: 'The aspiration was for every employee to truly see and feel that every activity he/she was engaged with every day was truly enhancing someone's life. As they became involved in doing this it all fed back into the business, lifting the bottom line while enriching people's lives.'

Authentic and confident leaders understand that all of the above and more are important, but none of it matters if the business isn't profitable and sustainable. 'You can't get away from the fact that at the base of it all is to create a sustainable, long-term, growing, profitable business. Otherwise you can't do anything; it all falls apart,' explains Donald.

At Nestlé they speak of 'shared value rather than social responsibility'. They feel that to survive in a long-term sustainable way they have to add value all the way through the value chain, from beginning to end – from the farmer who provides raw material to the end consumer. Everyone in the value chain must be successful; then follows the responsibility to add value to broader societal issues like gas emissions, water pollution and so on, which Nestlé is very involved with.

And so, an authentic and confident leader is very aware of the big picture and uses this to create meaning, purpose. All perceived meaning is contextual, which means that the greater a leader's context of the big picture, the greater the meaning.

Nestlé SA has not grown satisfactorily over the last couple of years. Donald is the man to make this happen, while simply being himself – authentic and confident, and then ensuring he surrounds himself with equally authentic and confident leaders.

||||||||||||||||||||||||||||||||||||||||||||||||||||||||||||||||||||||||||||||||||||||||||||||||||||||||||||||

CHAPTER 15

Seamless leader attitude to sharing

WITH
❏ *Tom Hamilton*
❏ *Raymond Ackerman*

Sharing in the sense discussed in this chapter is an advanced attribute of emotional intelligence. Sharing often holds the key to positive relationships and seamless leadership effectiveness.

Seamless leaders stand out because they adopt the principle of sharing. They share their all in serving humankind. They share their most precious feelings with others around them; they share their precious time unselfishly; they share their hard-won wisdom; they share encouragement and good humour and at times they share sharp rebukes in order to inspire others to excellence.

My father thinks back fondly of a partner he worked with years ago, Francois van Niekerk, who is a very successful entrepreneur and Christian philanthropist. He shared the highs and the lows of the company with the staff. He also went around discussing and sharing key issues with staff individually. My father remembers feeling somewhat special when Van Niekerk sought his opinion on an issue, not realising that he was also seeking the insight of others.

A sharing spirit tends to encourage others to share with seamless leaders. To learn from others is the essence of humility and wisdom.

There is much to be shared: Seamless leaders share their time, their talents, their experience and wisdom, encouragement, their feelings, desires, passions and concerns. Think of the opposite of sharing: selfishness, anger, secrecy, suspicion, negativity, smouldering resentment, hidden agendas and loneliness. These are not good attributes on which to build a personal legacy!

Sharing builds relationships: Seamless leaders realise that nothing builds a relationship better than a sharing attitude. Such an attitude tends to drill down into essentials, to be honest and to convey respect for others. After all, it is a powerful feeling to experience the trust of somebody else.

A sharing attitude is the antithesis of the fat cat syndrome: The fat cat syndrome is categorised by an overriding passion for position and power. It is often followed as night follows day by serious debt, and an expensive house in an expensive suburb. Family needs are often about fourth or fifth in line in terms of priorities. Fat cat syndrome sufferers strive after a social life of fun and self-indulgence. In order to bring about some kind of 'balance' they may as a gesture of goodwill support good 'remote' causes such as a clean environment and the need for transformation.

Each of these attributes and strivings mentioned above are legitimate expressions of living, but when they become more important to a leader than a positive and honest value system they tend to breed dishonesty, manipulation, corruption in many forms, secrecy, and negative corporate politics, excessive gambling, negativity, selfishness and unpleasantness of nature. By its very nature the spirit of sharing resists selfishness and self-indulgence.

Sharing is a multiplier: When a seamless leader shares he multiplies more seamless leaders and also equips them to multiply. I personally respond to a person who has a sharing attitude. The common expression 'to give of yourself' exemplifies a seamless leader's sharing attitude.

Sharing may have negatives: That which is not received well by others may cause damage to relationships. This means that when seamless leaders share they do it with a profound respect for others, or else their sharing may backfire. They realise that simply sharing their feelings in an emotional manner without the required respect for the values and sensitivities of others may have negative consequences.

A key to positive sharing: It is important to understand the nature of attitudinal modes. It is human nature to see life mainly through different lenses or windows. In practice this means that we tend to see things from either a negative or a positive perspective at a specific moment in time. Our perceptions may change from one mode to the other depending on various influences around us. The point that seamless leaders tend to remember is that a person is heavily influenced by the attitudinal mode he or she may be in and this can have a profound impact on how their sharing is received. Because they understand this principle they are patient when others are in a negative frame of mind.

Channels of excellence: This is a principle that boosts the ability of many seamless leaders to lift others around them. The expression 'channels of excellence' refers to interests and inclinations that stimulate our attention and open our ears and minds. The opposite is also true. People are receptive to different issues and interests and will therefore probably fail to respond positively to approaches that fall outside their interest range. This is a fact of human nature and the seamless leader recognises this reality. Showing an interest in the interests of others not only communicates a spirit of respect for that person but tends to establish a valuable bond that can serve as a channel of excellence. This is a good leadership principle to study and master! My mother has the amazing ability to share feelings with strangers at the drop of a hat. She somehow zeroes in on channels of excellence in strangers that draw them together like a magnet.

Sharing of things: Typically Christmas is perceived as a time to give and receive gifts. It is the motive that is perceived to *accompany* the gift that is the real blessing or curse in the eye of the receiver of that gift. All of us are sensitive to what we perceive as 'real motives' and we are often wrong in our deductions. Seamless leaders realise that the way they give gifts and the manner in which they convey respect for the other person are crucial to the success of their sharing.

Honest confrontation: Honest confrontation accompanied by a genuine motive is a mature way of sharing concerns and key issues with others. It is an essential element of seamless leadership.

The ability to share gifts of value with others is in direct proportion to the degree of preparation to share: Seamless leaders invest in their own abilities, skills, learning and attitude and therefore invest in their ability to share valuable gifts that they can give to others. They realise that the more prepared they are, the more they can share.

Students of all ages should bear this in mind when they prepare to write exams and tests. It is not just about the 'paper' that they are aiming for, but the knowledge and skills they are receiving in preparation to be sharers rather than takers. You cannot share that which you do not possess.

Nelson Mandela used many years of incarceration in order to empower him to share and to serve rather than to exert retribution. Look at the legacy he left as a result of his attitude to sharing and respect for others!

Seamless leaders possess the attitude of sharing.

Tom Hamilton – Headmaster of St Alban's College

Seamless Leadership Principles:

1. Note the sharing attitude in adopting another school.
2. See other seamless leadership principles like lack of fear to confront, emphasis on people and much more.

Tom Hamilton has institutionalised a 'Fontainebleau environment' at St Alban's College in Pretoria. There have been great leaders before him, but as said by a colleague: 'There is no doubt that it is he who has put St Alban's College firmly on the map of top South African schools. In this he has left his own mark and his own legacy.'

Some time back I spent an afternoon at St Alban's. Parents were taken on guided tours by students. 'The smell of the place', a positive and energetic atmosphere (see chapter 4 for an explanation of 'the smell of the place'), was tangible! Before formal proceedings started on the outside lawn where all the seats were taken, I sat down on the grass. Not even ten seconds passed before a young man offered me a chair. Before the head boy and headmaster gave their speeches I knew that great leadership had to be behind this energy. I was convinced in my mind that if other schools, businesses and even state-owned enterprises could create such an energetic culture they would flourish. Or is the energy a result of performance?

Much can be said about why Hamilton has been so successful. When asked to summarise what his success can be ascribed to in three principles, he highlighted the following:

1. **Put people first, always:** No matter what he is doing in his office, if there is somebody who wants to see him, no matter who they are, they can see him. He says: 'There is never a task that is too important

not to put a person first.' A former colleague states: 'It is clear that St Alban's is about relationships first and foremost; people are valued here.' And: 'He *sees* people – he understands that a happy teacher is a good teacher, so he is reasonable in his requests or refusals and he takes great pleasure in affording his staff opportunities for growth and renewal.'

2. **Being rigorous but not ruthless:** He is rigorous and knows what he wants. He knows what the standard is and demands it. And 'I challenge people to reach that standard,' he comments. If they don't, they know there is going to be some sort of response from him. He simply won't let it slide. He does not wait until it is time for the formal appraisal. Others comment that he has allowed talented men and women onto the team, but add that 'you cannot be a slacker on this team though – you need to lead, you need to grow and you need to intuitively love and want to nurture young men.' The standard is clear.

3. **Lack of fear to confront (candour and honesty):** He views confrontation as an opportunity for all involved to grow, 'irrespective of what the outcome might be, providing we approach it honestly,' Hamilton adds. He believes there is a degree of honesty in him: 'I am honest about who I am. Some of my staff members are paragons of virtue compared to me. They are almost saintly men and woman and I am not. I am loose and do all sorts of weird things that some of them must look at with disdain. I am fully aware that I am fallible and can get things wrong.' Yet, someone says of him: 'He has learnt to see the good in others despite their frail humanity. He understands intimately that he has made mistakes and allows others to do the same – he has a huge capacity for forgiveness and this is a wonderful example.'

Hamilton also explains: 'When I think you need to hear the honest truth I am going to give you a chance to hear it and I am going to hope that before you are out the door we are going to have a hug. If the honesty leads to you leaving the school I hope that when we next meet we will have a glass of wine or something together, that you'll feel "I have not diminished one bit in his eyes", in the sense of who I am as a person, a man or a woman, it's just that I couldn't work on his team any more.'

He has always had a striving towards high standards, except that in his earlier career it was at the cost of people – almost ruthless. 'It's never at the cost of people now,' he exclaims. But like all great leaders do, he puts the cause, organisation or purpose first, and 'if anything comes second it is the boys,' he says. He believes teachers are there to serve boys. However, 'we are all here to serve the school'. As someone comments, 'He talks to and with the boys. He laughs with the boys. He cries with the boys. Young and old alike know that he is human and thus, the "title" becomes irrelevant, but the respect for the man remains.'

When someone suggests something he always asks how the boys feel about that. What do they benefit from that? What about the customers, the parents who pay the fees? How will they benefit from that? Hamilton is convinced a lot of the staff see it that way.

It is said of the DNA of the school: 'The word "awesome" is like the nucleus of a human cell: stuffed full of metres of DNA. Unravelling that astounding string of biological bits illuminates what it is that makes St Alban's special. Here are some Albanian "nucleotides", transmitting genetic information from one generation of College boys to the next – DNA of positivity; DNA of significance, a step beyond success; DNA of innovation; DNA of relationship; DNA of difference and diversity.'

With this leadership and such a culture it should come as no surprise that St Alban's has for years given back to the community. They adopted a school in Mamelodi, as an example. The 'Fontainebleau Energy' is also starting to rub off there. In four years a 12 per cent pass rate has moved up to 82 per cent. How do they do it? 'We play soccer together, the kids do, the staff do, we braai meat together, we attend socials together. Whenever I go to leadership conferences or whatever, the Principal of that school goes with me.' They did nothing fantastic, just did simple things well: 'We taught, we were there on time, we were there on the days we said we were going to be there, we produced good resources, we followed up on what we said we were going to do and we added a bit of value here and there by coming out here to do stuff that we couldn't do there.' They further insisted everyone had to have email, start talking to each other by email, which 'completely transcends the here and now', says Hamilton. They simply treated people like they were really important. It is in essence the same sort of things they were doing at St Alban's. Hamilton explains: 'People are people, no matter where you're from, we're the same.' Their school cultures remain distinctly different, but Hamilton is convinced this high school 'is going to become one of those iconic places you'll want to be visiting shortly'.

And not surprisingly, it is said of Hamilton: 'Tom has been a great servant – he has grown with this school and has allowed it to thrive beyond him.' This is the legacy of a great leader, when what he has moved can thrive beyond him. In short, the leader of a school can make all the difference.

Hamilton comments on why public schools sometimes fail: 'Actually it's not about resources, it's about attitudes, I think. The thing that allows us to be a bit nimble and somewhat risky in a way is we're not afraid of failure, we're not afraid of embarrassment. We don't have a fear-of-failure mentality, we're willing to try things and if it doesn't all work out, as long as one or two or three do – that's a good return. We find in many State schools there's a sense that you don't want to be caught making a mistake so you just do the minimum, you just play it safe all the time. Here our teachers push the boundaries. Sometimes with the staff it's actually about trying to keep them in line just a little bit – saying hang on a bit, we're trying three new things this term so we're not going to try a fourth one. I don't think it's apathy in the public system, I think it's just, in some cases, a sense of hopelessness because there isn't strong leadership from government, from the department, from the local district leaders. Principals to an extent are also strangled, because if you even want to engender something new, something different, they'll say *what's in it for us?* The type of ethos you're going to get in a school like St Alban's or Pretoria Boys or Menlo Park is to give extra time to the students if they want it, but this isn't common in this country, it's not common. And it's not common because teachers don't see their primary role as education; they see it as the means of earning a living. Teachers in good schools and great schools don't see it as a means of making a living; they see it as a calling, a vocation. If I talk about the happiness that we've got in our school, it's not an overt desire or drive to achieve happiness. To my mind, happiness is a by-product of all the good healthy things that happen. If you set out to achieve happiness, there's some deception going on, there's something going on where perhaps just pretending you're happy is enough to get by. Happiness, when it happens, it just creeps up on you – it just means you've got good, strong, resilient, boisterous, healthy systems that take time to create'.

A perfect St Alban's leadership story

Seamless Leadership Principles:

1. Note the spirit of sharing that permeates the school – how students, a teacher, a parent and a pupil lead.

This is the perfect leadership story, emanating from St Alban's College, one of the greatest schools in South Africa and an exemplary leadership academy for the future leaders of our country and beyond. It is about a Grade 8 (Form 1) student who has been endowed with great abilities, but not with sporting or natural fitness talent, although he is probably a late bloomer. It is also about fellow students and a teacher who exemplified model leadership, and a mother who closed the loop. It is about every character in this example playing their part. It is a simple and true story that corporate, political, civic, sports, educational and other leaders can and must learn from.

As part of school tradition the different houses competed against one another and all the boys had to participate in running a 3 km race through school grounds. Our Grade 8 student struggled to finish or even jog all the way and being slightly ill didn't help either. As a result he had to walk part of the race while being lapped by many. He kept going. To his surprise his fellow Grade 8 students who completed the race went back to cheer him on and assist him to finish the race, walking alongside him to the end.

The next day our Grade 8 student was very stiff and sore and didn't feel like going to school. But he did, and it was here that the 'teacher leader' stood up and sealed the experience. He thanked all the boys for partici-pating in the race and then made special mention of our Grade 8 student who persevered and finished, even though he had to walk part of the race.

The mother was there to cheer our Grade 8 student on to go to school the next day and she got in the car with him to drive the 3 km route and relive the experience; allowed him to point out where boys started lapping him and at what point friends came back to walk with him.

So, who is the leader in this story? What makes this so perfect is that every actor in the story was a leader. The boys who went back showed great leadership by supporting a friend and cheering him on. They showed that life, and therefore leadership, is not just about winning alone but assisting the entire team to finish the race. They showed that everyone in the team is important. They cared. Ironically, when all Grade 8 students started 2014 with a camp and every one of them was paraded in front of a panel of Grade 12 students to field questions, our Grade 8 student answered the question: "Who in your group would you send on their way?" with "No one, because we are a team and should stand together." This was not everyone's answer.

The teacher demonstrated great leadership by recognising and highlighting not only expected efforts on the day but also the winning attribute of perseverance that will stand these young leaders in good stead way beyond school. His leadership was brilliant because he lifted the entire situation to a higher level.

The mother cared. She showed vision when she allowed her son to relive the experience; to offload; to recap; to review; to get closure. She helped him work through it and become stronger as a result.

And then, our Grade 8 student was also a leader because he had the courage to persevere and keep on going, to finish. His example was powerful. The example of leaders really matters! And, if it wasn't for him none of these leaders in this story would have had the opportunity to serve, share, respect, lead and grow character.

So what can experienced corporate, political, civic, sporting and other educational leaders learn from this true story?

I imagine a Mine Overseer (MO) or Mine Captain, even a Shift Boss (SB) on a shaft noticing his colleague, another MO or SB struggling to achieve production targets and after achieving his own, turning back to assist his colleague to finish the race, because he realises everyone on that shaft is a team, depending on one another to succeed.

I can imagine one executive on a leadership team walking into the office of a struggling fellow executive who has just had a horrible executive meeting, sitting down and sincerely asking: 'How can I help you?' as opposed to 'Let me know if I can assist', or even allowing his colleague to struggle on alone.

I can imagine the headmaster of a successful school where they have 100 per cent matric pass rate, and many more achievements, turning back and offering assistance to another struggling school to help them move towards the same achievements.

I can imagine the leaders of the MOs, SBs, executives and headmaster above sincerely congratulating these individuals for demonstrating what leadership is really about – *successful movement (achievement) ... together!*

And finally, I can imagine the down-and-out MO, SB, executive or headmaster humbly accepting assistance and allowing a colleague to share his energy, expertise, resources, for the good of the entire team, business, school, education system and future of a country, realising that this is a great opportunity for a colleague to serve, respect, care, lead and therefore grow. You see, sometimes we need to be on the other end of the leadership story – we need to be served. Then, the time will come when we will be the servant leader.

Raymond Ackerman – Founder and former Chairman Pick n Pay

Seamless Leader Principles:

1. Identify where Ackerman demonstrates a seamless leader attitude.

2. Try to identify more seamless leader principles. There are many to pick from, including:
   - ❏ Develop that remarkable drive to accomplish the extraordinary
   - ❏ Acknowledge 'luck' in your life
   - ❏ Believe that you can learn from people
   - ❏ Listening is a crucial aspect of a leader
   - ❏ Be accessible
   - ❏ Remember Napoleon's quote: 'Leaders are dealers in hope'
   - ❏ A leader must keep changing the organisation in line with modern standards, but he/she must not change integrity, decency and kindness
   - ❏ In these difficult times you must seek opportunity to breathe hope and positivity into your people.

I remember coaching a young up-and-coming leader who informed me that her husband had just been laid off at work. To make things worse she was surrounded by a situation in her workplace where colleagues were being laid off on a weekly basis, which meant her own future was not necessarily too certain.

Fortunately I could bring Raymond Ackerman into the picture – the man who built Pick n Pay, an exemplary company that today is a household name with hundreds of stores and tens of thousands of employees, recently awarded the prize for the world's best retailer.

When Ackerman was about 35 the company he worked for let him go, even though he had played a major role in building one of their business units, Checkers, from one to 89 stores. But, he was out on the street with a wife who was pregnant with their fourth child and no capital.

With the benefit of hindsight he believes it was the greatest thing that could have happened to him. At the time it was one of the most challenging experiences ever, but nevertheless turned out to be an exceptionally difficult situation with an extraordinary outcome.

Perhaps it all started because he, like all other individuals who have achieved great things, had a remarkable drive to accomplish the extraordinary. He remembers how, from a young age, that drive manifested in wanting to be in the school's first rugby and cricket teams; or wanting to become the head prefect. He was always striving to achieve – and he mostly did, despite incredible resistance, often because he was Jewish.

He believes this drive may have come from the association with his father, who was an amazing yet difficult man. He promised to go and watch Ackerman play rugby only when he played at Newlands for the Springboks. Well, eventually he did play at Newlands in a curtain raiser before a test match. But, his father was not there because he did not play for the Springboks.

Ackerman says about this: 'In a way it was harsh, but it made me strive and strive and strive all the time!'

Ackerman would also not have reached the extraordinary without remarkable luck or destiny. While running Checkers he received a call from Jack Goldin, who was not only eventually the founder of Clicks but also started Pick n Pay stores.

The call came when he was at his busiest and the stranger asked if he could visit the Checkers stores. He was about to open three little stores in Cape Town and didn't want to make fundamental mistakes with size, refrigeration and so on.

Why not simply shrug it off and decline without hesitation? In his own words 'something made me say yes, whether it was luck or intuition.' He told his secretary that even though he was so busy he would do it. He dropped what he was doing and took Goldin around – in short, he shared.

One year later when Ackerman was sacked he again received a call from Goldin wanting to sell his three Pick n Pay stores. He only wanted to sell them to Ackerman and no one else. The rest is history. Was this luck, destiny? You decide what to call it. Whatever it is, it happened because of a man deciding not to be big-headed; to be accessible, which goes hand-in-hand with another principle that helped him become an extraordinary leader – he associated with extraordinary individuals.

He really believes in learning from people, which has allowed him to be influenced positively by them. He says, 'Don't be big-headed; don't think you know everything. Quite honestly, nearly everything I have done or do comes from other people. It's not me being clever ... A lot of people are just not receptive to ideas from even the "lowest" person on the ladder ... Nearly everything we have done at Pick n Pay has come from an idea from someone overseas or someone local, by listening. I think that listening is a crucial aspect of a leader.'

Today Ackerman tries to see all who want to see him. He is accessible, without a doubt. I called his secretary expressing a desire to interview him and within a minute we had scheduled an appointment. This is an icon in business, and trust me he is still very busy, yet it wasn't difficult at all to access him. Most leaders at his level are not like this (I could give you many examples)!

Ackerman agreed with me that extraordinary leaders would be non-existent if extraordinary situations were not thrust upon them. Who would Francois Pienaar be without a World Cup? Who would Nelson Mandela be without apartheid? He added if he wasn't fired from the job at Checkers he would probably have remained a corporate man throughout his career. But an extraordinary situation was thrust upon him; he had an extraordinary drive; he allowed extraordinary associations to mould him; extraordinary luck happened, and the result is an extraordinary life. To think there was a time, many years ago, when Ackerman and his wife were encouraged by friends to leave South Africa. Back then there were so many perceived threats to one's possible bright future. But they stayed, and he is so grateful that they did.

During this period of leading, which spans decades, he believes much changed and much stayed the same, leadership being a good example. He referred to Napoleon's words: 'A leader is a dealer in hope.' He added: 'You have to be realistic, of course. But, you deal in hope because a negative person or a negative concept can just drag you down so easily.' Leaders in the sixties, seventies, eighties and nineties had to deal in hope. This has never changed.

He has seen structures like technology, systems and so on change, which affects the speed of decision making. But, some deep philosophies and morals have not changed. A leader must keep changing the organisation in line with modern standards, but he/she must not change integrity, decency and kindness.

In these difficult times his message to leaders comes back to hope. 'Seek opportunities to breathe hope into your people. Remind them that the current economic crisis may be here for a while, but it is going to go away; it is not the end of the world. One's attitude is incredibly important ... Breathe hope and positivity, because we have been through so much since Mr Mandela took over. So much that has happened is good. It is all very well just criticising the corruption or lack of delivery, but an enormous amount has changed. The next 15 years can be much stronger than the last 15 years ... I firmly believe that!'

|||||||||||||||||||||||||||||||||||||||||||||||||||||||||||||||||||||||||||||||||||||||||||||||||||||

CHAPTER 16

Seamless leader attitude to difficulties and leading in difficult times

WITH

❏ *Hlengani Mathebula*
❏ *Gary Crittenden*
❏ *Gary Player*

Seamless leaders never give up! They view difficult circumstances with gratitude and realise that these are what contribute or contributed towards who they are today. Difficulties or challenges trigger in them an even greater drive to succeed, improve, and create movement, as opposed to giving up or slowing down. They allow difficult times to develop their character, sense of context, wisdom, desire to build bridges and become authentic, rather than developing negative traits like hatred, grudges, revenge, giving up, dishonesty and negativity in general.

Difficult times move them towards innovative solutions, seeing opportunities and becoming courageous, rather than regressing, withdrawing, becoming more defensive and over-cautious.

During difficult times seamless leaders are aware of an inclination that most human beings possess: under pressure we are liable to default back to current and even past weaknesses, negative behaviour and those actions that seemed to work for us or relieved stress during previous stressful situations. If you had a propensity towards anger, then you will probably resort to it when pressure mounts. If your weakness is/was misappropriation of finances in some form (weakness for money), under pressure you may resort to unacceptable financial practices. If your past behaviour consisted of sexual promiscuity, or even an addiction to pornography, under pressure you may resort to the same behaviour. The same goes for addictions like drugs or alcohol.

Your weakness or negative behaviour may be as simple as being disorganised, having low self-esteem, certain prejudices, unhealthy pride and even an unhealthy need to be liked and accepted. I can go on with examples.

During good times these weaknesses and negative behaviours remain hidden, suppressed or under control. The same goes for an organisation – weaknesses in its system and offerings are hidden during times of plenty, but when times are very tough, these often surface and become amplified. This is a 'normal' human tendency that leaders are of course susceptible to, only they are often under more pressure and more visible than ordinary individuals and thus more liable to become headline news. While this condition has existed over the ages, the immediacy of information and media makes it seem more prevalent today. Seamless leaders are prepared.

They know their weaknesses, past negative behaviour, strengths, desires, deep-seated values, and much more. They know that personal reflection is crucial. They understand the current and potential barriers to their full potential. Where possible they eradicate weaknesses, but know they are vulnerable in those areas, especially during difficult times, which will become more frequent than ever before. In fact, this is the new reality.

They learn to absorb pressure: They understand that part of getting to know yourself is knowing how best to absorb pressure, how best to re-energise. There was a time when it was sufficient to work hard and at the end of the year go on a long holiday to re-energise, re-calibrate. Then some leaders caught the vision of somehow taking more regular breaks, because pressure and pace had increased. It seems that even this approach is not enough now, as leaders come back to the same pace and pressure, with inboxes filled to capacity, and within a day feel like they are back where they were. Because of the pace of our environment, more decisions need to be made quicker than ever before. So, leaders decide to take technology on holiday with them so as to mitigate pressure upon their return. But this tends to defeat the purpose. Seamless leaders have learnt to re-energise weekly and even daily, over and above more regular breaks.

They find a way to remain balanced, happy, connected to who they are and what their actual purpose is: Seamless leaders know that no human being can absorb extraordinary power, influence and affluence and keep their feet on the ground without conscious effort.

They become more confident and conscious about how they create successful movement: Far too many leaders depend on luck to create their movement. Seamless leaders are absolutely conscious about the process they implement to do it. They have complete clarity in their minds regarding this function of leadership. When one is not absolutely clear and confident about any process, what happens is that under pressure your actions resort to primitive behaviour – basic instincts like pure survival.

Confidence is trust in processes that work. A seasoned martial artist will, under pressure of defending against an attacker, act in a confident and composed manner, while someone who only recently learnt some tricks of martial arts will resort to ineffective behaviour like freezing, running away or swinging wildly once or twice and being so tired as a result that the attacker can push them over with one hand.

Under pressure, the leader who is not absolutely confident in the processes that lead to successful movement will resort to ineffective behaviour that followers just can't understand. The behaviour will be totally contradictory to the intelligence of the leader, who will cut costs wildly, act aggressively towards followers and even stop taking those universal steps that will and must result in effective movement forward.

The new reality is different. South Africa is different. The world is different. Choices we make today determine the leadership culture we create. And, the leadership culture determines what leaders we develop in the future. We must get this one right. We owe it to our leadership legacy.

It takes courage to develop good character that will respond positively and fearlessly under pressure. We have the privilege of having personal leadership conversations with leaders who respond positively to pressure situations. What a difference these people make to the fibre of our country at all levels of society!

May you learn to more fully appreciate and value your good character traits and work hard to eradicate those weaknesses that act as barriers to successful movement.

Remember that when we slip into a crisis management frame of mind we are in danger of losing the respect and performance of the very people we depend on to turn the situation around.

Hlengani Mathebula – Executive at Reserve Bank, former Managing Executive of ABSA Private Bank

IIIIIIIIIIIIIIIIIIIIIIIIIIIIIIIIIIIIIIIIIIIIIIIIIIIIIIIIIIIIIIIIIIIIIIIIIIIIIIIIIIIIIIIIIIIIIIIIIIIIIIIIIIIIIIIIIIIIIIIIIIIIIIIIIIIIIIIIIIIIIIIIIIIIIIIIIIIIIIIIIIIIIIIIIIIIIIIIIII

Seamless Leadership Principles:

1. Note Mathebula's amazing attitude to challenging conditions.
2. See other seamless leadership principles, for example –
   ❏ Seeing the positive in difficult conditions
   ❏ Failure is never an option
   ❏ Learning from diverse sources
   ❏ Seeing the big picture.

IIIIIIIIIIIIIIIIIIIIIIIIIIIIIIIIIIIIIIIIIIIIIIIIIIIIIIIIIIIIIIIIIIIIIIIIIIIIIIIIIIIIIIIIIIIIIIIIIIIIIIIIIIIIIIIIIIIIIIIIIIIIIIIIIIIIIIIIIIIIIIIIIIIIIIIIIIIIIIIIIIIIIIIIIIIIIIIIIII

On 29 October 2009 thousands of students wrote their 'Life Orientation' exam paper. One case study was about Hlengani Mathebula, who at that time was the Managing Executive of ABSA Private Bank, the largest Private Bank in South Africa. He was also the newly elected Chairman of the Black Business Executive Circle (BBEC) and Chairman of African Leadership Group.

I visited with him for two hours as he explained his humble beginnings; how he rose above them; how in fact they benefited him. His story inspired me and I trust it will do the same for you.

His childhood was spent in Limpopo, where his family was exceptionally poor. At a very young age he snuck into a truck that collected workers for hard labour on cotton, orange and mango farms, and though soon discovered, was not brought back for a month until the truck's scheduled return. During this period he experienced terrible discrimination. His personal scars of racism or discrimination contributed to moulding him into a leader with a passionate desire to build one prosperous nation, irrespective of the pigmentation of our skin; a secure future for our children and their children.

He was an entrepreneur at a early age, fixing shoes as a self-taught cobbler and taking photos at functions like weddings with an old camera – all to take himself to school. When such ventures were not sufficient he became a petrol attendant at a station that was about 18 km from his village. He did this at night until about 4 am, locked up and then walked back to be on time for school. Somewhere in the middle of the day he would leave class to take a 'power nap' inside the toilet, only to come back to a hiding because he had missed out on a class or two.

Mathebula went through high school without a uniform and his teachers did not even know this. To conceal the fact that he did not possess a shirt, he cut the collar off an over-sized cast-off and wore it underneath a grey jersey that he got from a NG Church bazaar. He did this during summer and winter. His first pair of shoes were size 9 police issue that he seized when a policeman threw his away. He was in Standard 9 (Grade 11) at the time. How ironic – his jersey from an NG Church bazaar and his first pair of shoes from a policeman.

Had he decided not to complete school one would have understood. Many of his friends dropped out because of difficulties. But Mathebula simply did not give up! In fact, he was mostly number one in his class and enjoyed it, even to the point of arrogance. This came to a head when another boy surprisingly overtook him, but his competitive drive took over and he restored the situation the very next term.

His response about his upbringing that describes his attitude most aptly is: 'Look, I was very fortunate, very fortunate to have been born in a poor family.' He believes that had he been born into a wealthy family he would not have learned the lessons he did. He would not have exerted himself the way he has; he would not have chosen the path he has chosen. He adds: 'The collective of all those experiences has built the Hlengani that today I am.'

Mathebula's life instilled within him a hunger for education, entrepreneurialism, ambition, resilience, hard work and many more attributes. He truly believes nothing is impossible if you set your mind to it.

After matric he really wanted to go to university and kept searching for a way, despite obstacles like lack of finances. Fortunately, as often happens when we have passionate dreams, opportunities drifted his way. The Dutch Reformed Church in Africa was looking for young men to become ministers. It was on that ticket that he went to university. Pointing his finger in the air and waving it from left to right, he said to me with absolute certainty: 'My single point of reference was that it didn't matter how I was going to go to university. I was going to go to university!'

For him, failure was never an option. For his first four months at university he lived on bread and Kool-Aid without sugar. He slept on his first ever bed. The funds he received were not enough for food. So, he collected empty cooldrink bottles and exchanged these for money. But, politics happened ... He got involved and was dismissed from the course. He boldly promised the academics that he would come back to complete his theology studies, which he eventually did. He completed his Honours degree in the field.

Where does this unconquerable drive come from? While some of it may have been inherent, he was raised by his unschooled, humble yet wise grandmother, who never stopped telling him that he would one day amount to greatness. If he came back from the bush with a long face because someone beat him in a fight she would analyse the altercation with him and show him that he could be the best. She inspired him to grow. She also taught him: 'The seeds of failure are sown at a height of victory or celebration.' In other words, at that moment when one is recognised and elevated into a leadership position, what one says or promises at that beginning point could lead to one's downfall. So, she taught him the best thing one can do when elevated is to keep quiet, listen, observe and then make an informed decision and comments.

Other great leaders also had a positive impact on his personal development. He sat at the feet of Beyers Naude after being dismissed by the church as a student. Naude explained that the same church dismissed him and that the manner in which Mathebula would handle the challenge would determine whether he would become something in this country.

When a militant Mathebula was the President of a Christian Student Body, Desmond Tutu sat him down and said: 'Look, young man, militarism is great, but the same things you burn you will have the responsibility to build.' What a lesson!

In conclusion, the following story describes how Mathebula thinks and who he really is. During a Christmas break he invited an Afrikaner friend to his home village for a couple of days. The friend had to participate in every aspect of Mathebula's humble past – eat what they ate, eat like they ate (pap with fingers), do what they did. There were no 'holy cows'. He wanted to strengthen their relationship beyond a superficial one where black and white are only comfortable with one another in the comfort of their Sandton mansions. He wants to build bridges. He wants an authentic country with authentic leaders, friends and colleagues, where we nurture relationships built on openness and acceptance of who we really are.

Gary Crittenden – former Global CFO Citigroup

Seamless Leadership Principles:

1. Note Crittenden's amazing attitude regarding challenging conditions and leading in difficult times.

2. See other seamless leadership principles that appear in this piece, such as –
   - ❑ The need for a grounded family
   - ❑ The impossible can become possible
   - ❑ Just do your best.

On the morning of 11 September 2001, Gary Crittenden, then Executive Director and CFO of American Express, stood at his 51st floor office window in downtown Manhattan, staring at the Twin Towers of the World Trade Centre. He was probably contemplating the challenges associated with a $1.2-billion loss for which many channelled their anger towards him. Not long before, the *Wall Street Journal* had fingered him as the weak link in their system, even though he had only been with the company for about seven months.

I am sure there have been times he wished he wasn't standing there at that moment, but he was and unfortunately became a witness to the terrible moment when the first passenger airliner crashed into the World Trade Centre. The eventual collapse of the Twin Towers damaged their building and logic dictated that his and the organisation's existing enormous challenge had just become even bigger.

But, as Crittenden says, 'leadership opportunities come out of difficult times'. One can only try to imagine the emotional and psychological effects on staff. Over and above the critical decisions that were already confronting the executives of American Express, they now had a range of new issues to consider, including whether or not they would move back into the same building. The possible consequences of this particular decision may have been underestimated by the executives, an obvious one being the potentially unwelcome psychological and emotional effect on employees of returning to a location associated with such horrible events. Remember that these were people who had to turn around a business with huge losses.

I wonder sometimes how many of the 'important' decisions leaders make end up being more far-reaching than originally anticipated – negative or positive? Well, they decided to move back in, thinking at the time that such a move would simply demonstrate support for the downtown Manhattan community.

What then happened is that the company's profitability started improving significantly, quarter after quarter, following their move back to that area steeped in unpleasant memories. American Express's people lifted the company out of its financial hole.

The lesson: Crittenden believes in the principle that when you fall off your horse, you get back on it right away! Perhaps the symbolism here is also worth emphasising. The physical building was repaired (healed) successfully and they moved back in. It seems this courageous step assisted employees, who were seeking emotional healing, and as they became stronger they – and I include top leadership – gained courage to take on the business challenge. But it was surely not easy. Crittenden explained that for a long time after the move, when he got into the elevator and pressed number 51, his thoughts raced back to that dreadful day when he could so easily have been one of the victims.

End 2007, beginning 2008, Crittenden found himself in another very tight spot. All I have to do is mention Citigroup, bail-out packages and the fact that he was the CFO at the time, and I am sure you will understand. They were in the eye of the financial storm!

What exactly caused this 'financial tornado' is a debate I leave for the appropriate experts. They can argue about whether managers were to blame, or whether certain 'tools' such as VaR (Value at Risk) modelling were responsible, or whatever. Crittenden's own view that no system should be too smart for its people is worth noting.

I was interested in what lessons leaders could learn from that experience he had. What did it look like inside that storm and how should you behave if you are the one caught up in something like it?

I travelled on a train from Washington, DC to New York City so that I could personally interview Crittenden. It was a bitterly cold and rainy day in a massive, daunting city. As someone noted, it was quite possibly the worst weather of the season thus far. The conditions seemed to hint at the magnitude of the challenge that lay before Crittenden and Citigroup – quite possibly the worst situation he or the company had ever faced.

What I found in the middle of the Citigroup storm was more than 300 000 employees worldwide who were, to varying degrees, on the edge, unsure, concerned about what tomorrow would bring. There were investors who watched doubtfully. Clients, customers and counterparties required reassuring and clear communications if they were to have the confidence to hang in there.

Closer to the centre there was a CFO with a situation thrust upon him that required great leadership and technical prowess. Current risk management models were being challenged and interrogated. The media wanted to know what was happening and due to the nature of the industry and the specific situation, he was often the face of the company. It had been a while since he had worked through so many nights. Decisions of unprecedented magnitude needed to be made in record time. There was pressure on other areas of his life that were also important to him, including his family.

Crittenden's sincere desire to be personal and caring towards Citigroup employees was hampered by the need to run from one high-level meeting to the next. Many of the things he wanted to do as a good leader had to be put on hold. So, what are the lessons we could learn?

Lesson 1: Try to remain optimistic. Amidst overwhelming challenges, Crittenden said it was fascinating to live through the financial crisis, to sit on the sidelines of history and see how things were playing out – in fact, to be participating in the game.

Lesson 2: Crittenden felt that one couldn't underestimate the need people had for stable beacons or a harbour during a time of crisis – somewhere, someone who provided a steady and focused message of hope. Not everyone in the business could fulfil this role, but those who could had to be more visible so that attention could be drawn to them.

Lesson 3: It was amazing how what seemed impossible could actually happen. One must be willing to accept highly unlikely outcomes in one's scenario and risk management planning and consider contingencies for those exceptionally rare events that could have dramatic consequences.

Lesson 4: Delegate to the next level those leadership actions you would want to do yourself. Let them know that if you were not so tied down you would be out there making personal contact with staff, then encourage them to do this.

Lesson 5: Acknowledge those staff members around you who demonstrate resilience. It is easy to fall into the trap of taking such employees for granted. Tell them that you have noticed and appreciate their resilience.

Lesson 6: Work on developing a grounded family. Crittenden said this experience was impacting his family. Fortunately, he had a grounded family. This is, of course, something that does not happen overnight. It takes years of quality time and proactively investing in each relationship. So start today!

Lesson 7: Just do your best! This is really my suggestion of what Crittenden could learn, but I think he already understood it at some level. He said that he wished he could find it within himself to do more of the important things that he would ordinarily do, but I sensed he was trying his best. For example, twice a week he rounded up his global reports for a half-hour conference call. They tried to discuss all the important issues during that meeting. He wanted to spend more time on those discussions, but this is what he could do right then.

In about the year 2000 Crittenden and his wife decided to 'hang up their spurs', as he put it, and perhaps serve a voluntary mission for their church. Then a friend approached him to take up the American Express post. He decided to put those spurs back on again! It has been an interesting and eventful ride from there.

I sensed at the time that he had been prepared well for that difficult and unprecedented financial crisis. What ultimately counted were great leadership qualities that included emotional and spiritual intelligence and resilience. After meeting with Crittenden, I thought he had these.

Gary Player – world renowned golfing legend

||||||||||||||||||||||||||||||||||||||||||||||||||||||||||||||||||||||||||||||||||||||||||||||||||||||||||||||||||||||||||||||||||||||||||

Seamless Leader Principles:

1. Look out for the passion Player has for life and how he has come to possess higher values.
2. Try to identify more signs of a seamless leader attitude in this piece. There are many to pick from, including:
   - ❏ Adversity can drive one to succeed
   - ❏ One of the principles of happiness and success is to love – really care and have compassion
   - ❏ Adopt a healthy lifestyle so that you can have energy
   - ❏ Patience is a great asset
   - ❏ One must have faith.

||||||||||||||||||||||||||||||||||||||||||||||||||||||||||||||||||||||||||||||||||||||||||||||||||||||||||||||||||||||||||||||||||||||||||

For me Gary Player represents energy, positivity, tenacity, endurance and understandably, confidence. Some of the values that drive him seem to be discipline, hard work, love, a desire to improve in every respect and a strong faith in God.

A senior leader in a business shared an interesting story with me. While on holiday in Plettenberg Bay, his son, who is a sports fanatic, came home from an evening with friends, very excited: 'Dad, guess who braaied for my friends and me tonight?' He answered for his dad ... Gary Player. Apparently Player's granddaughter had invited this group of friends over to their place and not everybody knew exactly who she was. When they arrived there she announced that she was going to ask her grandfather to braai for them. Well, Oupa agreed and only when he arrived did everyone realise that her grandfather was the legendary Gary Player. He did everything from building the fire to braaiing the meat. He has a zest for life, which I will add to my list of attributes above.

Together with two retired gentleman whom I admire a lot and whom Player allowed to sit in on the interview, I met the 74-year-old icon in the foyer of The Palace Hotel. He greeted us energetically and made us all feel welcome in an instant. On the way to his room the lift was a bit slow to arrive so we climbed the stairs. He comfortably climbed two stairs at a time, explaining that this was what he always did. I promptly changed the way I was climbing the stairs.

Player is arguably one of the greatest ambassadors South Africa has ever had. And of course he has managed to be this even though he is not perfect. Some perceive him as slightly arrogant while others view him as humble. Such opposing views are to be expected of one who walks in such utterly unique and almost unmatched shoes. Also, his incredible discipline and confidence can easily be mistaken for arrogance, in my view. Ultimately, transcending all opinions of him is the fact that probably everyone worldwide respects him and he deserves it.

I tried to understand whether he always sensed there was greatness in him – that he would accomplish something special in his life. He explained that his mother died when he was eight. His 17-year-old brother went to war and his sister went to boarding school. Dad worked long hours in the mines. Player had to wake up at 5 am, prepare for school and get there on his own by tram, bus and on foot. It took him about an hour and a half to get to school. In the afternoons he would attend his sports activities and go home to an empty house.

'I suffered a lot,' he said, 'which is the greatest thing that could have happened to me at the time.'

He was driven to succeed because of the adversity that he faced and because he had nothing. He explained, further, that to be successful you also have to have a passion and, in his own words, 'work your butt off'. This is what he had to do from a young age, and he continued this habit throughout his life. In fact, that very morning of the interview he rose at 5 am to hit some balls, even though his golfing career is over. He does this because 'I want to keep my body in shape and I want to see people, share love, discuss!'

He loves people! In fact he believes one of the principles of happiness and success is to love – really care and have compassion. That same morning, on his way to the driving range at 5:30, Player walked past the lady cleaning the passage floor, stopped and then thanked her for keeping the floor so clean every day. What a difference this would have made in her life, and he did not know her from a bar of soap. Almost everybody in this world would walk past the cleaner. At best some would greet her.

Player immediately owned up that acting like this is a gift God has loaned him. In fact, he calls it a gift of being a champion – champion of golf, champion of love. This gift he believes can be taken away at any time, and before he could earn it he had to be given suffering from a young age.

Being surrounded by difficult circumstances somehow placed him in that frame of mind where he subconsciously thought to himself that if he received a chance in life he would grab it. His first chance was going to a great school – King Edward VII. He commented that had he not gone to that school he never would have become a champion.

He refers to the 'little white ball' as another 'chance' that opened up unimaginable opportunities of appearing before more people across the world than any South African in our history.

Success for him is simply attaining your goal, whatever this might be. But, while striving towards this goal you are only truly successful if you are humble enough to have respect for other people and realise that you can always learn from somebody else. Being a champion is also about making a sincere effort: even if you do not necessarily achieve exactly what you set out to do, but the sincere effort was there, you are a champion.

His life experiences range from having dinner with every American President for the last 56 years to eating pap with his fingers in Soweto and with the workers who helped build the Sun City Golf course. Yet, after all his great experiences, in his view the single most important thing one can obtain in life is love in one's heart. This gives one the most happiness. In his words: 'If you asked me if I get more happiness from being the only man on the planet to have won the grand slam on the regular and the senior tours or from the love in my heart, I would say to you I get more happiness from having the love in my heart.'

According to Player, what really moves people is when you give them love, 'If you see someone on the veranda and you give them a smile.'

Gary Player believes that 'the great people in the world are those that have suffered and have love, like Mandela, Gandhi, Martin Luther King, Mother Theresa'. But, having love in one's heart with no energy to share it can be counterproductive and quite possibly depressing. Player works overtime to enjoy both in his life. He exercises very hard and eats as healthily as he possibly can. He feels so passionate about this principle that had I allowed him he would have spoken about healthy living for the entire interview.

I thought long and hard about his passion for this topic and then bought into it. One of the greatest blessings in life has to be energy. What can we do without it? I have heard many comments that successful people always have high levels of energy. In many cases the passion for what they do gives them a lot of their energy, as is the case with Player. But, if one really wants to make a difference, sustainably, one has to invest more into a lifestyle that enhances energy – diet, exercise, sleep, rest, etc. Passion for what one does can only maintain energy for so long.

In the weeks leading up to my conversation with Player he had visited 12 countries and 19 cities in 30 days. That required energy! He said: 'The word energy is one of the most crucial words in life today! If you have energy you are blessed and I find very few people with enough energy.'

What stops people from doing something about their energy levels? I asked. Player believes in two Ds – Dreamers and Doers. Most people are dreamers and not good enough at doing. He believes what often stops them from doing is laziness and being in a comfort zone.

One of his biggest frustrations is that 'in schools we don't teach children that you can have millions in the bank; you can have the best wife/husband in the world; you can have the best family; you can have everything that you like, but if you don't have your health you've got zero. This is my big frustration in life – that you have zero and people don't worry about that.' He cannot understand why schools must be purely about academics: 'Are we not trying to build a nation of energy, productivity?'

What advice would he give to a 21-year-old Gary Player, if he could? 'I think patience ... It is a great asset. The man gets on his knees and prays for patience and the Lord gives him tribulations, difficulties so that he will learn patience. In my life time I have seen few people with real patience.

Someone that truly has it, oozes with it. You stop at the robot and take two seconds to pull off and people behind start to hoot at you. So, if I had to look back and give the young Player advice I would say he needs to practise more patience.'

And his final advice to leaders out there? 'One must have faith. For me, the strength in my life has been my faith. Whether this means being a Muslim, a Christian, a Jew, does not matter ... You have to have a faith and not be conceited and think everything you are doing is you alone.'

He has often seen individuals ride the crest of success, thinking that they are doing it themselves, and then they move on, only to go into depression because they have not learned that what they had was a gift and 'everything shall pass'.

Is he concerned about leaving all 'this' (life and achievements) behind when his time comes? 'No, because I will go to a better place, but I am not in a hurry to go. This life is just a stepping stone.'

CHAPTER 17

||||||||||||||||||||||||||||||||||||||||||||||||||||||||||||||||||||||||||||||||||||||||||||||||||||||||||||||||||||||||||||||

Seamless leader attitude to highly sensitive and contentious situations

WITH
- *Malusi Gigaba*
- *Julius Malema*

Some time back, as I drove from the airport, I heard on the news about a 'war' between the government spokesman and the press. Some thoughts crossed my mind of the age-old truth that every single situation in life has two sides to it (and some believe three – yours, the other party's and probably the truth). In general, the situation between the spokesman and the press was no different. Sensing the views on both sides, but realising I did not know all the facts, I did not make a judgement but thought of a key leadership principle that, had it been applied, could have helped move the situation in a positive direction.

Seamless leaders catch the spirit of the quote by Martin Luther King Jr: 'Returning hate for hate multiplies hate, adding deeper darkness to a night already devoid of stars. Darkness cannot drive out darkness, only light can do that. Hate cannot drive out hate, only love can do that.'

King's words touch on a higher law of leadership, that the solution to a sensitive and highly contentious and even flammable situation often lies in doing the opposite of what is expected and even perceived as normal or 'natural'. Only after attempting to apply this higher law and being unsuccessful is it time to act tough, which could even mean going to war in some instances.

The late Nelson Mandela showed the way. Instead of returning hate for hate, he left prison with understanding, patience and forgiveness. Instead of supporting the abandonment of the Springbok emblem in the mid-1990s, he encouraged ANC leadership to keep the emblem. I am convinced that even Mandela did not always apply this higher law, because seamless leaders are human and it is therefore very difficult to do so consistently. Fortunately he seems to have done so when it mattered most. Jesus Christ was a perfect example of this principle. He said 'love your enemies, do good to them that hate you'.

After Eugene Terre'Blanche was murdered and many celebrated his death, a new AWB leader, Steyn van Ronge, was elected. I invited him for a meeting. Much to my surprise, to be honest, he agreed. I tried to convince him to step up to the plate and apply this principle, to motivate the AWB to 'retaliate' in a way opposite to what the world expected of it, to be a seamless leader.

Needless to say, Van Ronge unfortunately did not do this, or he could not convince his executive to follow the higher law of leadership. And the result is an almost non-existent AWB. Had they done so, in a sincere way, we are convinced it would have 'changed our world' towards a more seamless society that would have included improvement of the race relations that continue to trouble South Africa. But hope remains. In a leadership conversation with a fairly senior black leader he referred to a sensitive situation in which a white Afrikaans-speaking subordinate clearly undermined him. His natural response was a desire to discipline the man and show him who was boss. Not wrong, but also not seamless leadership. We discussed the higher law and he applied it excellently with a remarkable result. Their relationship improved dramatically and the employee started performing better than before.

One of the elephants in the room that is resisting national unity, that seems to chain us, hold us back emotionally and psychologically, is of course our racially divided past and its contribution to societal inequalities. While there are other contributing factors to our societal inequalities and poverty, the race issue plays its part without a doubt. In fact, most of us may be underestimating its negative influence on trust, respect and ultimately performance in all spheres of society. Almost every day I sit with black and white senior leaders one-on-one, and the race issue often surfaces as an obstacle to unity, in some form.

I have experienced conversations with leaders from all these opposite ends of the scale and in many instances listened to views on a road to national unity. The case for 'moving on' and putting our racially divided past behind us once and for all is a strong one. The case for still needing to redress the past is an equally strong one. It is true that many are involved in projects that assist in healing psychological and emotional scars of our racial past; it is equally true that not enough is being done. The opposite and different views are many, and mostly sound, depending on who one speaks to. It seems impossible to arrive at a united answer of what needs to be done!

Through all of this I have seriously contemplated what we as a nation can and should do to reconcile and somehow put our racially divided past behind us, in order to step up into a fairly unknown space where true unity and deep trust replace division and distrust. Collectively we have had a glimpse of this space, but we have simply not yet gained sufficient momentum for lasting change. In fact, many would be of the opinion that the momentum may very well be slowing down fast. We need something noble and extraordinary that transcends ordinary solutions, because our situation is not ordinary. Yet we live in a country with extraordinary potential, which we are not even close to accessing.

Following a conversation with Bobby Godsell I came to the conclusion that what we need is an individual or group willing to take the lead and 'do the big or honourable thing', to walk a higher road that somehow attempts to thrust this entire situation onto another and higher plane. To do this requires a radical, selfless yet simple approach, which is based on the deeply universal principle of atonement, *at-one-ment*, which means 'making one' (or whole), bringing together again that which is broken. But for this principle to be effective, at least two elements are necessary. Firstly, what needs to be made whole should seem almost impossible to achieve on its own, therefore needing some form of outside intervention to trigger the movement. Secondly, the 'outside intervention' should be an innocent party or parties that sacrifice immeasurably in a most relevant way.

Whether one is a Christian or not, a perfect example of an atoning act is the belief that many have that Jesus Christ, an innocent and perfect, sinless being, took all of mankind's sins upon Him. In other words, despite

His innocence He was willing to sacrifice His life and suffer incomprehensible pain for others' sins, taking punishment for what billions did or were yet to do wrong. This act takes full effect in someone's life on condition of, firstly, acceptance of the free atoning act, and secondly, that the recipients do what they can to make right – this is called repentance, that part where an effort is made to rectify or change. In other words, on the one hand the atoning act is free, but on the other hand it opens the door for the parties to do their part as well.

In the spirit of being part of the solution, not in an 'excuse me for living' way, for the preservation of our country and our children, and to restore broken trust between black and white, some brave, white and innocent, or largely innocent leader and/or grouping must rise up and openly, publicly, boldly acknowledge that South Africa's racially divided past has wronged and limited fair opportunities in life for our black South Africans. This courageous leader and/or grouping must recognise that while offering better opportunities for most white citizens, in most cases the system not only scarred many black South Africans psychologically, emotionally and economically, but also many white South Africans, at least psychologically and emotionally.

Remember, life is about SiPCOM – experiencing situation after situation and relationship after relationship, enjoying opportunities from which to exercise our sacred right of choice, while handling obstacles and challenges along the road towards one's full potential. But, decisions by some resulted in life opportunities being made available based on race, whilst contributing towards limiting this SiPCOM experience for black South Africans – and this was unacceptable, especially as far as their freedom of choice was concerned. In other words, many black citizens were held back on their path towards their full potential. Recognition and apology for the wrongs inflicted upon our fellow black South Africans also need to be offered on behalf of those who were directly responsible for establishing racially based regulations, including white South Africans who have passed on and, had they been here, may have appreciated the opportunity to stand and be counted.

One can only hope that such a formal and heartfelt apology, together with past and current amends, will open the door for all white South

Africans to demonstrate unsurpassed courage, should they so choose, by formally apologising to black South Africans. And, should they feel it necessary, in addition to what they may currently be sacrificing to our country, do something more to indicate remorse for what our racially divided past did to black compatriots. As mentioned earlier, many are already doing their part and may feel that such a formal apology strongly contextualises and gives meaning to their current acts of sacrifice. One trusts that such acts will be or are in the spirit of 'teaching a man/woman to fish' rather than simply 'giving the fish', in other words a gift that is accompanied by an effort on the part of the recipient, so as not to create an entitlement mentality across our nation. This act should also be accompanied by a lifelong commitment to ensure we will never allow this kind of injustice to happen again!

I do not presume to speak on behalf of black South Africans by telling them how to react, but I personally believe that when such a noble act is performed by one party the other party often reciprocates. So, while white South Africans should do this simply because it is the right thing to do, and should not have expectations of a specific response from black South Africans, what will probably happen is that most black South Africans will rise to the same level of nobility and accept the public and private apologies and acts of amends and forgive unreservedly. The act of atonement will then become effective in their lives as well, and together with white South Africans they too will probably be willing to commit to never again allowing any form of racism to happen in this country. In essence, this courageous act and sacrifice of white South Africans will likely be matched by how black South Africans embrace it. This will go a long way towards restoring broken trust.

Perhaps most white and even black compatriots will view this suggestion with absolute disdain. But they will miss the fact that embracing it places them in the same noble category as those leaders that society admires so much, like Mahatma Gandhi and Nelson Mandela. Both of them rose above ordinary solutions and followed a higher road that saved nations. They made noble acts like forgiveness (Mandela), not retaliating with violence (Gandhi), 'doing unto others as you want done to you', and other difficult acts that often go against our nature seem so doable, especially in hindsight. We cannot all become Mandelas and Gandhis who save nations, but we can act like them in our own spheres of influence.

If it is done courageously, honestly and with real intent, many will be released from these psychological, emotional and even spiritual chains that bind us and contribute towards holding us back as a nation; we will once again be an example to the world; we will show that this nation doesn't need legislation to fix it; it will unite and move closer towards its full potential.

The alternative is just too frightening to contemplate! In essence we will continue to pretend, distrust motives and create superficial unity through sporting events and other activities that offer a temporary feeling of unity, much like what happened in 1995 and 2010. But time and time again we will slip back – deeper and deeper – into the sad state of distrust, division, unresolved issues and expectations, and negative perceptions about one another. If this kind of action does not happen now, our only hope will lie in the rising generation, but the problem is that the ticking time bomb may not wait that long and our next generation is unfortunately being polluted by the actions and attitude of many from the current generation.

Malusi Gigaba – Minister of Home Affairs, previously Minister of Public Enterprises

Seamless Leader Principles:

1. Look out for the reactions of former President Mandela and President Zuma to how the Youth League wanted to act, and note the response from Gigaba.
2. Try to identify more signs of a seamless leader attitude. There are many to pick from.

My introduction to Minister Malusi Gigaba was at a function where he received an award recognising his fight against pornography, a passion driven by a desire to protect our children.

Gigaba has managed to move his way up the political ladder amidst challenging dynamics. In simple political language, he seemed to be in favour during the Mbeki era and now he is in favour during the Zuma era. To achieve this does not sit comfortably in any politician's skill set.

He believes the ability to navigate through political minefields takes both learnt skill and innate character traits. I will add a dash of luck and a level of authenticity.

Gigaba does not believe he is a natural street fighter. However, he re-alises that in politics the time arrives when one must step into the street and participate in a 'good fight'. He is never afraid of this, but his up-bringing and what he has learnt from various leaders of the ANC taught him always to remain calm under stormy circumstances. Keeping calm, he commented, allows one's 'thinking facilities to work according to how one wants them to'. This protects one from being dictated to by events or emotion and then saying or doing things one would regret afterwards.

Gigaba recalled a time in 1994 when there was violence in KZN and many of the younger generation were excited by it and the associated action. The ANC Youth League held several meetings with Jacob Zuma, just before the elections. Zuma remained calm and suggested they, as the leadership of the youth, should step back and ask themselves some questions: 'Does violence serve the country in the longer term? What damage does it do to your constituency?' He further reminded them that violence will come to an end, without a doubt, but that consistent and unnecessary exposure to it will result in deep psychological effects and other resultant behavioural problems like violent crime, and so on. He appealed to them to see the bigger picture and become advocates of peace.

This experience had a lasting impact on Gigaba. Association with other leaders like Nelson Mandela also influenced him as a leader. In 1996 the ANC Youth League Executive Committee was about to release a statement rejecting the Springbok emblem. President Mandela called them in and encouraged them to support the springbok emblem, since reconciliation would be threatened if they opposed it. He was both persuasive and instructive. Their Youth League NEC went away and decided that he was right. As the Youth League leader Gigaba called a press conference and expressed their support for the springbok emblem. Why change their views? Gigaba explains: 'Any young leader must be prepared to learn from those that have come before him'. They learned from President Mandela that day.

Gigaba's leadership approach was certainly influenced by his upbringing within a very strong family structure. Being the son of a minister and a nurse, he and his siblings were taught clear values. His grandmother, a very strong and loving person, also lived with and influenced them. Gigaba's father moved around as the church 're-deployed' him. This taught him to be accepting of new environments and also to look forward to them.

Surprisingly, there were no politics at home. Gigaba was exposed to politics through associations in the township. His parents decided that he and his sister had to go away to boarding school, possibly hoping that Gigaba would drift away from political influence. However, he became even more involved at university. While studying for his master's degree he started working for the ANC Youth League and this is where he remained.

In 1996 Gigaba was caught by surprise when he was elected Youth League President at the age of 24. He moved to Johannesburg and held this position for eight years, which means he was re-elected several times.

He was moulded by difficult life experiences. His younger brother died in a car accident in 2004 at the age of 22. While recovering from this tragic event, the following year his younger sister also died in a car accident. This was tough on the family, especially the parents. I have personally been affected by the death of my 21-year-old brother in a car accident and then a few years later the near death of my older sister, also in a car accident. My parents aged overnight and the impact on me was lasting. However, it was also a growing experience for all of us and I sensed this growth in the Minister.

Gigaba surely stares the greatest leadership challenge of his career in the face. As Minister of Public Enterprises challenges are and will be innumerable. From my associations with current and former CEOs of state-owned enterprises the following leadership questions should perhaps be confronted: 1) What is the overall 'philosophical' vision for SOE's – their core reason for being? 2) Why do so many CEOs of SOEs (especially the large ones) seem to fail?

Politicians, like all of us, are human beings with shortcomings. Walking away from my conversation with Malusi Gigaba however I felt hope. I also wished that he would climb the political ladder further, and he did ... and he will.

Julius Malema – leader of Economic Freedom Fighters and former ANC Youth League leader

Seamless Leadership Principles:

1. Notice his suggestions that correlate with the views above regarding the principle of atonement.

2. Notice his fearlessness. He is simply not afraid to raise his views and fight for a cause, even though at times he does not do it the seamless leader way.

3. Try to identify more seamless leadership principles and signs of a seamless leader attitude in this Q&A piece.

Q: How do you feel about your life so far?

Malema: Well, I have no regrets. I've lived the life of a political animal and I'm very happy that I've lived that life – I still live that life. I grew up in a township where most young people of my age surrendered to alcohol, drug abuse and criminal activities. In the majority, most of those I grew up with are either alcoholic, or jail birds, but I grew up differently. They would come together to smoke dagga and all manner of things including brew and all that; I was never part of that because it tells of the discipline of the organisation.

Q: What do you regard as the prime tasks and responsibilities of a great leader?

Malema: A great leader must listen to the people and implement the aspirations of those people. A great leader must be a good listener and be grounded amongst the masses, not be far ahead of the masses and call yourself leadership when you are very far from the masses because when you look back you are likely not to find those masses. A leader who does all those things, always getting direction from the people of our country – that person is a great leader. You can't listen to a faction, you can't listen to your business associates, you can't listen to your family members – once you're a leader you're a leader of everybody including those who don't want you. Your ears must be open to everybody, including those who don't want you; they must feel comfortable talking to you about what are their issues. That represents the calibre of leadership that we need – the leadership that is not in the pockets of capital because most leaders receive backs – when they ask for money they tell you don't put it into an account, they tell you don't give me a cheque – they take backs and once they take backs from capital there is no way they will tell capital where to get off because they are compromised.

Q: In your opinion are you successful as a leader?
Malema: You know, we have been very successful. To get the country talking is not as easy as that. People of note in big institutions, they give speeches where everyone is forced, who loves and is patriotic about this country, they are forced to listen to them, that when they are finished speaking no one can remember what they said. So we got this country talking, we got this country beginning to appreciate that compromises made before 1994 actually cost us a lot – we needed to find a way of taking our people out of poverty and we succeeded in putting that agenda firmly on the table – when President Zuma was speaking, there were areas when I closed eyes, it was as if the ANC youth leader was speaking, and for me that is clear success for the Youth League and we've succeeded in it.

Q: What leadership lessons have you learnt over the last year?
Malema: One lesson that I've learnt is that you must never rely on an individual in a revolution – you must rely on the wisdom in the revolution and the collective leadership of that revolution. Individuals change especially when they assume positions of power and they begin to show true colours. That's a lesson I have learnt.

Q: Knowing that lesson now, if you look back over the last year, what would you have done differently had you known this?

Malema: What we would have done is actually to elect leaders who work within the collective and who would then be able to nurture and give guidance to the youth instead of destroy them.

Q: How would you define your personal leadership style?
Malema: I don't have any personal leadership style. You know when you become the president of the Youth League you assume a particular leadership style by virtue of occupying that office. You come as an innocent young person but get to be transformed by that responsibility because it requires of you to be outspoken, to be radical and to be militant – to be uncompromising unless persuaded otherwise.

Q: So are you saying then that one's style is inextricably linked to the position, whether in the corporate environment, your business, Youth League?
Malema: Absolutely. When you are assuming a responsibility of ANC Chaplain General, you ought to behave in a particular way befitting the individual occupying that office. When you are the president of the Veteran's League, you behave in a particular way. So it's not about your leadership style: that office has been designed and whoever is going to get into it must fit into that design, otherwise you will not be relevant.

Q: You have displayed unique abilities to raise issues and be confrontational – are you a leader who is also able to listen to divergent views and build consensus?
Malema: Absolutely.

Q: You don't necessarily come across in the media as a consensus-driven leader; you just come across as confrontational.
Malema: I'm not confrontational. I'm a consensus leader. I am forthright, not confrontational, I'm forthright. When it comes to issues, especially political issues, I raise issues openly without fear or favour and without diplomacy – I'm not a trained diplomat, I'm a radical political activist – and my issues will come as they are and if you have a problem with them you can respond accordingly as well and diplomats, if they are worried about the diplomatic part, will find a way in putting diplomacy into them.

I am a youth activist, I'm not a diplomat. So I'm very forthright and I'm very honest and I hate pretenders – I know hate is a very strong word but pretenders are very dangerous because they've got the potential to derail the revolution. So I want people who say when they're in they're in. Not one leg in and one leg outside. Those who are opposed, they must be able to say no, we don't agree and then we need to engage from that point of view. I must be persuaded and people must be prepared to be persuaded as well by myself – I've been defeated many times on issues and I've always accepted well, ok, that's the direction we need to take.

Q: Did you from a young age sense that you were able to influence those around you to act or did that develop later?
Malema: I've always worked with comrades as a collective and every step of the way we're planning together. When we decided who must attack this way or that way we would all speak collectively and at the end you wouldn't even remember who said what – you feel like this is your contribution and you have to take up that task. My primary school was next to the high school, and there we would plan the strikes of that high school when we were in primary school and even when we graduated into the high school we went in with an attitude. So when we went there that first year we planned the strikes in that school, write placards and distribute leaflets everywhere else for what is going to happen. Then the same thing at high school: when I was in high school I used to sit and plan the strikes of tertiary institutions actively, because then I was in the provincial leadership of COSAS and we had what we called Progressive Youth Alliance which was SOSCO, a student organisation at tertiary level. In high school I was then elected class representative, SRC and from then I became the chairperson of COSAS's local branch and from then it all happened. It's always been there in the movement and we've always led from the front.

Q: How do you handle the attention and the stress?
Malema: The stress part of it I do not mind because when you assume a battle internally and even externally, it does not become a personal battle – it's a battle for everybody who supports the cause. The other thing that helps us is that we grew up under the leadership and we saw

how the leaders before us handled decisions. These leaders were able to soldier on. President Mandela, who ordinarily could have given up in prison, soldiered on for 27 years so why should you behave like a cry-baby and think there is something special happening to you? There is nothing special happening to you; it can happen to anybody who is assigned that responsibility.

Q: You seem fearless – I think that's one of the fascinations people have with you – more than other leaders who also have mandates, who also have a weight on their shoulders, in the same way you may have, but just in different capacities. Share with us your humanness – what are you fearful of?

Malema: I'm not compromised – other leaders are compromised. They've got skeletons in their own wardrobes. They know that taking a boast may well lead them to being exposed for what they really are, so I've got nothing to fear. I don't owe anybody anything. They try and scare me and put investigations against me, put all manner of pressures against me, but then I tell them, look, I never in my own conscious life took a decision to engage in a criminal activity and if you say you are investigating me about this or that let me get a day where I'll answer those allegations and deal with them. I'm not going to be threatened that you're being investigated and therefore you must keep quiet and go negotiate with the authorities quietly ... no. I'm not that type of a person. If I have done wrong, I should take responsibility for what I've done wrong but I'm not going to suppress my views and my ideas on the basis that you may be compromised and that if you keep quiet you run the possibility of being rescued. I strongly believe that leadership shouldn't find itself in a compromised position because it is those things that lead to a position where they are no longer able to articulate the mandate honestly and loyally because they are scared that certain things might come out.

We were born of fearless mothers and we grew up amongst fighters who were prepared to lose everything for what they believed in and who are we? Solomon Mahlangu was sentenced to death, on the day they were going to hang him, he never pleaded, even when he saw the rope before him, even when the rope was put on his neck, he made wonderful words to his fighting people – they must continue the struggle and his blood will nourish the tree that will bear the fruits of freedom. This is a man who has got a rope around his neck. So you don't have a rope, you don't run the risk of going to prison for your ideas, you are not going to be killed for your ideas, nothing is going to happen to you, but you still suffer from the fear of the unknown. Let them do what they want to do. The ideas are out there, they are being debated, and even if I'm buried tomorrow those ideas will not be buried with me. Others are even quoting those ideas without quoting the source.

Q: How would you describe the legacy that you want to leave – you personally?

Malema: That question for me ... I don't think it arises. I am still very young to be asked questions about legacy – I thought legacy was for old people who when they pass on, would want to be remembered, those type of things. I'm still too young to be talking about legacy. We are economic freedom fighters and we want to be remembered as economic freedom fighters, having changed the living economic conditions of all people.

Q: I must be honest, I struggle to see you as a 31-year-old – you're far beyond your years because of your experiences. It shouldn't be a surprise because you've had a full life; you've been in the presence of mature, seasoned, street-wise leaders in your life.

Malema: You know, I never grew up with people of my age – I've always interacted with very old people, some of whom qualified to be my parents, but we became friends somehow. When you don't handle certain things in a correct manner, by virtue of their age and experience, they take you on there and then and want to workshop you in how certain things must be done. So I guess sometimes it's so because of the people we grew up with. Then I came to interact more with people of my age when I got elected into structures of the ANC – then we were the same age – but we're not friends, we're not close, we meet at meetings but then after that we go separate ways and then I retreat to these older friends. So I've had those interactions with them, that's where all these things come from.

Q: What's your vision for the future of South Africa?

Malema: We need an equal society, a proper well-resourced society. We don't need an Alexandra and Sandton. We need to live equally in this country, peacefully and happy. Our society into the future can only be an equal society through economic freedom. There must be decisiveness, we are not calling for anarchy, and we are not calling for the collapse of the economy. Those who are opposed to the proposals we have put forward, let them put alternatives. People stand up there in the podium and say the Petroleum Act guarantees that minerals are in the hands of the State, but the same State is taking those minerals into private hands through licensing and individuals don't benefit. Let's share the wealth of the country. Let us de-racialise the economy. We have no problem with the white man, but the white man must be prepared to share. Let's de-racialise the economy of this country and let those who volunteer begin to give to others – not use our democratic laws to want to perpetuate the apartheid inequalities with arguments like *I've got a right to private ownership, I can accumulate as much as I want – there's nobody who can do anything about it, I'm protected by the constitution.* Wait for the day those people are going to participate in an uprising, you must tell us where's the constitution, because then you can't stop them, not the judiciary, not even the army, not NATO – it will never stop the masses. So before we experience an uprising let there be a genuine debate on the table on how do you redistribute. We can't have one family controlling so much you know, so much influence on the economy. I want to be sitting here one day and get a call from the Oppenheimers or these ones in Stellenbosch, they must say to us can you identify an informal settlement, we want to go there, demolish those shacks and build proper houses. If they want us to start to listen to them they must stop theorising and take practical action – we've been talking for quite some time now.

Q: Let's say that's right, I see the spirit of what you're saying – but what about teaching a man or a woman to fish rather than giving them the fish? So we don't just give free houses and grants and just give give give. One of the best things that ever happened to the Afrikaner was the taking away of 'easy' opportunities. Now they must go out and fend for themselves and build businesses, so there's a positive for the Afrikaner who perhaps has had it easy, essentially. That's the concern I have – the mentality about 'give it to me' – it doesn't build character – but there is a case for somehow redistributing.

Malema: How am I going to fish with an empty stomach? There is nothing wrong with you saying to me – here's fish – but these fish, you can even get more by doing one, two, three. I am giving an example of houses in an informal settlement but in the same informal settlement we must build everything else that must take place for it to be called a residential area. You must build schools, you must be able to identify kids in those areas who have potential, take them to the best schools, and in that way you are also giving them the rod to go and fish. But those people do not have any hope. They don't see any possibility of a bright future unless something drastic happens. An example is a township that has just turned 100 years – those rich families in Stellenbosch – in celebrating 100 years of Alexandra, they can come here and make a contribution and say we want to turn this place upside down, with 500 million contribution from those families, it's nothing to them. Each one of them comes and pledges 100, 100, 100, put it together. Why not say they must give black people tenders, they move in here, they must demolish this place, build the best city ever in Alex as their contribution to a democratic SA with a commitment to sharing.

Q: Would that work in the bigger picture of teaching skills, of making sure people don't have that entitlement mentality?

Malema: We don't want to create a welfare state, that has never been our intention, hence we said to President Zuma when he became president, part of your legacy will be to produce well-qualified young people, can you put aside money in your own budget – you've got that capacity? Take 10 000 students from the country every year, to go and learn in the best countries while we are still transforming our education system here. We can't wait for this system to be transformed; we don't have that luxury, let's take others out of the country to be equipped with the necessary skills, 10 000, and then bring them back. Each year 10 000 go, then by the time you leave your office in five years you would have graduated not less than 50 000 young people who are now in the service of our country. Nobody cares to listen, but when we take microphones, all of us, and we say skills development, we must ensure our young people have got skills, but no practical programme to say this is how we're going to do it. The Ruperts can do this without Zuma.

Q: What place in society do you see for minority voices – whites, coloured etc? Now I am sitting in front of you today as a white Afrikaans-speaking male. But I am a white South African who has friends leaving this country, thinking there's no future. I'm staying here to be part of the solution. So when I hear Julius Malema stand up and say we must take back the land for our people or we must put money back for our people, a lot of those statements, I get the strong feeling I am not included, but excluded. And that creates a lot of alienation. Not everybody has the opportunity to sit with you here like I am, but the guys out there, South Africans out there, they feel excluded, they feel that race relations are going backwards rather than forward.

Malema: No no no no no ... the white minorities, not even coloureds and Indians, I do not even begin to hear those fears amongst them – they're just scared of nothing. If we wanted to do anything to them we would have done it in 1994. We had all the reasons, but look, we are not anti-whites, but we can't ignore what happened historically and they need to come to terms with that. The sooner they appreciate that they have caused us so much pain, the better. They need to know that. They must never behave like nothing happened. That's the problem, they want to behave like nothing happened, and they want to say to people, put everything behind – we can't, we can't. Never ever try to push us to put everything behind because you're going to force us to pretend to you and once we have to pretend the anger in us is going to boil. And then it will explode.

Q: So how do we confront that? How do we really clear up the race issues?
Malema: They must open up, this is their country, they too should feel comfortable and never feel attacked when we speak about redressing the imbalances of the past. They must open up and one of the ways of opening up is to accept that Apartheid has caused us this trouble we find

ourselves in now. Then they need to ask themselves a question – how do I contribute? We are speaking to all those who own the means of production. White working class belongs to our struggle. They must come and join us to fight for equal distribution of wealth in this country, and when we say equal distribution of wealth we don't refer only to blacks – we refer to the white working class who have got nothing. They can't be celebrating rich people.

Q: I asked a waiter yesterday – a black waiter – while I was having lunch, what would you want to ask Julius Malema? And he said 'Are you going to be the next president of South Africa?' What would you say to him?
Malema: (Lots of laughter) No, that question doesn't even cross my mind. Like I told you I have been involved without any expectations and even now I do not expect anything. People of my age and people that I have led, actually are now in government and leading in positions of responsibility. It's not easy to be a President of South Africa; it's not an easy task. It shouldn't be either – it comes with a huge responsibility. And I love my privacy, I love my parties, I love chilling and walking freely without any restrictions.

CHAPTER 18

||||||||||||||||||||||||||||||||||||||||||||||||||||||||||||||||||||||||||||||||||||||||||||||||||||||

South Africa and the world's seamless leadership journey

Not long ago our leadership icon Nelson Mandela was at the forefront of our minds. It may be appropriate to reflect on what we have done, or can do, about his leadership legacy, and even consider moving South Africa and the world's leadership legacy to the next level.

There is no doubt that if great leadership had not been demonstrated in our country's recent past, South Africa would have been a very different place. This is something to be proud of. Having said that, there is obviously a strong case to be made for ineffective leadership having brought about or exacerbated many of the daunting challenges we currently face.

I want, however, to suggest that what we have not done is to capitalise effectively on our Mandela leadership legacy by moving it to the 'next level'. As a result, we may very well have moved backwards to some degree.

Some time back a senior ANC leader explained to me that when Jacob Zuma became President of the ANC and then South Africa they expressed one core desire – 'Madiba legacy revived'. Perhaps this meant a legacy of forgiveness, openness, inclusiveness, giving rather than taking, service (Mandela Day), sharing, respecting, performing, approachability, unity, and much more.

From a leadership point of view, when you look at the behaviour and performance of some top politicians and societal leaders, the success of the above desire can be questioned.

Of course we all want to revive the magic of the Mandela era, while rounding it off with an equally magic touch of tangible delivery for real and sustainable change. Is this remotely possible if a culture of full ownership does not permeate our society; if we expect politicians to solve everything; if the leaders we follow cannot be followers themselves?

And I pose this question: among whom is Nelson Mandela's legacy to be revived? Surely not merely the political leaders in South Africa and beyond? Our current level and frame of reference is one of a leadership legacy that was built by politicians, struggle heroes and others who demonstrated an attitude that made it possible to carve out a future together. The rest of us became mere recipients of this leadership legacy, and ordinary South Africans may have distanced themselves from it. This is a mistake.

The next level to which we should move is where this leadership effectively filters to the masses and where more ordinary citizens stand up to assist the politicians in leading their own countries towards a destiny of excellence. However, to reach a point where ordinary citizens truly believe that they are leaders, even though they are not moving within the highest echelons of political structures, is a challenge.

There is a perception that one is a leader only when appointed to a formal position. Yet ironically everyone has an opinion about leadership, how to lead, about good or bad leadership. Is it because everyone has been led somewhere in their lives? Is it because every single person is being led at any given moment in time? Is it because every person is in fact a leader?

I believe it is all of the above, but more specifically I want to address the largely undiscovered truth that almost every person is in fact a leader. I have stated a clear case in this book that leaders are in the business of movement – themselves, others, attitudes, ideas, organisations, countries and so on. A primary function of a leader is to generate movement, more commonly referred to as change, growth, development, improvement, and so on.

If you are in agreement, then the following is also true. If you are a regular day-to-day parent you are leading your children towards a certain belief system or value system, coping with life, and teaching them skills, which means you create movement. If you are a junior supervisor in an organisation you strive to move your staff to perform better and you are striving to improve the output of whatever you do, which means you are leading. I could go on ... So, nearly every person has an opinion about leadership because nearly every person is a leader – they just don't necessarily realise it, because society is confused about what a leader is.

Please understand that the debate is no longer about who is a leader, because we all are! The debate is how to get people to accept and believe that they are already leaders – and then how to consciously be one every day, moving our society towards one of a value system of excellence. Every time you stand up and do what is right and excellent, you help to move the value system in the right direction and therefore lead, even if no one sees you. Also remember that a great leader is always a great follower. One cannot be one without the other.

We need to support more fully a spirit of service while overcoming debilitating practices like entitlement, as briefly touched on by James Ritchie in chapter 6. Dallin H Oaks, a former US Supreme Court Judge, said the following about entitlement, which is certainly one of the barriers to elevating our leadership legacy: 'The worldly aspiration of our day is to get something for nothing. The ancient evil of greed shows its face in the assertion of entitlement: I am entitled to this or that because of who I am – a son or a daughter, a citizen, a victim, or a member of some other group. Entitlement is generally selfish. It demands much, and it gives little or nothing. Its very concept causes us to seek to elevate ourselves above those around us ... The values of the world wrongly teach that "it's all about me." That corrupting attitude produces no change and no growth.'

We would do well to internalise this statement by Thomas S Monson, which is in line with my earlier quote by Martin Luther King Jr: 'Vice never leads to virtue. Hate never promotes love. Cowardice never gives courage. Doubt never inspires faith ... Times change, but truth persists. When we fail to profit from the experiences of the past, we are doomed to repeat them with all their heartache, suffering, and anguish.'

Admiring Nelson Mandela as a leader is one thing, but learning from him and his experiences and following his example is another. May we honour him by doing the latter!

Perhaps what makes this difficult is that we live in one of the most dynamic communities in the world, faced with sombre realities as well as great opportunities. On the one hand, each of us at a moment's notice can list many serious challenges facing us on a daily basis. On the other hand we can also think of the amazing degree of freedom in our country to choose and to become.

To be happy or satisfied here is not only a matter of upward mobility and money. Obviously these two principles may be important and even crucial considerations, but we could be doing ourselves a lot of harm by thinking that they are the real basis of satisfaction and happiness.

In our country presently, and probably most other countries across the globe, the *fat cat syndrome* (discussed in chapter 16) is a dominating factor in the lives of many leaders who really believe that this is the answer to all their desires and dreams. Such an attitude is often reinforced by the spirit of negative entitlement that also seems to motivate far too many of our leaders. The irony is that those individuals and seamless leaders who develop a work-, family- and values-based ethic are often in a much better position to achieve upward mobility and increased income than those who are predominantly motivated by the fat cat syndrome. The time may be rapidly passing in our country where people are given significant positions of power and money simply because of political correctness. A new generation of qualified and more experienced leaders are competing in the market place. It was easier in the immediate past to get by with an entitlement attitude that is not necessarily backed by good character and experience.

The secret of optimising our existing situation with a positive and seamless leader attitude may be far more profitable in the long run than to be continuously seeking after position, power and more money.

The following story is told by Dieter Uchtdorf, a former Chief Pilot at one of the largest airlines in the world. During a conference there was a need to move a large piano to a room in another part of the complex. Many gentlemen were standing around not knowing how to move this delicate and heavy instrument. One of their leaders asked the men to stand close around the piano, and then for each of them to 'lift where you stand'. It was as simple as that; each of the men did their part and the piano was moved satisfactorily. We can each of us learn 'to lift where we stand' instead of always looking for the great break over the horizon.

There is something very attractive in a person who is geared attitudinally to 'lift where they stand' in the sense of making positive use of the environment he or she is in presently, and magnifying the opportunities around them. This does not mean that we should not apply for a more attractive job. Often doing so may be the best for us, but the fact remains that our ability to optimise our existing opportunities in a positive manner is a major contributing factor in our personal progress towards seamless leadership.

When we develop a positive seamless leader attitude towards our environment we may well find that the people around us are not all that bad! The bosses are not necessarily the enemy, and life is certainly far more enjoyable than before. We become part of the solution rather than just another person who is part of the problem. The spectacles through which we see things generate the building blocks of our futures and happiness.

Speaking from experience over many years, we can assure especially the young reader that our attitude towards life and a value-based ethic is an overriding factor in our careers, family and personal happiness. The irony is that a person who is driven by an honest set of spiritual values will in most cases be happy in most positions without necessarily detracting from their legitimate ambition to move forward towards their full potential.

Ultimately our legacy is about the values we truly believe in. When we allow ourselves to slip into a set of values that is selfish and short sighted, we will pay a price that may in some instances be too much to bear. Our media reflects on a daily basis the price we are paying in our community for the fat cat syndrome that cares only for position, power and money.

Fortunately our experience over many years is that there are many who are anxious to rise above the fat cat syndrome and strive towards a more values-driven society, which is a breeding ground for seamless leaders.

Asking questions

If becoming a seamless leader is such a long-term project, how does one ensure it remains a quest? Well, mankind's quest for knowledge is mostly triggered by questions. We see this in small children who often pester us with a multitude of questions. Why? When? What? Where? Who? The asking of questions is a necessary prerequisite to obtaining knowledge and to continuing our discovery of seamless leadership.

Seamless leaders, who are often also quality teachers, are always on the lookout for students or followers who ask questions, because they know such individuals are the ones who are normally the most receptive to knowledge and attitudinal change. Encouraging a questioning mind and heart is the essence of effective teaching and learning.

Ordinary leaders at all levels, from the home to universities to the world of different professions and business, are tempted to resist questions because they are 'inconvenient' and tend to disrupt the flow of the lesson of the day – and because these leaders often favour the practice of 'telling' rather than teaching. A key reason why such a vast percentage of knowledge gained during formal academic studies is mostly lost to us is because we were not driven by sincere questions as much as the need to study, write and pass exams.

Most people, somewhere in their lives, ask the really great and important questions – what is the meaning of life? What is my mission in life? What is my relationship with God? And then, for different reasons, they may stop asking these questions and get caught up in the demands of daily living. Perhaps this happens because they never came to realise that the level of their emotional and spiritual maturity is determined by the level and sincerity of their questions. Or, perhaps somewhere in their lives they came to the important realisations, but then allowed them to fade again.

One of the unavoidable consequences of not developing an attitude of asking and then seeking answers to the important questions is that we settle for some form of mediocrity and never move from ordinary to good, to great, to seamless. We ask the wrong or at best the 'good' questions, not consciously realising that it is impossible to become 'great' by asking 'good' questions and that great questions lead to great answers, which invariably lead to great results. Then, universal questions lead to universal, bigger-picture answers, which fall into the domain of seamless leadership. So, we will struggle to become seamless leaders if we shy away from asking the universally applicable questions.

In today's competitive and pressure-filled world a leader or individual cannot afford to slip into the rut of mediocrity or simply remain 'good'.

Obviously there is a time to 'tell' (instruct, convey information, make decisions, express opinion, and so on). However, when you add the 'seamless questioning' approach to your relationships and way of leading, you enter a higher seamless leader level of leadership that involves counselling with those around you, which prompts initiative, team work and creativity, and tends to foster a culture of caring.

Impossibility thinking

To become a true seamless leader you have to continue lifting your thinking and questioning to a higher level. In today's world it is no longer the art of 'possibility' thinking and doing that makes the difference, but the art of 'impossibility' thinking and doing. As I engaged leaders on this specific theme the following three attitudinal categories evolved:

1. You go about your daily job and when perceived impossibilities confront you or are placed before you, you allow these to stifle or slow down your movement, or you simply reject it as outright impossible and revert back to your experience only.
2. As you go about your daily job and perceived impossibilities confront you, you seek a way to turn these into possibilities, though you also wait for impossibilities to come your way. You are willing to challenge your experience.
3. You proactively go in search of so-called impossibilities and then make them possible. Seamless leaders fall into this category.

While most individuals or leaders may have a 'one or the other' attitude, it is, strangely enough, also circumstantial. In one area of your life you may proactively seek out the impossible and make it possible, while in another area you have little confidence and fall into the trap of playing the waiting game.

Those who achieve amazing movement or feats have to enter the realm of 'impossibility'. This is a lonely place to be, because it is uncomfortable;

it is frowned upon or ridiculed; it increases the risk of failure; it can be stressful. But, its rewards and results are often handsome, admired and even revered in history.

Individuals like Steve Jobs, Adrian Gore, Raymond Ackerman, Richard Branson, Mahatma Gandhi, Nelson Mandela, leaders featured in this book, and many others somehow achieved what seemed impossible to most, within their own world. Their attitude is or was not one of waiting but of proactively going in search of what others may perceive to be impossible and then sacrificing much, working very hard, mostly long hours to make it possible.

Leaders in today's fast-paced, stressful, challenging environment have to move from mastering the art of possibility thinking and doing to mastering the art of impossibility thinking and doing, while striving to be a seamless leader. But, many are so bogged down by the challenges that confront them they don't have time and energy to take themselves and their people into that space of the 'impossible'. Fortunately there are exceptions and these individuals keep alive the possibility of achieving the impossible. At the same time, in today's competitive world, organisations that don't have leaders leading them towards the impossible may not last long.

The natural inclination of a leader of a struggling business or division is to return to basics, just to bring back normality or stability. While this may not be wrong, and even correct in the very short term, more and more, leaders who cannot sell the 'impossible' to their organisation will not create a strong enough 'opposite pole' to attitudinally draw their people away from the 'struggle pole'. The day-to-day reality of struggling then tends to weigh much heavier than the alternative position of something greater, and therefore the scale just does not tip towards a more attractive future. Before long the organisation slips back into the struggle space, where it subconsciously starts believing it deserves to be. In short, a back-to-basics campaign on its own is simply not a strong enough magnet to counter the struggle pole.

In the past, when the environment wasn't as dynamic and fast paced, a leader had the luxury of time to lead a business through a recovery period without necessarily creating that opposite pole of an 'impossible' achievement, inadvertently leaving this for later. The challenge is that while the organisation moves through the recovery or 'back-to-basics' period to consolidate, a competitor with a leader who takes them towards the 'impossible' continues to leapfrog ahead and could very well get out of reach of the struggling business. The latter may never catch up!

To help you shift towards the attitude of proactively searching for the impossible, and to kick off with the art of 'impossible thinking', ask this question: *What in my mind is impossible to achieve, but I wish it wasn't?* It should be something you need to be 'not impossible' for your leadership responsibility or business to move forward. It is that impossibility that – when you are honest with yourself – you believe cannot happen, but you need it to be possible. List one, two or three of these, then start working on the most relevant one until it starts looking possible. Ask questions like: Why is this not possible? In other words, confront the negative perceptions head on. Then ask why it is possible – engage the positive perceptions by building hope and possibility. As you honestly ask and answer these questions you will start lifting your belief that it is possible and before you know it you will put directions and structures in place to move closer towards the impossible. Something in the universe conspires to work in a person's favour when he or she courageously and consciously engages the perceived impossible

If you are in a position of authority and influence, realise this: 'If many employees on all levels of your organisation do not start actively seeking opportunities to make the impossible possible, your organisation may not survive in the new world, because it will not be dynamic enough.' It needs this kind of thinking in order to have the ability to move fast enough, capitalise on opportunities quick enough, and react to change almost immediately. Consider a monthly award across the business for the employee who made the impossible possible, however small or large this may be. Then, turn your impossibility achievers into heroes. Reward those who seek the impossible and make it possible. This will go a long way towards building a culture of achieving the impossible.

'Begin with the end in mind,' said the late Dr Stephen R Covey. You decide the level of your 'end', which then determines the standard of every other action and behaviour that follows.

Our challenge to everyone across the globe is this: in your roles – father, mother, employee, citizen, manager, politician, community leader or whatever – stand up for what is right, adopt seamless leadership, or 'Mandela Leadership', in some form and help move your country and this globe forward to a better place. If not for yourself, do it for our future generations. Be part of the solution rather than the problem; focus on taking ownership and creating effective movement where you stand!

Acknowledgements

To all the leaders with whom I have associated over the years, who somehow contributed towards the body of knowledge that we share in this book, whether quoted herein or not; whether leaders of large organisations or not.

To South Africa, a wonderful, beautiful, exciting country that somehow always rises to the occasion, though at times we are somewhat bipolar – ranging from being manic, energetic and confident to depressed, self-conscious and unsure about our capabilities.

To the late Nelson Mandela and other key leaders who set the pace, turned our nation away from a path of sure disaster to one of democracy, hope, freedom for all – a place where all will be able to achieve their full potential.

To Ellis Mnyandu (Editor, *Business Report*), for being a visionary and making a national platform available on which I could place many of the leaders in this book to debate and showcase leadership. He has made much possible since becoming involved because of a passion for our South African leadership legacy.

To Theo Garrun (Editor, *Star Workplace*), for believing in me and allowing me to start publishing leadership content many years back. His contribution helped take our mission to another level and to affect many lives positively.

To my beautiful wife and children who patiently stood by me as I carved away at this book and sacrificed many special hours with them.

To my colleagues at Leadership Platform who have supported and inspired me to keep at it; who often shared valuable insights that added huge value to this book.

Adriaan Groenewald
February 2015